C00 962 869X

D1428927

Architecture
in Play

Architecture
in Play

Intimations of Modernism in Architectural Toys

Tamar Zinguer

University of Virginia Press

CHARLOTTESVILLE AND LONDON

University of Virginia Press
© 2015 by the Rector and Visitors of the University of Virginia
All rights reserved
Printed in the United States of America on acid-free paper

First published 2015

9 8 7 6 5 4 3 2 1

Library of Congress Cataloging-in-Publication Data
Zinguer, Tamar, 1965–
    Architecture in play : intimations of modernism in architectural toys / Tamar Zinguer.
        pages   cm
    Includes bibliographical references and index.
    ISBN 978-0-8139-3772-4 (cloth : alk. paper)
    1. Architectural toys. 2. Play (Philosophy) 3. Architecture and
recreation. 4. Architecture and society. I. Title.
    GV1218.5.Z56 2015
    720.1'03—dc23
                                        2015001628

Frontispiece: House of Cards/Wolken Kuckucks Haus, Charles and Ray Eames, published by Otto Maier (Ravensburg), ca. 1961, photolithographed paper laminate.

Illustration facing table of contents: The Little Toy, Charles and Ray Eames, manufactured by Tigrett Enterprises (New York, Chicago), ca. 1952, paper-fibre board, metal, covered copper wire.

For Maiolica

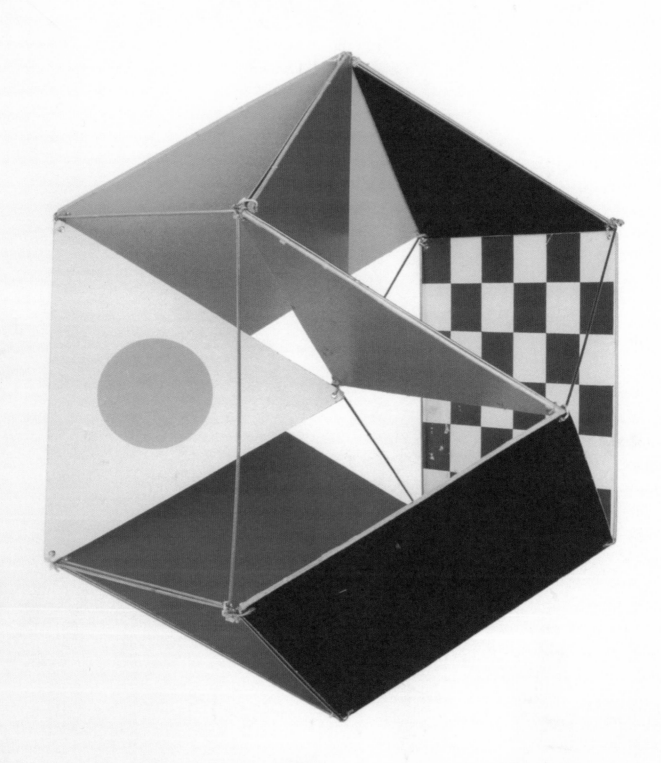

Contents

Acknowledgments viii

Introduction 1

1. Kindergarten Gifts, circa 1836 19

2. Anchor Stone Building Blocks, 1877 53

3. Meccano, 1901, and Erector Set, 1911 97

4. The Toy, 1951, and House of Cards, 1952 145

Conclusion 195

Notes 213

Illustration Credits 241

Index 245

Acknowledgments

I remember, as a child, finding perforated metal pieces in the shed at the back of my grandfather's backyard. It wasn't until years later that I realized they were Meccano parts that must have belonged to my father when he was growing up in British Mandate Palestine. Toys crossed seas and bridged over cultures, and these rusty "bribes et morceaux"—these "odds and ends," testimony to some past events, in the language of Claude Lévi-Strauss—would eventually take me on a long voyage of discovery. Meccano and the other architectural toys in this book were unknown to me at the start of this project, yet my research and writing have led me to some great, formidable places, and to meeting generous, inspiring people.

At Princeton, where this book first took shape as a doctoral dissertation, I am grateful to numerous individuals. First and foremost, Beatriz Colomina, as dissertation advisor, never failed to show her interest and enthusiasm. I am deeply grateful for her insights and unwavering support of my project. She always offered a motivating intellectual challenge, while her own work continues to provide great inspiration. Stimulating and thought-provoking exchanges took place with other professors during my studies. They have all contributed to the formation of this work. I thank Hal Foster, Antoine Picon, George Teyssot, and Mark Wigley, whose discerning observations have stayed with me. I thank Spyros Papapetros, whose keen perception, during my last year at Princeton, was significant to the completion of my study. I am also thankful to Spyros for his continued friendship and support since that time, through all the steps leading to the completion of this book.

During my years of teaching at The Cooper Union, I was lucky to have Anthony Vidler as dean. He was ever attentive and positive, and his architectural writings and vision were inspirational always. It was in conversation with him about my work that the word "intimation" was first spoken, and it has since become an integral part of the project. I thank him for his continued support of my writing and teaching.

I could not have undertaken and completed this work without the financial help and support of various grants and institutions. I am indebted to the Canadian Centre for Architecture (CCA) in Montreal. Since the most important architectural toy archive is housed at the CCA, this work could never have been realized without the free reign I was given with the collection. I am deeply grateful to Phyllis Lambert and Nicholas Olsberg for their interest in my work and welcoming hospitality, as well as for the generous support through a predoctoral fellowship. I am also grateful for the support, knowledge, and friendship of Rosemary Haddad, who made my stay at the CCA memorable.

I also gratefully acknowledge the Lemelson Center for the Study of Invention at the Smithsonian Museum of American History, the Mrs. Giles Whiting Foundation Fellowship in the Humanities, and the Center for American Studies at Princeton University for the predoctoral fellowships I was awarded.

I have gained from presenting parts of this book at the annual meetings of the Society of Architectural Historians, the College Art Association, and the Association for the Study of Play. Presenting the work in various formats helped crystallize my thought and writing. I am grateful for the invitations to lecture at the Lemelson Center for the Study of Invention, at Cornell University, the University of Tennessee at Knoxville, the University of Pennsylvania, the University of Minnesota and Hochschule RheinMain in Wiesbaden, Germany.

Portions of chapter 4 appeared in another form as "TOY" in *Cold War Hothouses,* edited by Beatriz Colomina, AnnMarie Brennan, and Jeannie Kim (Princeton: Princeton Architectural Press, 2004). That essay was translated into French and published in *Azimuts: Revue de Design,* no. 25, special issue on Design and Mathematics, June 2005. I thank the editors for these opportunities.

My students at The Cooper Union who, in the last four years, took the "Architecture in Play" seminar have shared my enthusiasm for architectural toys and have consistently proved that playing with blocks can be very enjoyable regardless of electronic progress and smart interface. I thank them all for consistently inventing and making beautiful objects to play with. Besides attesting to the power of play, these moments have deepened my joy in teaching.

Detlef Mertins was always ready to listen with interest to my discoveries on play and toys. I will miss our exchanges and his great erudition. I thank Nancy Later for her editorial comments and Georg Windeck, who has lent support throughout with very precise German translation, following the tremendous help of Anna Kathryn Schoefert earlier in the process. Holger Kleine invited me to present this work extensively in Germany—it has been an invaluable experience. I thank them all for their lively interest.

I am thankful to the University of Virginia Press and to my editor, Boyd Zenner, for her keen interest in my project and for her enthusiasm and support from the start. I am also thankful to Angie Hogan, Susan A. Murray, Morgan Myers, and Ellen G. Satrom of UVA Press, who helped bring this project to completion. Two anonymous readers took great care and time to read the manuscript and provided insightful observations. I am very grateful to both. The publication of this book is also made possible by a generous grant from the Barr Ferree Foundation Publication Fund, administered by the Department of Art and Archaeology at Princeton University.

The extensive images I collected during the years of research entailed a different kind of work during the last few months. I am most grateful to Elizabeth O'Donnell, who as Acting Dean has been very supportive during this last phase of my project. I am also grateful for the assistance of The Cooper Union archivist Steven Hillier and of Pat McElnea, as well as for the support of the staff of The Cooper Union Library. I am also indebted to my assistants Derrick Benson and Jianjia Zhou for their tireless help when they were needed. I thank the collectors Jim Gamble, George Hardy, Andrew Jugle, and Paul Tambuyser for their enthusiastic support with images and information.

My mother, Ilana Zinguer, has always provided great encouragement and insight. I greatly appreciate her patience and constant advice. She has provided an exemplary model of scholarship that is hard to follow!

Finally, I am deeply thankful to Sylvester Wojtkowski, who has been tremendously patient and greatly supportive of my endeavors. He has diligently shifted his attention from reading my chapters to focusing on real block structures on the living-room carpet. There, a House of Cards and some Froebel's Gifts have been played with repeatedly and renamed "Mommy's work toys." I dedicate this book to Maiolica, my growing partner in play constructions.

Architecture
in Play

Introduction

"Why don't you play with your playthings, my dear? I am sure that I have bought toys enough for you; why can't you divert yourself with them, instead of breaking them to pieces?"[1] The book *Practical Education,* written in 1801, was the first to recommend building blocks as beneficial toys, possibly to counteract those destructive acts that its Irish authors Maria Edgeworth and her father, Richard L. Edgeworth, observed. In the opening chapter, devoted to toys, the writers noted: "We have found that two or three hundred bricks formed in plaster of Paris, on a scale of a quarter of an inch to an inch, with a few lintels, &c. in proportion, have been a lasting and useful fund of amusement."[2]

No such plaster brick has survived, but since the end of the eighteenth century, architectural toys—blocks and constructions sets—have provided evidence of the social and economic life of their periods, and have become a locus of confrontation between technological culture and education. Designed by adults for children, they have created an intersection between generations and have reflected changing attitudes toward childhood and the home. Unlike full-scale architecture, architectural toys have an ephemeral existence. They exist for the player for a few moments or a few years, and then they are forgotten, destroyed through play or by accident, misused, and lost, always holding the potential to be reconstituted anew in other forms at other times.

While some building blocks have imitated their surroundings, reflected stylistic inclinations, and incorporated technological changes in their "systems of construction," others have represented built structures more abstractly, their play with architecture more suggestive. Nevertheless, all architectural toys share a complex of similarities, following Ludwig Wittgenstein's claim that all games belong to a "family," establishing a network of relationships and describing notions of "family resemblances."[3] They usually consist of kits of parts that form miniature spatial constructions and can be manipulated, taken apart, and then reconstructed. They also have an imprecise function: they are disassembled and assembled again, present variations and possibilities, and their function is, in fact, to be created anew at each occasion. Their use is unpredictable and always entails a sort of deviation. The playful use of architectural toys consists, many times in fact, of their misuse.

The recent interest in Froebel's Kindergarten Gifts, designed in Germany in 1836 by Friedrich Froebel (1782–1852), arose from findings about the presence of these toys in the early childhood of many of the pioneers of modern art and architecture. Frank Lloyd Wright first wrote about the inspiration provided by his early toys in his autobiography, published in 1943. He linked his architecture to the crystalline formations he must have created as a child with the geometrical wooden blocks—a series of cubes, spheres, and cylinders that were gradually broken down to smaller parts. He remembered playing with the Gifts his mother had bought for him at the 1876 Centennial Exhibition in Philadelphia, and recalled "the smooth shapely maple blocks with which to build, the sense of which never afterward leaves the fingers: *form* becoming *feeling*. . . . What shapes they made naturally if only one would let them!"[4]

Accounts of other architects' play with the Froebel material followed. The young Charles-Edouard Jeanneret (Le Corbusier) had attended a private primary school, the "École Particulière" of Mlle. Colin in Neuchâtel, for at least three years.[5] Louise Colin, a graduate of the Froebelian Normal School in Neuchâtel, advertised in local papers that her school "would follow the new method, which is applied to the present lifestyle and adjusted to current industrial needs. The intellectual development of her students would not be neglected," she promised, as she would "provide a moral and intuitive education with Froebel material."[6] This early Froebelian apprenticeship was recounted by Le Corbusier to explain the formal similarities between his plans of La Ville Radieuse and some works made by kindergartners with Froebel's Occupations. Charles Eames, who attended a kindergarten based on the Froebel system, also held his play "with elementary blocks of spheres and cones and pyramids and different kinds of exercises" accountable for his interest in structure;[7] and Buckminster Fuller testified to his use of Peas-Work (Froebel's nineteenth Occupation) in kindergarten and related this play experience to his intuitive structural knowledge.[8]

In *Inventing Kindergarten,* Norman Brosterman provided an extended list of famous graduates of the Froebelian system, which by the 1880s had spread throughout Europe. Georges Braque attended such a school in Argenteuil-sur-Seine, Paul Klee in Bern near Neuchâtel, and Wassily Kandinsky attended one in Florence, where his parents had stayed for a few years.[9] Furthermore, Johannes Itten had trained to be a Froebelian kindergarten teacher, and Piet Mondrian and Josef Albers were elementary school teachers likely to have been familiar with innovative pedagogical methods. A formal link between the Froebel kindergarten system and the origins of modernism can be drawn since the geometrical aspect of the school projects of late-nineteenth-century kindergartners evoked the works of modernist architects and artists. Was it their geometrical form, or the new aspects of play that were conducive to such invention? The new setting of Froebel's class, where the focus was on the child's well-being, as well as the dedication of time apart to play have certainly had an impact on early childhood education.

In *Architecture in Play,* I explore architectural toys that, like the Gifts, were part of numerous childhoods and have imparted lasting knowledge to the players. This is not simply about the formation of a modern object, but about the formation of a young player, a child, who through play could cultivate building instincts and aesthetic habits. As, in time, this player would become a maker creating his own buildings and environments, this early play with blocks establishes the important interchange among means of production, play, and architecture.

Following the first chapter, which focuses on the abstract, geometric Kindergarten Gifts, the second chapter examines Anker-Steinbaukasten (Anchor Stone Building Blocks) that were designed in 1877 in Germany by the architect Gustav Lilienthal (1849–1933) and his brother, the mechanical engineer and flight pioneer Otto Lilienthal (1848–1896). Heavy little bricks made of cast stone in three different colors could be fashioned into castles, forts, and churches by following detailed drawings and with very careful stacking. A quarter century later, Meccano (1901) was invented in England by Frank Hornby (1863–1936), and a decade after that Erector Set (1911) was invented in New Haven, Connecticut, by Alfred C. Gilbert (1884–1961); these two construction sets constitute the focus of the third chapter. Meccano comprised metal slats perforated along their lengths with holes, while the parts of an Erector Set looked like miniature steel girders. When connected with screws, nuts, and bolts, both sets yielded skeletons of innovative engineering works—bridges, cranes, and skyscrapers, as well as numerous other structures presented in the instruction manual for the young engineers in training. These remained the most popular building toys for a couple of generations. The Toy (1950) and House of Cards (1952), designed and manufactured in California by the husband-and-wife designer-architect team Charles Eames (1907–1978) and Ray Kaiser Eames (1912–1988), are investigated in the fourth chapter. Both toys were made of cardboard and presented the possibility of endless combinations—open-ended play with abstract, colorful, and lightweight structures.

Like Froebel's Gifts, all construction sets designed between 1836 and 1952—a period of increasing industrialization and mass production—could be taken apart, disassembled, combined, and then recombined. And just as the Gifts were innovative for their time, the other sets, too, stood out among contemporary toys in their form and novel use of materials. The toy designers came from diverse fields—mineralogy, mechanical engineering, aeronautics, business, and architecture—yet all chose to impart object lessons to children through building. All these toys became widely known, either through educators and their writings or through commercial advertisements, and were readily available to the general population. Manufactured for many years, each became the quintessential toy of its generation. House of Cards is still being manufactured today just as it was designed in 1952, the year of its creation.

Josef Hoffmann, the Viennese Secession architect, designed Fabrik (Factory) in 1920 (fig. 1). Rectilinear blocks, painted gray and black and gridded with windows all around, together with narrow arcades and two chimneys located this small factory in the realm of industry. The little flowers painted in a regular pattern on the box and on the blocks confirm Hoffmann's shift in interest from the arts and crafts and manual fabrication to industrial production. Another toy, Dandanah, The Fairy Palace, was designed by the architect Bruno Taut in 1921 and comprised sixty-two glass blocks: cobalt-blue glass columns, red and yellow

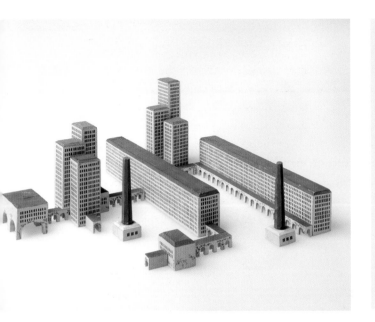 

Fig. 1. Fabrik (Factory) with box cover, Josef Franz Maria Hoffmann,
manufactured by Wiener Werkstätte (Vienna), ca. 1920, painted wood.

glass spheres, small green and orange cubes, and other clear, gem-cut glowing
stones (fig. 2). Akin to jewels, the blocks appeared like precious stones embodying
the fantastic potential of crystalline configurations, reminiscent of Taut's drawings in *Alpine Architecture* (1919) and the colorful fantasies of the Crystal Chain
(1919–21), the illustrated correspondence among architects and artists solicited
by Taut and dedicated to advancing architecture through crystal and glass ico-
nography.[10] To anyone who wished to play, the set suggested the use of crystals as
building forms and exemplified Taut's prophecy of an architecture made of glass.
These two sets were never intended for a large distribution—only one Fabrik
was ever made, and Dandanah was manufactured in a small edition—seeming
rather like an afterthought, as if revealing a bee in the bonnet of their makers.[11]

Lincoln Logs were designed in 1917 by the architect John Lloyd Wright, Frank
Lloyd Wright's son; yet the set bore no relation to the aesthetic philosophy of its
designer (fig. 3). This set comprised miniature wooden logs that were notched at
their corners and combined to form over and over again one American log cabin.

Fig. 2. Dandanah,
The Fairy Palace with
box and instruction
manual, Bruno Taut,
manufacturer unknown,
1919, colored cast-glass.

Lincoln Logs found great appeal with the general public—perhaps specifically because of the simplicity of combination and the vernacular architecture it portrayed—and prevailed as one of the most popular construction sets ever since its initial production.

Dollhouses—playful architectural environments—offer "large" interior spaces in which to play with miniature domestic artifacts and objects. Dollhouses, however, do not present a system of construction, as they cannot be dismantled and play with them focuses on domestic activities rather than on "building." Neither dollhouses nor souvenir buildings are investigated in this study. Souvenir buildings became popular in the nineteenth century with the rise of tourism and before the advent of photography. As miniature mnemonic devices, they could be easily taken from any memorable site and carried away in one's pocket. As playful as the souvenir houses seem, they commemorate existing structures and as such are meant to be held, contemplated, and collected rather than manipulated and dismantled. Architectural models, on the other hand, are constructed at different stages of design, then taken apart, rebuilt, and reworked numerous times. Even in this digital age, they provide helpful means to envision larger projects. Although their making and appearance can be playful, they are not examined in this book either—in the hands of architects, models are tools

Fig. 3. Lincoln Logs, John Lloyd Wright, manufactured by J. L. Wright Incorporated (Chicago), ca. 1930, patented 1920, stained wood and cloth tape.

rather than objects of play designed for children. Overall in this work, I consider construction toys to be playful kits consisting of individual parts that can assemble into something larger and architectural. And while some computer games allow the construction of virtual structures on the screen, I deem manual manipulation to be a defining aspect of the building toy. Artistic and playful practices, such as origami, also entail manipulating and building by hand, but the focus in this book is on a physical kit of parts with a set of elementary rules, which an inventive user could arrange and rearrange to create an architectural form.

In 1928, Walter Benjamin wrote a review of the book *Children's Toys of Bygone Days* by Karl Gröber, published that year. Impressed by the toy's transmission of history, Benjamin wrote: "The perceptual world of the child is influenced at every point by traces of the older generation and has to take issue with them."[12] And indeed, the technological and structural developments of the latter part of the nineteenth century manifested themselves in play and in miniature form on the early-twentieth-century living-room floor. While architectonic ideas, scientific thought, innovative materials, and new means of production have informed the building sets, changing ideas of play and education have also led, across time, to transformations of the blocks. In accordance, two main frames of reference provide the context of this investigation: evolving architecture and technology from 1836 to 1952, and changing notions of play during the same period, notions that are in play with each toy and that change with every generation.

Following the Enlightenment and fuelled by rapid political, economic, and cultural changes during the nineteenth century, architecture became a ground for daring experimentation. Its relation to the past was constantly questioned and debated, its "styles" were probed in a scientific manner, and competing visions sought to respond to the challenges of a rapidly changing world. Such was the architectural climate surrounding Froebel's opening of the first kindergarten and his invention of the Gifts. Further industrialization and emerging technological and artistic interests affected the urban landscape—as well as all walks of life—and contributed to the development of unprecedented public structures, which were paralleled in the world of play and mimicked by building toys such as the Anker- Steinbaukasten. By the dawn of the twentieth century, greater ease of travel and emerging notions of leisure further transformed the built environment—with the introduction of such means of transportation as trains, ships, and airplanes. Toys echoed these technological inventions—although not with quite the same tempo—through material changes and the inclusion of small motors. Meccano and Erector Set testified to the enthusiastic acceptance of these technological changes. Calling for the unity of aesthetic standards, the Modern movement looked toward a new architectural future while seeking to eradicate the past. Following World War II, however, these universals established by modernist architects were again questioned, and in the hands of designers, toys, too, became tools for demolishing the established rational precepts and formal absolutes. The toys designed by Charles and Ray Eames in the early 1950s thus reflected this new formal richness. Hence, in the span of a century, building blocks came to reflect the changes in the built world and became a means to experiment with educational and technological principles: architectural toys have embodied the intersection between pedagogy and means of production.

During the nineteenth and early twentieth centuries, the design of toys also went through drastic transformations. Before the mid-nineteenth century, all toys were produced by the handicraft industry. Since at the time the different crafts were segregated by guilds and strict regulations, each toy was manufactured based on its specific material and fabrication. The woodworkers made blocks and carved wooden figurines, and the candle makers made wax dolls: the toy was often a by-product made from the residual materials of the production process. There was thus a close link between contemporary technological processes and the material composition of toys. The shop was adjoining the home, and with no kindergartens yet existing, the child was present at the production sites of toys.[13] Later, fewer restrictions on the division of labor and the advent of industrialization allowed for new ventures to form specifically for toy making, which in turn enabled the fabrication of toys that incorporated a range of materials and different methods of manufacture. Thus, whereas earlier toys, made of leftover materials, represented the child's isolated and marginal status, a change occurred when toy design and manufacture became an independent industry, paralleling the fact that children were now acknowledged as a distinct social group. With the advent of pedagogical theories in the late eighteenth century, childhood was recognized as a paramount phase in life, and children were accepted as a vital force for the future of society.

The choice of case studies also reflects the centers of world toy production. Leading up to the twentieth century, Germany was the largest exporter of toys, due to the availability of wood from the Erzgebirge mountain area. Following the defeat of Germany in World War I and the rise of industrialization and mass production, the center of toy production shifted to the United States. Although my focus on German and American toys was not motivated by these economic and commercial factors, it certainly reflects them.

Notions of play, too, like the design of toys, changed with time; and while some universal themes unite all play, different concepts of play have altered the nature and design of toys. The changing understanding of play has affected toys in general and more particularly the ways architectural toys have articulated and transformed the built world.

Play belongs in the category of "tacit knowledge." It elicits a response that is at once immediate, intuitive, and universally understood. Furthermore, the nature of play, which involves competing aspects of reality and fantasy as well as truth and illusion, allows for diverging definitions of the concept. It is precisely this immediate yet ambiguous nature of the concept of play that has enabled old definitions to be actual and relevant, and that has allowed play to retain a major role in contemporary thought. During the twentieth century, the play discourse spread to many disciplines, including biology, anthropology, sociology, psychology, education, economics, political science, cybernetics, physics, and mathematics. Moreover, play is now understood to function differently in different cultures and different historical contexts; it is no longer considered a universal phenomenon. In architecture, the discourse on play has been limited, but it is an emerging topic of investigation.[14]

Play was acknowledged as an important part of education for the first time in *Émile* (1762) by Jean-Jacques Rousseau (1712–1778); the freedom afforded by play could release the potential of children, Rousseau theorized. Play resurfaced as an explicit philosophical topic with the rise of German idealism. At the end of the eighteenth century and in the wake of the Enlightenment, Friedrich Schiller (1759–1805) introduced play as part of a rational mentality that opposed prerational notions of play as defined by Plato, based predominantly in games of power and competition. Schiller linked art and aesthetics with nonviolent rational play concepts.[15] That moment, marking the beginning of the modern understanding of play, corresponds to the period in which toys were first designed with pedagogic intention. Since play was associated for the first time with education, it gradually acquired permissibility and thus concrete form. Following that defining moment, the design of toys in general, and of architectural toys in particular, could be illuminated by theories of play. For the first time in 1836, Froebel's Gifts concretized a pedagogy that provided tools to understand the natural and built worlds. Whereas the other architectural toys presented in this book did not embody a pedagogical theory as precise as Froebel's, their manipulation nevertheless was intended to impart concrete object lessons to children during a time in which play became increasingly recognized as central in education. Throughout the years, these toys—each with its own goal and instructive purpose—allowed children to handle, and learn from, small pieces of the real world.

Only in the mid-twentieth century have historians and philosophers defined the characteristics that unite all play. *Homo Ludens: A Study of the Play Element in Culture* (1938) by the Dutch historian Johan Huizinga and *Man, Play and Games* (1958) by the French sociologist and philosopher Roger Caillois have provided a historical overview and sociological perspective that form the foundation for all subsequent elucidation of the play concept.

Huizinga demonstrated that play was a foremost factor in life and culture, and as such he designated man as a player, just as man was a doer or a thinker. Huizinga studied the play of different periods and civilizations, and in *Homo Ludens* he defined the important characteristics that distinguished play from the rest of life's acts. First and foremost, Huizinga wrote, to constitute play an activity could not be imposed but must be voluntary. As such, the main trait of play is that it is superfluous and free: play in fact embodies freedom. Furthermore, play presents "a stepping out of 'real' life into a temporary sphere of activity with a disposition all of its own."[16] It is secluded and limited, both in terms of space and time: "Play is distinct from 'ordinary' life, both as to locality and duration,"[17] as it takes place in a playground that physically demarcates the space of play. Inside its borders, the rules of the game hold. Within this playground, Huizinga explained, extreme order rules, and "the least deviation from it 'spoils the game.'"[18] Thus, just as any other act of play, building with blocks could be described as "a free activity standing quite consciously outside 'ordinary' life, as being 'not serious,' but at the same time absorbing the player intensely and utterly."[19]

Whereas Huizinga studied the qualities common to all play, Caillois, in *Man, Play and Games,* set out to classify the characteristics of different games and define their cultural significance. Caillois named four main kinds of play—*agôn, alea, mimicry,* and *ilinx*—depending on the aspect of the game that was most dominant: competition, chance, simulation, and vertigo, respectively.

Although mimicry includes all games of make-believe, it is the kind of play that is most readily carried out with construction toys. "For children, the aim is to imitate adults," Caillois wrote; "this explains the success of the toy weapons and miniatures, which copy the tools, engines arms and machines used by adults. . . . Acts of mimicry tend to cross the border between childhood and adulthood."[20] But as children immerse themselves in an imaginary world, mimicry alone cannot describe play with building toys. Agôn, which stands for the kind of play that is competitive in nature and is usually seen in sports, also exists in games exercising memory skills and ingenuity. "The practice of *agôn,*" Caillois wrote, "presupposes sustained attention, appropriate training, assiduous application and the desire to win."[21] Thus agôn, which usually implies rivalry between two players, also represents a competition of the self with cultural norms. The acts involved in playful constructions—tasks requiring manual dexterity and patient perseverance—thus present "the conflict . . . with the obstacle," and as Caillois explains, the influence of agôn is again necessary to act as catalyst for one's repetitive endeavors, to surpass oneself in the self-imposed obstacle.[22] Furthermore, Caillois continues, there is a "subtle complicity" between competition and mimicry. Just as in sports where "for non-participants, every *agôn* is a spectacle,"[23] the building of a miniature skyscraper is an act of mimicry that becomes a small feat of prowess and a spectacle for the young builder, who proudly shows his construction to the adults.

In addition, Caillois explained, in each of the four categories of play the different acts could be placed along a continuum, one side of which would represent carefree, uncontrolled exuberance that Caillois termed *paidia,* while the inverse tendency, *ludus,* represented play with binding rules, play requiring patience, skills, and application.

Involving both mimicry and agôn, play with construction sets could thus be mapped along the paidia-ludus continuum as well; between play with rules and imperatives and unruly acts of play. Play with construction toys is naturally aligned with ludus as "it provides an occasion for training and normally leads to the acquisition of a special skill,"[24] Caillois writes, "requiring application . . . and reflecting the moral and intellectual values of a culture."[25] Furthermore, he adds, "*ludus* is also readily compatible with *mimicry,*" as "in the simplest cases it lends aspects of illusion to construction games such as . . . the cranes or automobiles constructed by fitting together perforated steel parts and pullies from an Erector set, or the scale-model planes or ships that even adults do not disdain meticulously constructing."[26] But great pleasure in play could also be attained through paidia—the unruly act—since following precise instructions for hours in a miniature building task would be no fun. And so, after long and painstaking acts of building with construction toys, paidia could come into play and would present what Caillois termed the "primitive joy in destruction."[27] In a short and powerful destructive act, one could knock a "building" down and break it apart.

An extension of these acts of play, toys have constituted an integral part of our lives. Yet surprisingly little literature has been devoted to these familiar objects. Books about toys are largely comprised of anthropological studies based in socioeconomic research exposing a variety of play cultures in different geographical regions. Accounts of play sessions with toys have also proliferated in psychological studies, attesting to gender differences, learning abilities, pedagogical achievements, and more. Other books about toys as memorabilia or collectibles, which were published as aids for avid collectors by other collectors, abound in manufacturing details and technical information but fail to provide a critical historical overview. Altogether, studies about the design of toys have related them to other "material objects of childhood"—the furniture, play rooms, and play equipment that were of interest to architects. The studies focusing on construction toys, however, consisted primarily of observations based in educational and psychological practice.[28]

Lately, aspects of play in architecture have mainly been ascribed to computer games, engendering a myriad of studies about the nature of the "space" of games and the space of play. Rarely illustrated, those texts expose complicated chains of events based in a theory.[29] No study, in fact, has looked at the space of construction toys. In an architectural world so immersed in digital production, the act of playing with miniature parts—until recently the only means to model space—deserves our attention. Architectural toys have not yet been completely relegated to museums, hobbyists, and collectors. It is an opportune time to recognize their place in our culture—lest they be lost, they should now be appreciated and recorded.

Altogether, the few histories of toys that were written throughout the twentieth century pale in comparison to the colorful artifacts themselves and the animated sessions of play they inspire. How to describe the invention and manufacture of toys and simultaneously to relate the use of an object whose key features were to elicit amusement and fun has seemed to elude most history writers.[30] In contrast to those books, a few short essays written by authors and philosophers in the span of one hundred years have addressed issues common to all toys and have conveyed the childlike enthusiasm one experiences with the playful artifacts, as well as the universal fascination that toys elicit. And while throughout this book the different theories of play relevant to each period are addressed in relation to each toy, the concluding chapter addresses literary writings as well as aspects of play relevant to all architectural toys.

These short writings—by Baudelaire, Benjamin, and Barthes, among others—reveal the artifacts with the excitement and freshness of a session of play, and while a similar approach may be difficult to sustain in a formal and cultural analysis of toys, this study nevertheless attempts to embrace the attitude of discovery and surprise that has prevailed in those literary pieces. Each chapter in this book takes as a starting point the physical object—the toy. And while handling small elements taken from disparate wholes, assembling lightweight materials to make temporary constructions, and dismantling and breaking down are aspects of play with all of the toys discussed here, each case study has called for a different exploration. Each chapter attempts to uncover the inventor's original intentions in designing the toys and considers the reception of the toys in the first few years following their invention, during which they can be seen as actively playing out contemporary theories of play and architecture. Some of those intentions have been clearly stated, as in the case of Friedrich Froebel, who explicitly described his philosophy of play and education and precisely prescribed how to handle his blocks. In other cases, when toy designers have left no clear testimony, I follow different avenues to investigate the toys, trying to trace the motivations that have led to their creation. The toy is then seen to act as the repository of the interests and concerns of its inventor.

In the case of Anchor Blocks, the varied interests of the Lilienthal brothers have helped construct a worldview that has encompassed endeavors as disparate as flight and cooperative living. In the case of Meccano and Erector Set, whose inventors were mainly interested in business—Alfred C. Gilbert, for example, explicitly shunned books and libraries—I have related the toys, their instruction manuals, and advertisements as closely as possible to the then current technological culture and pedagogical climate. As for the toys designed by Charles and Ray Eames, it was again possible to rely on writings by the designers themselves as well as those by contemporary journalists and critics. Media, in the case of these last toys, became a player, as Charles and Ray Eames were very conscious of the image that their toys, or any work of theirs, projected. All in all, I attempt to trace the toy designers' motivations for placing architecture in the hands of children. As if in a session of play, I free-associate between cultural currents and design ideas that are contemporary with the toy's production, and relate the objectives of the toy with current theories of play and pedagogy. Implicit intentions are then uncovered by interweaving technological progress, pedagogical theories, and educational development. Each chapter presents a particular relationship between the toy, play, and the environment and uncovers singular relations between educational theories and means of production. The only rule I have followed in this study is that all associations are contemporary with the toy's inception. No theory is applied to the toy's reading that has temporally succeeded its invention.

This book is based on my study of many architectural toys, the physical objects at the archives of the Canadian Centre for Architecture (CCA) in Montreal. Since its founding in 1979, the CCA has gradually acquired a large collection of architectural toys that to date includes close to one thousand artifacts made from the eighteenth century to the present. During the 1990s, a series of exhibits entitled *Toys That Teach, Buildings in Boxes, Toys and the Modernist Tradition,* and *Toys and Transport* showcased toys from the collection according to different themes. Detailed cataloguing situated the toys historically and geographically with a precision that set an example for future exhibitions of toy collections.[31] Profusely illustrated catalogues accompanied each exhibit, with essays that focused on the related topics. For the first time since addressing the impact of Froebel's Gifts, architectural historians looked at the intersection of building toys and architecture. Clearly lacking a tradition of such writings, the essays in each exhibition booklet addressed the different artifacts—Bauhaus toys, pink Lego castles, or stereometric blocks—in relation to a relevant context, be it the modernist tradition, gender issues in architecture, or the study of drawing and mathematics. Read individually or in sequence, these writings have not looked at the building toy in relation to architecture over time and with a historical perspective.

At the CCA, handling numerous kits of parts of a variety of materials and forms starting with a toy of 1785, I was able to pinpoint the crucial moments of invention that have encapsulated both novelty in play and a clear interplay with architectural developments—moments that seemed most relevant for a first comprehensive study of this nature.[32] With four different materials—wood, stone, metal, and paper echoing construction with wood, masonry, steel skeletons, and light transportable structures—all four case studies reflect contemporary concerns and changing attitudes toward form, structure, and permanence. I manipulated, played with, and studied the physical objects, and from them all associations—cultural, technological, and material—ensued. Each of the chapters has a distinct structure, presenting a full description and history of each toy and then analyzing the several related discourses that have contributed to the toy's production and design, such as crystallography, aeronautics, and history of technology. In each case, I have researched the history of the different scientific and technological discourses at the time of the toy's inception, at different archives in the United States and Germany, and brought original material to highlight the specific aspects from those discourses that had an impact on the philosophy and practice of the designer.

This study stops short of the advances in plastics that led to the creation of Bayko (made of Bakelite and manufactured in Great Britain in 1934) and Lego (manufactured in Denmark since 1949), which have further altered the world of block building. Lego especially has played an important role in numerous childhoods. The small, plastic shape that connects tightly to another has presented a kind of pixel, a small unit from which entire scenes—people, animals, vehicles, and buildings—could be created. A crucial development during that period was the beginning of television programming for children. In due time, this would contribute to transformations, both in the structure of play and its imaginative content. Deserving a study in their own right, plastic construction toys often mimicked and represented the mediated environment and its characters rather than directly reflecting changes in the built world.

Following a visit to a toy exhibit at the Märkisches Museum in Berlin in 1928, Walter Benjamin wrote that the show included, according to him, "not just 'toys,' in the narrower sense of the word, but also a great many objects on the margins . . . such a profusion of wonderful games, building sets, Christmas pyramids, and peep shows."[33] Given that toys in general and more specifically construction toys have occupied players for hours on end and for generations, their marginalization as objects of study is difficult to comprehend. In this study, these "objects on the margins" become the main players. The different construction toys expose various aspects of the building culture that led to their inception—the forms, materials, and technologies. The chronological exposition of the toys also reveals how the built environment was handled and manipulated, and how acts of "construction," and hence "constructiveness," were valued as educational activities for children. What is the impact of tinkering with morsels of the environment? Does the handling of small parts most readily present a dialogue with historical figures, or could building and demolishing those same small structures instill change and inspire new architectural principles departing from classical orders, including characteristic columns and established proportions? Could models of play with architecture provide an indication of how we have viewed the world?

Although this book does not discuss whether construction toys can, or did, influence one's predilection for architecture and the arts the way Froebel's Gifts are said to have done, the different chapters do assess whether the interplay of architecture and play offers a new worldview. Architectural toys survey the world, classify and divide the environment, and provide tools to re-create its organization. The toys introduced in this book present a preoccupation with architectural history and its representation. In play, parts can be assembled into familiar architectural ensembles, but also into unknown combinations, potential architecture that has yet to happen. So while play involves manipulating historical bits and pieces, and presents materials and technologies not yet implemented in full-scale design, play happens in the present; play takes time here and now.[34]

Altogether, from the mid-nineteenth century to the mid-twentieth century, the period considered in this book, notions of time greatly changed. The pace of life gradually increased, while the experience of time and space shrank. Play with small architectural structures and with miniatures of the environment has always taken a long time, allowing one to experience a time that negates the flow of lived time.[35] Time slows down while one plays with a miniature, and one must have time to access the miniature. As Gaston Bachelard once wrote about engaging in daydreaming: "People who are hurried by the affairs of men will not enter here."[36]

Intimations of modernism can thus be found in a series of building toys. Lightness of building materials, repetitive parts, modularity, accelerated speeds of construction, and greater versatility—these are all aspects of "progress" that the sets embody. But the toys also embody iterations and repetitions of past forms. It is the simultaneous play with history and with notions of progress that the architectural toy enables—touching, handling morsels of architecture, and imagining new environments. It is as if through acts of play, conventions of architecture, building, and construction can be overturned, taken apart, and deconstructed.

Detail of fig. 22. (See p. 50.)

Kindergarten Gifts, circa 1836

Ironically, the Kindergarten Verbot—a decree issued by the Prussian government in 1851 that called for the closing of all Froebelian kindergartens—was instrumental in propagating these progressive educational institutions outside of Prussia during the 1860s. The kindergarten's inventor, Friedrich Froebel (1782–1852), had trained numerous teachers in the tenets of his progressive educational system, mainly women who, following the decree, became unemployed. Still committed to the mission of their teacher, they sought work in other countries, thereby disseminating Froebel's method. By 1851, a Froebelian kindergarten had opened in London. It was followed by kindergartens in Italy, the United States, Russia, Ireland, and Canada; by 1876, a Froebelian kindergarten had even opened in Japan.

In the United States, a series of opportune events precipitated the spread of the kindergarten system. The German émigré Edward Wiebé wrote the first English-language kindergarten manual based on numerous conversations he had had with Froebel's widow, with whom he was acquainted, prior to his move to Springfield, Massachusetts. He had tried to arouse the interest of his neighbor Milton Bradley (1836–1911) in this kindergarten material but with no success.[1] Bradley, the head of a factory that produced children's games, subsequently heard the American educator Elizabeth Peabody (1804–1894), who had opened the first English-language kindergarten in the United States in 1860, lecture enthusiastically about her discovery in Germany of Froebel's early childhood educational practices. From that moment on, Bradley dedicated his entire enterprise to the manufacture of educational toys based on the Froebelian system. When the Gifts and Occupations—Froebel's innovative object lessons—were officially presented at the 1876 Centennial Exhibition in Philadelphia, classes had been taught with the kindergarten material for more than ten years.

Froebel's progressive educational system was distinguished not only by its intrinsic educational methods but also by the physical setting it required. The dedication of a space apart, which was to house large tables whose slate surface was inscribed with a one-inch grid, and the provision of ample room for each child to work were revolutionary during a time when many children still spent their days working shifts in factories alongside adults. Those children who received formal instruction were frequently subjected to harsh disciplinary measures and tedious lessons consisting largely of rote memorization. Froebel's system of education, whereby the children occupied themselves analyzing, constructing, and making, offered something radically different. Despite its humanitarian outlook, Froebel's system had no root in religion proper. To some, if only because it did not mention the church in its curriculum and teachings, Froebel's system seemed to promote atheism. As a result, the kindergartens were fiercely opposed by the church, which eventually led in 1851 to their closing in Prussia.

Froebel insisted that children of all religions and economic backgrounds should benefit from the kindergarten's education, since without equal opportunity from an early age, humanity could not achieve any kind of progress. He also fought adamantly for the inclusion of both genders in the classroom and for the training of women as kindergarten teachers, and he was ridiculed for this as well: "Does Herr Froebel mean we shall eventually have women university professors?" questioned a (male) participant at a teachers' conference at which Froebel lectured during the 1840s, causing the rest of the assembly to break into uproarious laughter.[2]

Froebel was involved with education for the greater part of his life. He intended to study architecture but took up botany, mineralogy, and mathematics instead. Early in his career he worked as a private tutor and, realizing that education was his vocation, trained in early childhood teaching with the Swiss pedagogue and educational reformer Johann Heinrich Pestalozzi (1746–1827) in Yverdon. He also pursued advanced studies in crystallography—the scientific study of crystals and solid minerals and their geometry—at the University of Göttingen but subsequently returned to teaching, drawing material from his studies to further the education of man. Froebel's aim as a teacher, he explained, was to "give man the means to find himself."[3] He believed that a desire for activity was innate in every child. In 1836, at the age of fifty-four, he created an industrial enterprise called the Institute for the Fostering of the Creative Activity Drive, which manufactured toys. These were the Gifts and Occupations, which provided tools to encourage activity in the child. They represent the synthesis of Froebel's research and study and the culmination of his efforts. Children played with these toys in his Institution for Self-Education, which opened on June 28, 1840, and preceded the founding of Froebel's first kindergarten.[4]

In the kindergarten, the sequence of play began with the introduction of ten consecutive Gifts, so named because they were meant to draw out and develop a child's innate capabilities—his or her natural "gifts." This was followed by the introduction of the ten Occupations, fashioned after common employments of the period (crafts and handiworks), organized in a logical order.

The Gifts consisted of three-dimensional geometrical solids: sphere, cube, and cylinder. They first were presented whole and then were gradually broken down, from a solid to planes to lines and, finally, to points. The ten Occupations were subsequently introduced and used in reconstructing the three-dimensional objects in reverse sequence—from points to lines to planes and, finally, back to a solid. Only after a child became intimately acquainted with a set of relationships and assimilated them did he or she move on to the next, more complex, mathematical and spatial set. The Gifts provided a means for the child to observe and discover relationships between the part and the whole; the Occupations allowed the child to reconstruct "the world" based on these observations, to express the interrelationship of parts, and proceed to his or her own inventing (figs. 4–7).

A Paradise of Childhood: A Manual for Self-Instruction in Friedrich Froebel's Educational Principles, and a Practical Guide for Kinder-gartners, written by Edward Wiebé and originally published by Milton Bradley in 1869, included precise instructions for the use of Froebel's play material, the Gifts, which it labeled briefly as follows:

1. Six rubber balls covered with a net work of twine or worsted of various colors.
2. Sphere, cube and cylinder, made of wood.
3. Large cube, consisting of eight small cubes.

Fig. 4. Kindergarten Gift no. 1, Friedrich Froebel, manufactured
by J. L. Hammett Co., ca. 1898, wool.

4. Large cube, consisting of eight oblong parts.
5. Large cube, consisting of whole, half and quarter cubes.
6. Large cube consisting of doubly divided oblongs.
[The third, fourth, fifth, and sixth gifts serve for building purposes.]
7. Square and triangular tablets for laying of figures.
8. Sticks for laying of figures.
9. Whole and half rings for laying of figures.
10. Material for drawing.[5]

In the process of breaking down the solid to planes, lines, and eventually points, the first six Gifts decomposed into other, smaller solid forms; the seventh Gift was composed of planes, such as those surrounding a cube, whereas the eighth Gift featured lines that delineated the cube's edges. The whole and half rings of the ninth Gift demonstrated that lines could also be curved. Although with the first nine Gifts the children were to delineate form with given geometries, or, as the manual labeled it, "drawing with bodies,"[6] with the tenth Gift—"Material

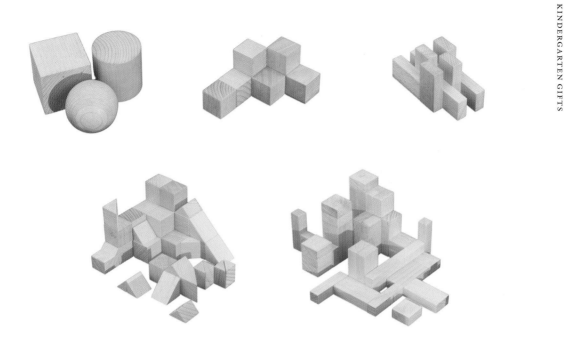

Fig. 5. *Top row from left:* Kindergarten Gifts no. 2, 3, and 4; *bottom row from left:* Gifts no. 5 and 6. Manufactured by Froebel USA, ca. 2000, maple.

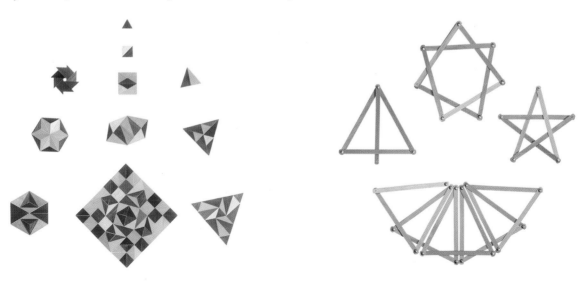

Fig. 6. Kindergarten Gift no. 7 (*left*), manufactured by J. L. Hammett (Boston), ca. 1880, stained wood; and Bradley's Kindergarten Material, Gift no. 16 (*right*), manufactured by Milton Bradley and Co. (Springfield, Mass.), ca. 1880, wood.

for drawing"—they were allowed to draw lines and points by themselves, leading to greater abstraction. Drawing on the "net-work of engraved lines" inscribed on the slate tabletop, Froebel maintained, would reduce the amount of frustration the children would experience before they mastered the task of forming verticals, horizontals, and curves on their own. In addition, executing each exercise on the gridded surface ensured that "everything [would be] done with a great deal of precision": for Froebel, this would impress upon the children the fact that "order and regularity in all the performances are of the utmost importance."[7]

Froebel's Occupations picked up where the Gifts left off. Wiebé's manual listed the Occupations as follows:

11. Material for perforating.
12. Material for embroidering.
13. Material for cutting of paper and combining pieces.
14. Material for braiding (or weaving).
15. Slats for interlacing.
16. The slat with many links.
17. Material for intertwining.
18. Material for paper folding.
19. Material for peas-work.
20. Material for modeling.[8]

The first Occupation emphasized the point. With the introduction of a piece of gridded paper to be pricked by a needle, the kindergarten manual explained, "We have descended to the *smallest part of the whole*—the *extreme limit of mathematical divisibility*."[9] From there the line was reintroduced, and the gridded paper was used for embroidering, to connect the perforated points with lines made of thread. Construction in two dimensions thus progressed from the point to the line and, starting with the thirteenth Occupation, was extended to the plane.

Three-dimensional forms were introduced with "Material for paper folding," the eighteenth Occupation. "Material for peas-work," the nineteenth Occupation, constructed "outline solids"—hollow forms "outlined" by means of sticks (lines) and peas (points), which functioned as joints. As early as 1896, Milton Bradley described those forms in the preface to his edition of *The Paradise of*

Fig. 7. Occupation no. 19, Peas-Work: Compositions of Cork and Wire, ca. 1880.

Childhood as "the forerunners of the wire models now so highly prized by all teachers of drawing, in illustrating the principles of perception."[10] This delineating the edges of three-dimensional forms prepared the way for the last, most difficult task of all, prescribed by the twentieth Occupation: modeling three-dimensional forms freehand, out of clay. Children were instructed at first to produce geometric solids, such as spheres, cones, and cylinders, followed by more complex forms made by combining parts of these regular solids.

Although Froebel employed all twenty Gifts and Occupations in the kindergarten, he described only the first six Gifts at any length: the majority of writing about these materials was done by his followers.[11] Some activities, such as "drawing on a grid" (the tenth Gift) and "perforating" (the eleventh Occupation), were already in use as part of drawing education in Germany during the 1830s; while "weaving" (the fourteenth Occupation) and "interlacing" (the fifteenth Occupation) were common crafts of the period. Froebel's innovation was to introduce these prevailing practices as part of a rational spatial sequence and to teach them to the very young.

The first six Gifts and the rules of play assigned to them embody Froebel's educational logic. Most importantly, no free play was to be allowed in the kindergarten. Froebel believed that by beginning with the simple and progressing to the more complex, the child would understand the relationship between the part and the whole, and thus would be better able to appreciate the unity of all things. "Only that which proceeds from the simplest, smallest, and near can develop from and explain by itself the manifold, great, and distant," Froebel explained.[12] The first six Gifts in particular would demonstrate the essential attributes of nature and would train the child to comprehend an object in its altered states of phenomena, as well as in different positions and arrangements. Through this "dismembering and reconstruction and perception of real objects," Froebel maintained, "true *knowledge of Nature and the outer world,* and (especially) clear *self-knowledge,* early come to the child."[13]

Froebel's first Gift is a ball. It is the beginning of all things, complete in itself and yet exemplifying many things through its geometry: it is one, the point, and the universe. It is representative of "rest and movement, of totality and unity, of that which is all-sided and that which has but one surface. It unites in itself the visible and the invisible (its middle, its axis, etc.)" (fig. 8).[14] Since the ball arouses the child's impulse to activity and brings about a desire for play, it can be given to a six-week-old child, when it will become his connection to the outside world. It can also be used in the kindergarten as an introductory toy to be played with under the guidance of the instructor, since no free play is allowed, even with the ball. Froebel stresses that the ball is "highly important from the intellectual, sentient, and moral side . . . as a moral means of preservation, as a talisman; since by the provision of the ball for free and full use, the child is preserved from ill-humor, and from all the moral diseases which proceed from it."[15] "For the genuine educator," Froebel summarizes, "the ball is just as necessarily given as the first plaything for the child, as the spherical form of the earth is for the first step of the geographer."[16]

The second Gift includes a sphere, a cube, and a cylinder, all made of wood

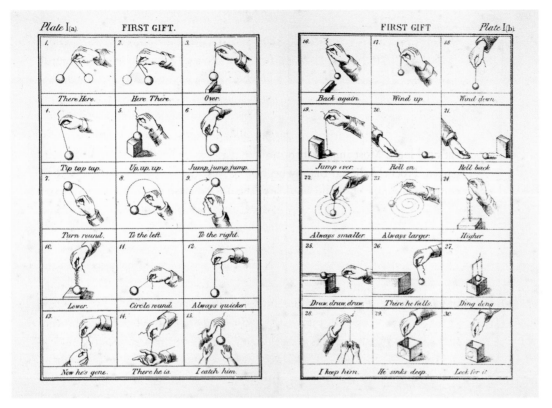

Fig. 8. Suggested exercises with the first Gift. From Johannes Ronge,
A Practical Guide to the English Kinder-garten, 1855.

(fig. 9). This Gift is considered the basis of the kindergarten system, as the forms embody for Froebel both the "Unity of Life," a visible reality capable of being experienced at all times, and the "Law of Opposites"—two of the guiding principles of the educator's pedagogy. The three wooden solids must be presented to the child all at once, but the sphere must be handled by the child first. In contrast with the sphere of the first Gift, which is made of rubber covered with wool, the sphere of the second Gift is hard to the touch. For Froebel, the sphere represents, as no other form can, "the three-fold principle underlying the education of man, i.e. *unity* or completeness; *variety* or all-sidedness, and *individuality* or that which marks the highest development of man."[17] His view of the form is mystical: the sphere has no limits, unites everything, and represents the origin of all diversity. This oneness, however, cannot exist in nature without its

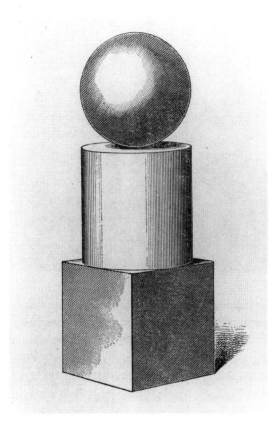

Fig. 9. Kindergarten
Gift no. 2. From
*Steiger's Kindergarten
Catalogue,* 1900.

opposite, as every action creates a reaction: it is this "Law of Opposites" underpinning Froebel's pedagogy that influenced the physical form the Gifts took. Soon after being presented with the sphere, Froebel explains, the child "wishes for, and the nature of the sphere requires, an object which is its pure opposite."[18] This object, Froebel asserts, is "the many-surfaced, many-edged, many-cornered, firmly resting, firmly standing, not easily movable cube, idle, as it were, only able to be shoved and thrown, but incapable of actual rolling."[19] When confronted with the cube, kindergartners are asked to identify first its similarities with the sphere, followed by its differences. The various parts of the solids are named: the edges of the cube are designated as being straight lines, and the faces of the cube as being squares.

In order to maintain the child's interest and force him to mark the contrasts between opposites, teaching had to include an element of surprise. Each successive investigation had to contain an element of change; otherwise, Froebel feared, learning would cease. But that rule, too, called for exceptions. Learning through opposites required a mediator, Froebel thought, since opposites could be reconciled only by finding a third entity that would bridge their differences. The translator and annotator of Froebel's autobiography explained:

> The true synthesis is that springing from the thesis and its opposite, the antithesis. Another type of the formula is this—
> proposition—counterproposition—compromise.
> Understanding by "compromise" (*Vermittlung*) that which results from the union of the two opposites, that which forms part of both and which links them together.[20]

ARCHITECTURE IN PLAY

Thus, "when the wonder and pleasure of the cube have been indulged in long enough," the teacher is to introduce the cylinder, or, "as the children call it, 'the roller,'" which will serve as the mediator between the sphere and the cube (fig. 10).[21] Again, similarities and differences are observed: the cylinder can roll easily, like the sphere, but can also stand firmly on its side, like the cube, "uniting round and straight."[22] Looking at these objects having "properties in common," the child is instructed "to observe how everything can be classified under one of these three forms," so that gradually "out of this feeling develops the perception of unity in the midst of diversity."[23]

All three solids are penetrated by different axes: three axes penetrate the cube (through its diagonal, its face, and its edge); two axes traverse the cylinder (through its base and its side); and a single axis bisects the sphere (through its central axis). Sticks and strings are provided in order to hang or hold the solids

Fig. 10. Kindergarten Gift no. 2, manufactured by Milton Bradley and Co. (Springfield, Mass.), ca. 1870, wood.

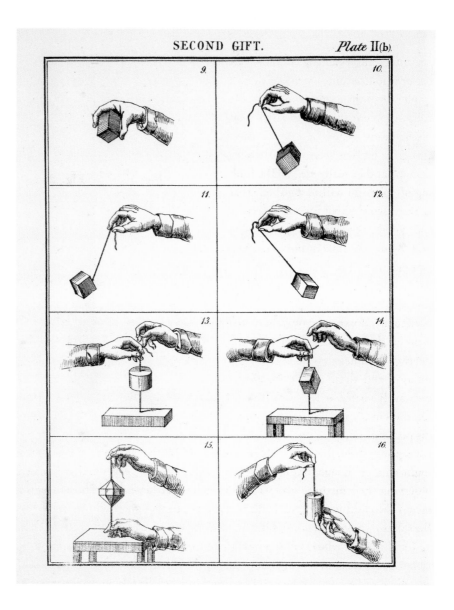

Fig. 11. Suggested exercises with the second Gift. From Ronge, *A Practical Guide to the English Kinder-garten.*

(fig. 11). The "unity of all forms" can then be perceived when the rods provided are inserted through one of the axes in the solids and the form is rapidly revolved. Then, "curious, semi-transparent shapes may be seen which will create an interest in geometrical forms."[24] If the cylinder revolves from the middle of a curved surface, for example, a "ball is seen with a shadowy rim around it." While revolving, the cube seems to change into a cylinder or a double cone; the cylinder, into a sphere within a sphere, or a double cone in a sphere (fig. 12). Through these observations, "the child learns that things in motion seem very different from what they really are."[25] "The finding of one form within another," that is, the discovery that the ball is seen in the cylinder, the cylinder in the cube and the double cone in both the cube and cylinder, "brings out the unity of the second gift."[26] "The invisibly visible lines are here again for the child, in a particularly instructive way," Froebel writes; "the connection between the never visible lines always hidden in the interior, and those which are always outwardly visible as edges."[27] This vision, according to Froebel, is "important for the child's intellectual development, particularly for the development of his power of imagination, and for the development of the inner perception and conception of the invisible."[28] It is the second Gift that Froebel considers most important. Although the solids remain whole and are not yet disassembled, observing their intrinsic geometries intimates a possible future breakdown; it incites the child to imagine the formation of an interior, the inner structure of the solids—the core aspect of subsequent Gifts.

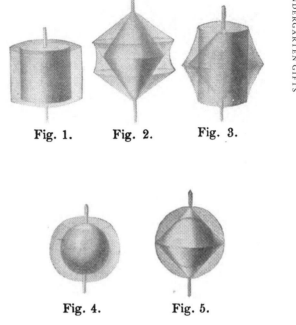

Fig. 1. Fig. 2. Fig. 3.

Fig. 4. Fig. 5.

Fig. 12. Suggested exercises with the second Gift. From Edward Wiebé, *Paradise of Childhood: A Practical Guide to Kindergartners,* 1869.

The third Gift consists of a cube divided into eight small, one-inch cubes (fig. 13 *top*). This toy stands in contrast to the previous undivided solids and responds, according to Froebel, to the child's natural instinct for taking things apart. As with all of the Gifts, a question-and-answer session takes place as the object is introduced:

> The teacher asks:—
> "What do you see now?"
> The answer is . . . "a cube."

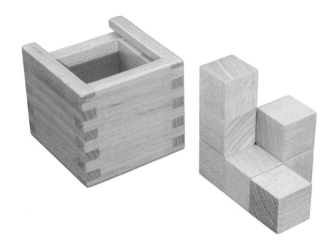

Fig. 13. Kindergarten Gift no. 3, with "Forms of Life" (*left*), "Forms of Knowledge" (*middle*), and "Forms of Beauty" (*right*). From Wiebé, *Paradise of Childhood*.

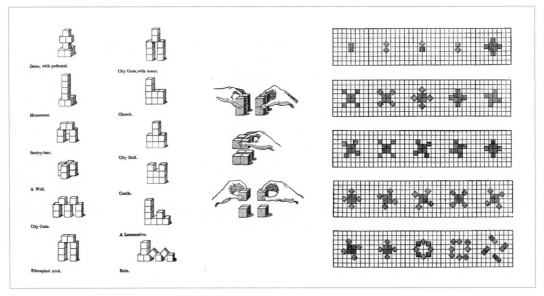

One of the scholars is told to push it across the table. In so doing, the parts will be likely to become separated, and that which was previously whole will lie before them in fragments. The children are permitted to examine the small cubes; and after each one of them has had one in his hand, the eight cubes are returned to the teacher who remarks:—

"Children, as we have broken the thing, we must try to *mend* it. Let us see if we can put it together as it was before."[29]

The kindergarten teachers are told that "the desire to look at the interior of things is the germ of the fullest development, the beginning of the formation of the scientific mind," and that "the best knowledge cannot be attained without division or analysis of a whole. . . . An arbitrary division cannot give clear ideas, so a regular division, according to certain laws is necessary."[30] The third Gift is thus divided once on all sides, into eight equal parts. The child delights, according to Froebel, in the multiplicity of the Gift, the eight parts being smaller but precisely like the whole, which is why he called this Gift "the children's joy."[31]

The third Gift is the first toy used for building purposes. With this Gift and with all the Gifts and Occupations that follow, the children build three types of forms: "Forms of Life," "Forms of Knowledge," and "Forms of Beauty." "Forms of Life" represent "objects which actually *exist,* and which come under our observation as the works of human skill and art," such as a train, a chimney, or a chair (fig. 13 *bottom*).[32] The children are asked to represent things they can observe around them: most typically, man-made objects found at home. In contrast, "Forms of Knowledge" do not represent objects but instead relay different properties and relations of numbers, such as fraction, order, and proportion by the particular arrangements and groupings of the blocks. Through "Forms of Knowledge" the children learn about halves, quarters, and other terms, as these bring "to our *knowledge* the fact that groups or bodies can be looked at and contemplated, first of all, in respect to their *form*, *size* and *position*, but secondly, in respect to their *combination*."[33] "Forms of Beauty" do not represent things like "Forms of Life" do, but they represent, as Froebel explains, "not only something, but something very delightful, without, however, being a something, an object, a thing of outward use in life."[34] "Forms of Beauty" resemble flowers or stars— symmetrical figures that would be "figures representing only *ideal forms,* yet so regularly constructed as to present perfect models of *symmetry* and *order* in the arrangement of the parts."[35] Children are guided by the instructor to create a center point and organize around it the different parts of the form. The child starts with a simple arrangement of blocks and changes it "by means of a fixed law"—a law that states that "every change of position is to be accompanied by a corresponding movement on the opposite side. In this way, symmetrical figures are constructed in infinite variety."[36]

The fourth Gift consists of a cube identical in size to the third Gift. As with that cube, the fourth Gift's cube can be divided into eight equal parts. However, to introduce change these eight parts are rectangular in shape, their "length, breadth and thickness . . . bear[ing] the relations to one another of four, two and one"—the proportions of an ordinary brick (fig. 14 *top*).[37] With these parts, the different compositions may cover a much larger surface and enclose a space much larger than the cubes of the previous Gift. Again, the teachers are asked to "let the scholars compare one of the small cubes of the third gift with one of the oblong blocks . . . not[ing] the similarities and differences." "If they can comprehend that notwithstanding they are so unlike in *form,* their *solid contents* is the same," Wiebé's manual maintains, "an important lesson will have been learned."[38]

Two additional rules are then applied. The first one states that every part of the Gift must be used; "otherwise the material is wasted."[39] Froebel explains, "If all the given material is used the relation of the part to the whole is kept constantly before the mind and eye of the child; each part being of value only as it helps to make the whole complete."[40] The second rule states that "as much as possible the following form must be so developed and shaped from the preceding, that what is already formed must serve in a certain respect as the foundation and means of representation of the following form."[41] With the "Forms of Life," a story is told to accompany play with the forms: for example, a table and two small benches are constructed to provide a place for a family to have dinner; the same elements are then transformed to make two larger benches upon which the family may sit in the yard after dinner, and so on. A gradual transformation of relationships between shapes and sizes should take place among the "Forms of Life," "Forms of Beauty," and "Forms of Knowledge," thereby emphasizing a harmonious disposition of parts (fig. 14 *bottom*).

The fifth Gift consists also of a cube, but one larger than the third and fourth Gifts. Just as the cube of the third Gift is divided once in every direction, the cube of the fifth Gift is divided twice in all directions, creating three tiers of nine squares each, or twenty-seven cubes altogether (fig. 15 *top*). As this division would have only multiplied (rather than diversified) the child's play, Froebel found it necessary to introduce a new element. Thus, he subdivided some of the cubes on the diagonal. Three of the cubes are divided into half cubes, and three others, into quarter cubes, so that altogether the fifth Gift consists of thirty-nine individual pieces. Here, for the first time, the triangle is introduced. The children find it to be "a great treasure for the development of forms," in that it opens up new possibilities for creating combinations, especially with the "Forms of Beauty"

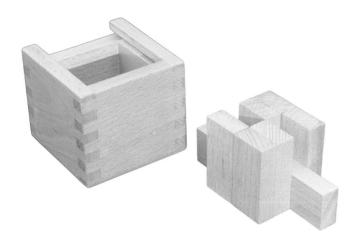

Fig. 14. Kindergarten Gift no. 4, with forms of life, knowledge, and beauty. From Wiebé, *Paradise of Childhood*.

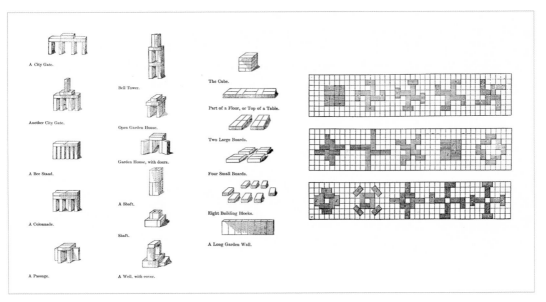

(fig. 15 *bottom*).[42] Froebel focuses great attention here on "answer[ing] the claims of symmetry," noting that children "should again and again be reminded that nothing belonging to a whole is, or could be, allowed to be superfluous, but that each individual part is destined to fill its position actively and effectively in relation to some greater whole."[43] In order to comply with this law, the children are instructed to perform movements with various parts of their forms simultaneously. This would "render more intelligible to the young mind, that real beauty

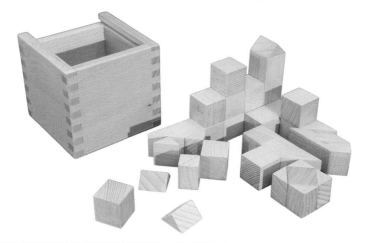

Fig. 15. Kindergarten Gift no. 5, of life, knowledge, and beauty. From Wiebé, *Paradise of Childhood*.

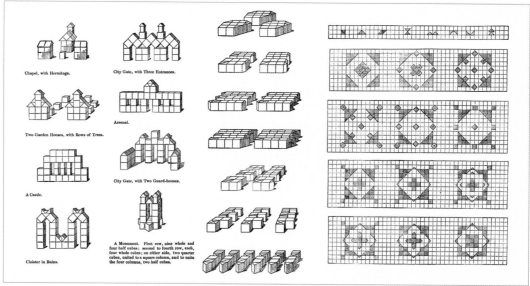

can only be produced when one opposite balances another, if the proportions of all parts were equally regulated by uniting them with one common center."[44] After becoming acquainted with the basic combinations afforded by the new forms of the divided cube, the children compose forms that have both an internal and an external part.

Although all Gifts could make all forms, the fifth Gift, with its triangular, prismatic shapes, lent itself more easily to the constructions of "Forms of Beauty."

Fig. 16. Kindergarten Gift no. 6, with forms of life, knowledge, and beauty. From Wiebé, *Paradise of Childhood.*

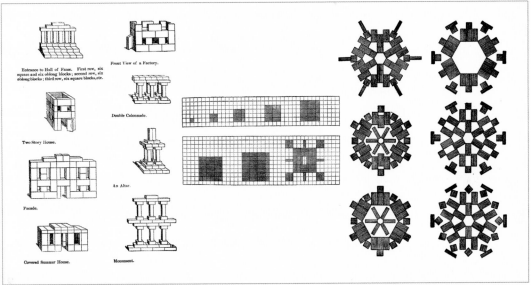

In contrast, the sixth Gift was deemed "more suitable for the construction of life forms than any of the previous ones."[45] A cube the size of the fifth Gift, Froebel's sixth Gift is divided into twenty-seven oblong blocks of the same dimensions as those of the fourth Gift. Of these twenty-seven, eighteen are whole, six are divided into two squares, and three are divided lengthwise to form six columns, resulting in a total of thirty-six individual pieces (fig. 16 *top*). The virtue—or "peculiarity"—of the sixth Gift, according to its creator, is that it enabled the child to represent "hollow spaces and columnar erections" (fig. 16 *bottom*).[46] In this manner, kindergartners begin to accomplish the important task of breaking down the solid into planes and lines, and handling the sixth Gift requires a different, more delicate touch, since the pieces are lighter and create much larger structures that can be easily destroyed. With this Gift, the kindergarten teachers are told: "We reach the end of the two series of development given by Froebel in the building blocks, whose aim is to acquaint the child with the general qualities of the solid body by his own observation and occupation with the same."[47]

When comparing them to other toys of the beginning of the nineteenth century, one is struck by the Gifts' stark geometry. While wooden building toys were prevalent in Germany, never had a toy been thought out so precisely, nor the pedagogy of play been formulated with such great clarity. Other contemporary wooden toys consisted of rough blocks, indeterminate in size or fashioned into more descriptive building elements. Smooth geometrical solids, when used in the classroom, were intended for a much older audience, to support the advanced study of stereometry or crystallography. Froebel's Gifts constituted the first building blocks meant for systematic pedagogical use by a two-year-old child, carried out in a novel kind of setting.

A synchronicity of events—developments in pedagogy and discoveries in science—led to the shaping of the Gifts. Friedrich Schiller's acknowledgment of the paramount importance of play in education contributed to the seriousness with which playing with the Gifts in the kindergarten was taken. The Gifts were made as precisely as tools; indeed, they could be seen as tools for the mind, meant to elicit through play constructs that were as precise as nature's own. They were not considered merely pastimes but rather as aids for developing cognition. The "play impulse" was, according to Schiller, a cognitive faculty of primary importance to the individual, as with it, man could navigate the sea of impressions and sensations, understand them, and make manifest their form. The Gifts thus embodied the "play impulse"—the mediator that bridged the "sense impulse," or life, and the "form impulse," or shape. Froebel's Gifts could be seen as tools to handle sensations perceived in nature and the external world, and through play, the Gifts could help organize and make comprehensible what until then had been only dimly sensed. As Froebel himself explained in *Pedagogics of the Kindergarten:* "The outermost and innermost ground of all phenomena of the earliest life and activity of the child is this: the child must bring into exercise the dim anticipation of conscious life in itself as well as of life around it; and consequently must exercise power, test and thus compare power, exercise independence, and test and thus compare the degree of independence."[48] The mathematically precise correlation of the various Gifts attested to the very specific relationships that Froebel wanted to convey. He was especially impressed in his studies of botany, crystallography, and mathematics by the similarity of and continuity between all phenomena, extending from the vegetal and animal worlds to that of man.[49] The specific organization governing all form (as it was known at the time) should be conveyed, he believed, to the very young.

A contemporary of Froebel's, the German philosopher and educator Friedrich Schelling (1775–1854), attempted to define what he considered to be the eternal, fixed, and unchangeable force of nature—the Absolute—that in the early stages of his thought he called the "World's Soul." There was, according to him, a common foundational force in nature that shaped discrete elements with determined parts. "*In nature,*" Schelling wrote, "*what bears the character of individuality must be an organization,* and vice versa."[50] Formative processes, best represented by crystallization, were examples of individuation and organization of matter. Although each process was propelled by a different set of forces, all were manifestations of "an ideal content that was derived from the Absolute."[51] A variety of different configurations and individual structures existed, yet a similar principle of individuation and organization acted in all of them. Schelling's philosophy of nature was explained in his *Von der Weltseele* (*On the World Soul,* 1798) as follows: "In all life everything that either itself or by the hand of man received a certain figure should be considered an individual. Each solid body, therefore, possessed a kind of individuality, such that each change from a fluid to a solid state was connected with a crystallization, that is, formation with a certain figure."[52] According to Schelling's formulation of the formation of matter, in crystals—so regularly and aesthetically structured—the implications of the "spirit" of nature were most clearly visible.

Froebel's thoughts on the formation of matter closely followed suit. Attempting to grasp the interconnection and unity of all phenomena, the Gifts were to follow the laws of nature. Each figure was to be derived by reciprocal and opposite moves, mutating and taking shape from the preceding form. By instructing young players in the crystallographic rules of polarity and reciprocity in solids, Froebel strived to ingrain in their young minds the inherent structure of all things, which he called the "Unity of Life." The thought of giving children very precise geometrical solids to observe and handle coalesced in Froebel, it seems, as the creator of the kindergarten experienced firsthand the advances in crystallographic studies that were taking place at the time.

It was to study the "Unity of Life"—"the inner law and order embracing all things"—that Froebel enrolled at the University of Göttingen in 1811, where he took courses in natural history, physics, mathematics, and mineralogy.[53] It was clear to him at that time, following the Naturphilosophie movement in Germany, that the natural sciences were the foundation and cornerstone of all life phenomena. In a treatise he wrote that year—*Sphaira*—he "strove to find the basic form which of itself creates an equilibrium within and between everything that exists."[54] He was dissatisfied, however, with the views held at the university regarding "fixed form"—crystallography and mineralogy—and decided in 1812 to move to Berlin to work with Professor Christian Samuel Weiss (1780–1856). The origin of some of the principles (such as the inclusion of opposites and compositional symmetry) that underpin Froebel's rules of play can be traced back to Weiss's innovative contributions to the science of crystals.

Weiss was a medical student at the University of Leipzig, where he received his doctorate in 1800 at the age of twenty. Interested in the sciences, he went on to study mineralogy in Berlin with Dietrich Karsten (1768–1810), Prussia's counselor of mines. It was under his direction that Weiss translated into German Abbé René Just Haüy's *Traité de minéralogie* (Treatise on mineralogy, 1801), a work that represented a major development in the science of crystals.

Prior to Haüy's discovery, a crystal was believed to be composed of identical microscopic particles whose cohesion resulted from an attractive force existing within them. This was the molecular theory of crystalline matter. Microscopic observations revealed that the tiny particles came in a variety of geometric shapes, and the accepted hypothesis was that the particles were superimposed upon each other in a number of different ways. It was Haüy (1743–1822) who developed the mathematical relationships between the variety of crystals and the identical microscopic particles of which they were composed—their constituent forms.

Haüy's structural theory rested on the determination of the shape of the basic building block of different substances. A crystal was mechanically divided, or split, until the resulting geometric configuration remained similar, however small the broken pieces were to get. He called these configurations *constitu-*

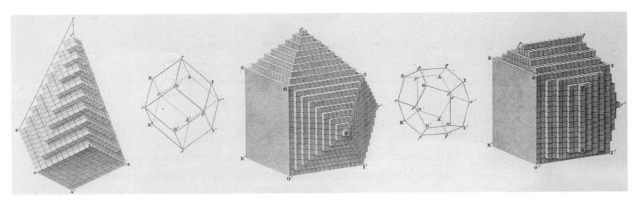

Fig. 17. Abbé René Just Haüy's illustrations showing the construction of a crystal with the Law of Decrement. From René Just Haüy, *Traité de minéralogie*, vol. 5, 1801.

ent molecules (molécules constituantes) and later renamed them *primitive forms (formes primitives)*. He assumed that a crystal was formed from a nucleus in the shape of a primitive form that, together with other primitive forms called *integrant molecules (molécules intégrantes)*, would yield numerous configurations. This construction would follow the Law of Decrement (*décroissement*), which stipulated that every crystal face could be understood as being built upon the nucleus from lamellae of the integrant molecules and decreasing in size according to simple mathematical rules (fig. 17).[55] The starlike shapes produced by his method would not be seen, in reality, because of the microscopic size of the molecules producing the lamellae. He professed that, since nature had formed crystalline matter in accordance with basic principles of arithmetic and geometry, their relationships should be found to be simple. The work of the crystallographer then entailed the determination of the simple mathematical relationships that existed between the primary forms (nuclei and integrant molecules) and the multitude of different crystal formations (the resulting secondary forms). He claimed that the measurements of angles, done until then with the reflecting goniometer, were isolated observations not appropriate for the formulation of a theory. The progress of science entailed the synthesis of theory and observation, aspects that no one, according to Haüy, had previously attempted to bring together.[56]

Haüy believed that his theory of crystalline matter was complete. His system, however, could not explain the geometrical formation of some crystals, among which was the octahedron. When he adjusted his Law of Decrement to include the octahedron, he stated that this concept—of subtractive molecules—was

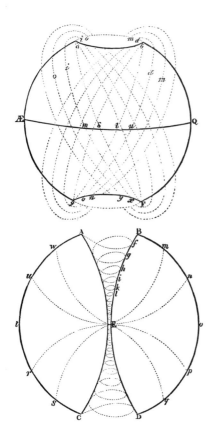

Fig. 18. An "elementary particle" with polar cones, Emanuel Swedenborg.

"designed to have a definite geometrical meaning only and [that] no physical significance should be attached to it."[57] Some of Haüy's students and followers, who best knew his research and its procedures, had qualms about his theory, which seemed quite arbitrary. Its mathematical simplicity and the discrepancies between his calculations and the goniometer's findings led to the system becoming discredited.

Weiss worked with Haüy in Paris in 1808 and thus was familiar with his research. Weiss's own work advanced the understanding of crystals through the analysis of their external symmetry, which in turn was believed to reflect the crystals' internal order. Understanding crystals through their external symmetry resulted from viewing the structure of matter from the polar rather than from the molecular point of view. According to the polar theory, the structure of matter was understood in terms of "dynamic forces of attraction and repulsion inhering in poles."[58] Immanuel Kant (1724–1804) and Schelling, whose works greatly influenced Weiss, adhered to the polar theory of matter.

Kant referred to the polar theory in his "dynamical explication of the concept of matter."[59] According to him, "matter is divisible to infinity, and indeed into parts each of which is again matter."[60] Such matter is impenetrable as "the consequence of repulsive forces of each point in a space filled with that matter."[61] However, such matter requires a force of attraction; otherwise "matter by its repulsive force alone . . . would disperse itself to infinity [and] all space would be empty."[62] According to Kant, the polar concept of matter arises because "forces which are opposed to the extensive ones, i.e., compressive forces, are required for the existence of all matter."[63] Without these two forces—repulsion and attraction—no matter would be possible. Viewing matter by way of opposing forces counteracted the assumption of basic bodies of a determined figure, an assumption that was a fundamental premise of the molecular theory of matter (fig. 18). It is with the polar viewpoint that Weiss revised Haüy's work and provided a radical novel concept of crystal classification.

It was during his years at the University of Leipzig, between 1796 and 1798, that Schelling wrote *Ideas for a Philosophy of Nature* (1797) and *On the World Soul* (1798). In both books, Schelling expounded his dynamic conception of nature that included the polar concept of matter. In *On the World Soul,* he wrote: "It is the first principle of a philosophical doctrine of nature *to go in search of polarity and dualism throughout all nature.*"[64] Following Kant's dynamic construction of matter, he argued that matter that appeared inert was in fact in equilibrium of forces that stood in polar opposites to one another: "Matter and bodies . . . are themselves nothing but products of opposing forces, or rather are themselves nothing else but these forces."[65] Therefore, "attractive and repulsive forces constitute the *essence* of matter itself."[66] He was critical of Haüy's formulation of primitive forms since, according to him, it could not be proven that such a form was the most basic and not in itself a crystallization of some other, earlier matter: "All crystallizations [in Haüy's understanding] are to be regarded as secondary formations, which arise from the various aggregations of unalterable primitive forms, because such a derivation does allow mathematical construction; yet, this is merely a clever game, because it can in no way be proved that so simple a form is itself not secondary."[67]

Weiss was a medical student at the University of Leipzig during Schelling's years there. They became friends, and Weiss became greatly influenced by Schelling's ideas of nature. It is with these views of natural science in mind that Weiss proceeded to translate Haüy's *Traité de minéralogie.* At the end of the translation, published in 1804, he included an article of his own entitled "The Dynamic Conception of Crystallization." Referring to the thought of Kant and Schelling, he explained how crystallization could be described based on the polar theory of matter. According to Weiss, only poles existed in an absolute manner—not matter. Poles sustained their existence only because repulsive forces separated one pole from another. Different crystals resulted from the interpenetration of two or more poles, and during the crystallization process, the different poles constituting the matter in question were restrained in varying degrees. Attractive forces worked against repulsive forces, causing some poles to shorten and others to even unite. The directionality and strength of the different sets of poles resulted in the solidification of faces at specific angles to one another.[68]

Although it was criticized at the time of publication, Weiss's theory was truly innovative. It did not involve primitive forms since, following Schelling, he believed those to be secondary. It did not involve integrant molecules, either,

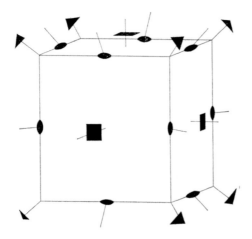 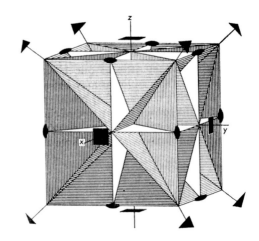

Fig. 19. The thirteen axes of symmetry shown by a cube (*left*) and the crystallographic axes of a class m3m crystal (*right*). From F. C. Phillips, *An Introduction to Crystallography*, 1971.

which assumed a microscopic, starlike structure on the face of the crystal. His theory introduced "directionality" in the analysis of the crystal, and it is this vectorial quality of crystallization that led him to develop the different axes of crystal symmetry (fig. 19).[69] In his dissertation, *De indagando formarum crystallinarum charactere geometrico principali* (Dissertation on the determination of the geometrical character of the principal crystalline forms), Weiss delineated the concept of crystallographic axes and the relationship of the different faces of the crystals to them.[70] Every crystal, he wrote, had an axis that was its principal dominating direction, but some crystals, like the cube, had three such axes, giving those crystals a higher degree of regularity. Weiss classified all crystals according to their number of axes, their angular relation, and their proportional length. Based on the number of axes and their relations, he identified different crystal symmetry systems. The cube and the octahedron, which Haüy could not classify, Weiss identified as belonging to the system he called "spherohedral" in light of his reliance upon spherical trigonometry to analyze these structures. He also listed and classified many previously "problematic" minerals: still in use today, his classifications are considered correct by modern standards. In contrast with Haüy, who disassociated geometrical findings and physical significance, Weiss thought that the symmetrical systems he proposed were not geometrical constructs alone but natural divisions, reflective of the forces producing the crystals and relating to the refractive qualities of matter.

Froebel was Weiss's assistant at Berlin's Mineralogical Museum between 1810

Fig. 20. Johann Heinrich
Pestalozzi teaching a large
group of orphans to draw.

and 1812, during the time that Weiss made his important discoveries. The Gifts reflect Froebel's desire to impart the existence of polar forces and symmetrical formations in nature to kindergartners, not in order to teach them specific scientific principles, but to show them what he termed the "Unity of Life"—the inherent structure of all things. Scientific laws were relayed through the systemic rules of handling the "Forms of Life, Beauty, and Knowledge." The way Froebel chose to convey this knowledge to kindergartners was through the observation and manipulation of abstract objects, broken down slowly, in incremental stages.

It was Johann Heinrich Pestalozzi (1746–1827) who introduced the observation of primary forms and their breakdown into elementary parts as a pedagogical tool for the instruction of the very young, and it was during his stay with Pestalozzi in Yverdon, between 1808 and 1810, that Froebel determined to make parts of Pestalozzi's method his own. It was not until the beginning of the nineteenth century that the potential of drawing as a subject in the general school curriculum was recognized. Pestalozzi instituted pedagogical drawing, claiming that drawing was essential for the growth of every child, that it should be granted equality with other subjects in the elementary school, and that it could be taught simultaneously to a large group of children (fig. 20). Although Jean-

Jacques Rousseau and, before him, the Moravian educational reformer Johann Comenius (1592–1670) had recommended the inclusion of drawing, it had never been developed as a full-fledged subject. When drawing was taught, it was usually in a studio on a one-on-one basis, with the methods of instruction mostly involving copying.

To communicate his method, Pestalozzi, together with his assistant Christoff Büss (b. 1776), prepared an elementary drawing manual. Published in 1803, *ABC der Anschauung* could be best translated as "An ABC of Observation [or 'of Sensory Impression' or 'of Sensory Intuition']."[71] The basis for drawing, according to Pestalozzi, was precision of observation. Looking at nature, the child was confronted with a multitude of objects. The role of the teacher was to "elementarize" those objects for the pupil, that is, to break down nature into its constituent forms. Only through such simplification would children be able to assimilate all that was in front of them and become alerted to the concepts of unity, plurality, and number.[72] The fundamental means of teaching these concepts was the straight line, and drawing simple forms derived from it, such as the square, was rehearsed. The square was the foundation of all forms; Pestalozzi based his entire drawing method upon its division into parts. All formal relations were reduced to comparisons of straight lines, whose proportions were to be gauged by eye (fig. 21). The children were to draw "a series of measured subdivisions of the square . . . arranged according to simple, safe and clear rules, and include the sum total of all possible sense impressions."[73]

Drawing instruments were forbidden by Pestalozzi, and only through constant repetition was perfection to be achieved. The children were not permitted to draw anything that did not consist of simple lines and curves but were encouraged to draw the lines they had rehearsed freely. Every drawing was erased, with a new one begun in its place. All was to be accompanied by simultaneous verbal exclamations: "I draw a horizontal line," the pupils would chant. Deliberate mistakes on the part of the teacher were designed to elicit shouts from the children: "No, No that can't be!"[74] "It is unbelievable," Pestalozzi wrote, "how this freedom within the limitations of the use of their imagination instills at the earliest age simplicity, order and taste, sharpens the ability to gauge by eye (*Augenmass*), and lays into their hands quite early a high level of executive skill (*Kunstkraft*)."[75] Such drawing exercises thus provided a guide for children to "convert dim sense impressions into clear ideas."[76] After completing *ABC der Anschauung*,

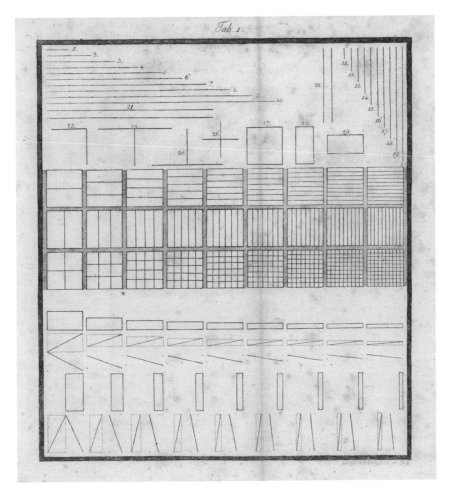

Fig. 21. A plate representing the pedagogical system devised by Pestalozzi to instruct drawing to elementary school children. From Johann Heinrich Pestalozzi, *ABC der Anschauung*, 1803.

Büss reflected: "Now, suddenly, all things that I saw stood between lines which defined their outlines. In my perception, I had never divided the outline from the objects. Now, in my imagination, they freed themselves from it and fell into measurable forms, from which every deviation was distinct to me. But as at first I saw only objects, now I saw only lines."[77]

Pestalozzi's innovation rested in the concept of *Anschauung*. To him, nothing was more effective than bringing the child in direct, unmediated contact with the "object of the lesson": "The *Anschauung* of nature itself is the only true source of human teaching because it provides the only foundation of human understanding."[78] The task of the teacher, then, Pestalozzi explained, was to logically organize the confusing impressions of the child, which he has gathered when confronted by the various objects around him:

> The world . . . lies before our eyes like a swirling sea of bewildering *Anschauungen;* the task of teaching, and its whole art, since our development through nature herself is not sufficiently rapid and unimpeded, is to remove this confusion which lies in our *Anschauungen,* to differentiate the objects which they present, to bring together the similar and the related again, and thereby to make everything clear to us and elevate the *Anschauungen* to perfect clarity and distinct ideas.[79]

The philosophical reference book *Encyclopädisches Wörterbuch der kritischen Philosophie,* published in 1797/8—at the same time Pestalozzi was developing his method—provides a contemporary definition of *Anschauung.* Based on a Kantian notion of space, its author, Georg Samuel Mellin (1755–1825), describes the various ways in which an accurate mental picture of an object could possibly be formed. According to him, verbal descriptions could form a mental visualization, whereas actual images could further clarify such a mental picture. Only direct contact with the object, however, could lead to agreement between the real object and the object in one's mind. When in direct contact with an object, *Anschauung* (or sensory impression) has two components. The first is *sensory representation (sinnliche Vorstellung),* in which a person receives direct sensory input, which is then perceived as representing an external object. The second component of *Anschauung* is *intuitive representation (intuitive Vorstellung),* in which a person recalls a past experience, or a form familiar from the past, thus inferring something beyond what would readily be available to the senses. Thus, according to the *Encyclopädisches Wörterbuch,* true *Anschauung,* which is the perfect correspondence between external stimulus and mental impression, precedes thought; as the art historian Clive Ashwin explains, one's "sensory impressions must subsequently be ordered by the understanding to make sense. At the stage of *Anschauung,* the representation is only an appearance (*Erscheinung*); the mind has not yet got to work on it."[80]

In 1793, Pestalozzi met with the German philosopher Johann Fichte (1762–1814), who introduced him to Kant's writings. It is possible that Kant's notion of space, as developed in his *Critique of Pure Reason* (1781), influenced Pestalozzi's conception of pedagogical drawing. Kant distinguished between the different appearances of an object. According to him, the perception of objects resulted from our sensory impressions. However, he wrote, "that in the appearance which corresponds to sensation I term its *matter,* but that which so determines the manifold of appearance that it allows of being ordered in certain relations, I term the *form* of appearance."[81] The appearance of matter is the quality of an object that is received as an external stimulus. Other appearances, however, such as form and space, are qualities that cannot be perceived as external sensations but that exist in one's mind as "pure intuition," a priori. According to Kant, "space is not an empirical concept which has been derived from outer experiences." Rather, "space is a necessary *a priori* representation, which underlies all outer intuitions . . . which necessarily underlies outer appearances."[82] Space "is the subjective condition of sensibility, under which alone outer intuition is possible for us," and "the form of all appearances can be given prior to all actual perceptions, and so exist in the mind *a priori*."[83] Both form and space act "as a pure intuition" and "can contain, prior to all experience, principles which determine the relations of these objects."[84] Thus, according to Kant, the perception of both space and form can be comprehended as the result of an innate structure that configures the fabric of the human mind.

In pedagogical terms, and following Kant's definition, the knowledge of space and form cannot not be taught but merely awakened, as space and form were considered to be innate concepts in the child's mind. Thus, Pestalozzi's method was to arouse "intuitions of form" through the observation of a carefully ordered sequence of formal elements—geometric forms of "a priori inevitability."[85] These were to slowly and gradually increase in complexity, so that the constant, gradual assimilation of forms would go unnoticed by the child. Consequently, the method adopted in *ABC der Anschauung* "was intended to suit the course of nature, namely here inner and outer human development, that these formal elements were not given to the child from outside, as it were, and derived from objects empirically, but that even they could be found in the deepest nature of man itself."[86]

Following Pestalozzi, Froebel embraced this method: that the material to be learned should be ordered in a logical sequence, that no stage should be attempted until the preceding one had been completed perfectly, and that there should never be a sense of urgency in learning. And, also following Pestalozzi, Froebel gave

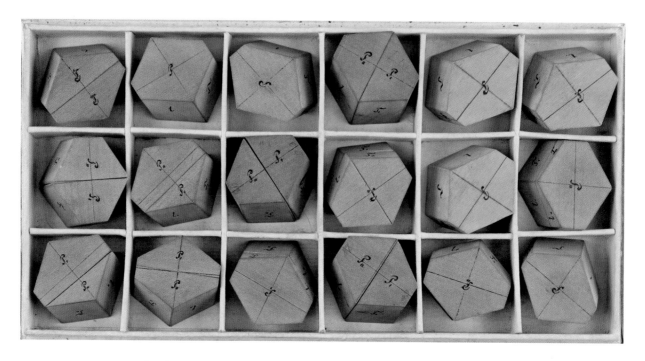

Fig. 22. To explain the principle of "twinning," G. E. Kayser made these eighteen crystal models that rotate around an axis for his teacher, Christian Samuel Weiss. Berlin, 1834. Weiss was Froebel's teacher and mentor.

kindergartners geometry. Solid forms, disassembled into crystal-like parts, were to evoke the child's innate intuition of space. Whereas Pestalozzi broke down two-dimensional forms (the square and its constituent parts), Froebel emphasized forms in three dimensions. He broke down solids, but he also emphasized synthesis and reconstruction. He was the first to introduce, in *The Education of Man* (1826), drawing on a grid, or net drawing (*Netzzeichnen*), as a pedagogical method.[87] According to him, both horizontal and vertical were key concepts essential to the processes of perception and representation, which is why all Gifts were to be handled on the grid. But to him the grid had yet another meaning. Froebel suggested that the German word for retina, *Netzhaut,* meaning literally "grid skin," was related to the way in which forms were naturally perceived by the eye, an intuition that could be reinforced by drawing upon a grid. Although the resemblance between "retina" and "grid" in German was held to be accidental, Froebel's connecting of the two revealed his personal ideology.

Observed, manipulated, and played with, the Gifts were meant to alert the child's imagination to the possible third dimension. Symmetrical forms of beauty, numerical forms of knowledge, and ordinary forms of life were compositions extending the innate, three-dimensional grid believed by Froebel to be

ARCHITECTURE IN PLAY

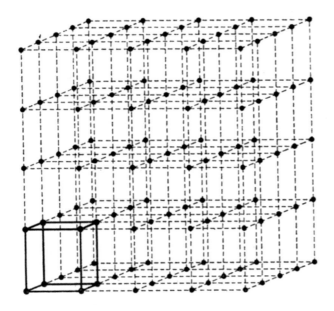

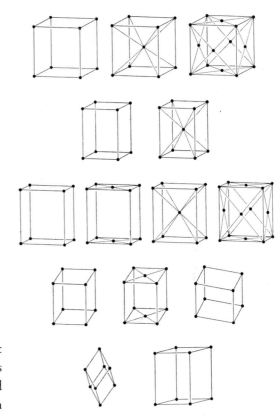

the underlying order of all spatial intuitions. Like the first six Gifts, his three-dimensional lattice had a scientific basis in crystallography. This notion of the "innate grid" seemed to predict the more general system of crystal classification occasioned by the discovery of symmetry by Weiss (fig. 22). Weiss's own discoveries provided the basis for the establishment of the spatial lattice by Auguste Bravais (1811–1863) in 1848, wherein different spatial lattices, based on the crystals' external symmetry, related to the pattern of the crystals' internal structure and to their chemical constitution (figs. 23, 24).

Handling Froebel's Gifts, manipulating again and again the regular solids in a prescribed fashion, thus promised to awaken in the child a structured understanding of the solid world. The unity underlying all phenomena would be comprehended through the crystalline shapes, first by looking and grasping them whole, guessing at their invisible inner structure, before actually taking them apart. A gradual, orderly breakdown could only elicit a structured reconstruction. The constructive logic of the Occupations, reversing the Gifts' prescribed sequence of decomposition, would thus position the creative works undertaken by man as a logical extension of the work of nature.

Fig. 24. A cubic space lattice. From Phillips, *An Introduction to Crystallography.*

Fig. 23. The fourteen Bravais lattices. From Phillips, *An Introduction to Crystallography.*

Detail of fig. 30. (See p. 59.)

Anchor Stone Building Blocks, 1877

Stacking was the essence of play with wooden building blocks, the most prevalent construction toy in Germany from the late eighteenth century through the nineteenth century. One of the earliest recorded building blocks sets was offered for sale in *Bestelmeiers Magazin,* a mail-order toy catalogue: article 51 consisted of 16 wooden blocks, while article 388 comprised 300 blocks painted red and yellow (fig. 25). Subsequent sets dating from the mid-nineteenth century were comprised of geometrical solids and distinctly architectural elements such as arches and columns. The basswood elements of Der fürstliche Palast (The prince's palace), manufactured circa 1850, could be assembled with a panel-and-slot system to form variations of a manor house (fig. 26); the stamped basswood pieces of Das Gartenhäuschen (The little garden house), made in 1870 by an unknown manufacturer, connected with tongue-and-groove joints to form a single gazebo; while Der kleine Holzkenner (The little wood expert), manufactured in Vienna in 1870, combined a number of geometrical solids with Greek columns and arches. The compositions were always limited by the architectural style of the building parts, and none of the existing blocks had supplemental sets or additional pieces that together would allow one to build more than a limited number of structures in a deliberately prescribed manner.[1]

Anker-Steinbaukasten (Anchor Stone Building Blocks) offered a different kind of play altogether. The blocks were invented and first manufactured in Berlin in 1877 by Gustav Lilienthal (1849–1933), an architect, and his brother, Otto Lilienthal (1848–1896), a mechanical engineer and a famous pioneer of aviation.

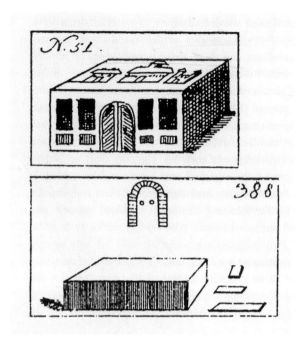

Fig. 25. Wood building blocks, models no. 51 and no. 388. From *Bestelmeiers Magazin,* 1803.

The sets contained small, dense ceramic stones made of a mixture of sand, chalk, and oil. The weight of the stones allowed for the building of taller and bigger structures, and the multiplicities of combinations allowed for open-ended play that was then unprecedented. Proportioned like miniature bricks based on a 20-millimeter module, the blocks came in a variety of geometric solids and architectural elements. The blocks' three colors—reminiscent of brick, limestone, and slate—rendered those structures realistic. All sets—from the smallest, containing 18 bricks, to the largest, containing more than 3,000—included precise instructions that detailed every course of stone and prescribed an exact order of construction to build picturesque civic architecture—medieval castles, forts,

Fig. 26. Two models out of the nine possible combinations made with Der fürstliche Palast (The prince's palace), manufacturer unknown, ca. 1850, wood with brass and bone hardware.

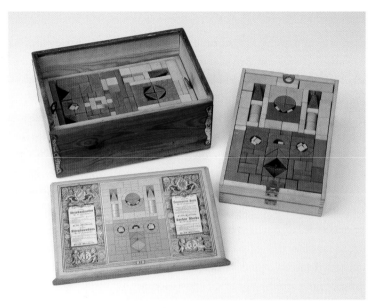

Fig. 27. Anker-Steinbaukasten (Richter's Anchor Stone Building Blocks), manufactured by F. Ad. Richter and Company (Rudolstadt, Germany), man-made compressed and dyed sandstone in three different colors. [*Top left*] Set no. 12, 1912. [*Top right*] Model of a church built according to the building instructions of set no. 8, 1885. [*Bottom right*] Model of a cathedral built according to the building instructions of set no. 34, 1900 (GK-NF).

and Romanesque churches (fig. 27). The constructions made with the blocks emulated existing structures, yet they could also be used to break apart historical models and invent new spatial combinations. The instruction booklets emphasized that "balance is important" and illustrated the significance of closely following the drawings.[2] Preliminary exercises trained the player through building a town gate, a fountain, or a war monument—all planar compositions, masonry-bearing walls with small window openings, emulating an architecture that preceded the advent of steel and (modern) concrete construction. Building a larger structure was a painstaking challenge involving patience and perseverance, since no joint or glue fixed the stones together, and only in set no. 14, after extensive training, would one get to build a medium-size castle.[3] An equally demanding task, exercising precision and a sense of order, was to pack up the stones in their box to form intricate tiling compositions—abstract two-dimensional organizations.

The brothers Lilienthal were familiar with Froebel's blocks, as Gustav Lilienthal had been responsible for illustrating Froebel's manuals. They would have certainly been aware of the abstract pedagogical concepts the Gifts were intended to convey. Nevertheless, in developing the small stones, they consciously created a realistic building set that would more closely imitate the historic style of their environment. In an old engineering manual, they found a formula for brick making that included quartz sand, chalk, and linseed oil, and they began experimenting. Gustav conceived of the blocks, their numbers and forms, and designed the miniature structures into which they could be assembled; Otto constructed the presses and the molds.[4] The original sets were small and assembled just a few models; the instructions consisted of detailed plans showing every course of stone and an axonometric view of the entire structure, a format that was kept throughout the years of the stones' production.

The brothers initially attempted to manufacture the sets in their own workshop and sell them in stores around Berlin. Without the funds to purchase advertising, however, Gustav later noted, the toy had no chance for success: the most the brothers could do was build a model with the stones in every shop's window. Thus, in 1880, after futile efforts to break into the market, and in dire straits financially after having invested their entire savings in the project, the Lilienthals sold the formula for the blocks and the rights to their manufacture to Friedrich Adolf Richter (1846–1910), the thriving businessman and owner of the publishing house that printed the educational tracts and manuals Gustav Lilienthal had illustrated. The subsequent interactions between the Lilienthals and Richter would reflect the fierce contest for control over this newly found play-ground: the lucrative meeting point between architecture and pedagogy, play and new means of production.

A powerful entrepreneur, Richter had achieved, through questionable means and aggressive salesmanship, great success in the pharmaceutical industry selling healing ointments "from America." Through his publishing house, Adolf Richter Verlag, Richter issued an illustrated newspaper in Leipzig—the *Leipziger Illustrierte Zeitung*—that prominently featured his manufactured products. Following the growth of his business, Richter moved to Rudolstadt, in the countryside near Jena, where he could avoid the restrictive pharmaceutical laws of Leipzig, and also where the Lilienthals' stones could be manufactured in a large factory.

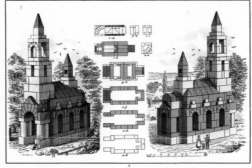

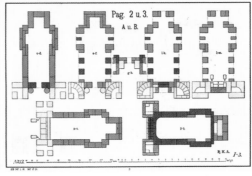

There, from warehouses located near the rail lines, he operated his mail-order business of medicinal formulas and building blocks. Although founded purely on profit-making grounds, Richter's company juxtaposed therapeutic ointments and toys so directly as to reinforce the links that had already been established, both in the United States and Germany, among play, self-help, and healing.[5]

In Richter's experienced hands, the blocks became an immediate success. Within a year of acquiring the Lilienthals' Patent-Baukasten, he officially renamed them Anker-Steinbaukasten (Anchor Stone Building Blocks) and patented their formula and configuration as sets in various European countries.[6] In the art department of his publishing house, architects test-built models with the stones and then drew them up for inclusion in a booklet that accompanied each set, in plan, section, and perspective, following Lilienthal's original examples (fig. 28). Perhaps most significantly, Richter also instituted innovative packaging techniques to market the blocks more effectively. He made the sets additive: each set could be expanded through the purchase of a supplemental set of blocks. A player could start with the smallest set to build relatively simple structures, and slowly acquire additional pieces to build more complex and elaborate ones. Rich-

Fig. 28. Anchor Stone Building Blocks, pages from instruction manual of set no. 8, 1893 (GK-NF).

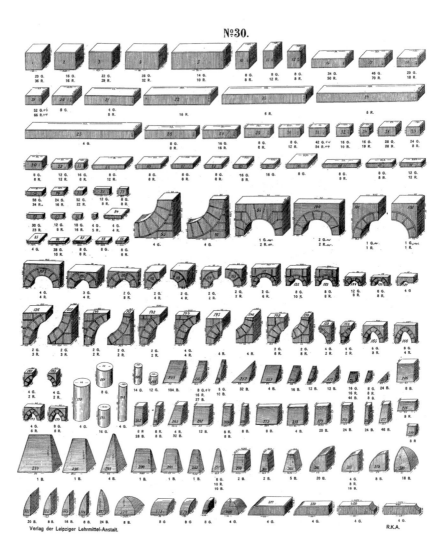

Fig. 29. An insert depicting the stone shapes supplied with set no. 30 of Anchor Stone Building Blocks.

ter also instituted a fixed price for the stones, a further standardization of the system. The incremental nature of the sets and the fixed price per piece were revolutionary concepts in the world of toys and appealed to buyers, who could gradually collect up to 1,200 different pieces, depending upon their individual skill, level, and budget (fig. 29). Additionally, lost or missing stones could be replaced, and entire sets could be ordered by mail. All of these innovations were publicized through a massive advertising campaign facilitated by Richter's own publishing business (fig. 30).[7]

The Lilienthals were not oblivious to the blocks' success, nor to Richter's accruing wealth. Gustav Lilienthal, demoralized by the sale of his patent and the overnight flourishing of Richter's business, left Berlin to work as an architect for the railroad company in Melbourne, Australia. There he continued to investigate ideas about the building blocks' production and experiment with an alternative mixture for the stones. During that same period, in Berlin, Gustav's brother, Otto, developed a design for a steam-driven machine that could form and press batches of blocks, thus automating their production. A patent issued to

Fig. 30. Advertisement poster for Anchor Stone Building Blocks, Vienna branch of the Richter Company, 1917.

Otto Lilienthal in 1884 for the steam press prompted Gustav to return to Berlin in the hope of reentering the toy business. The brothers crafted different kinds of mixtures using casein (a protein in milk used to make cheese) and Aestz (an acidic metal powder), and in 1885, Gustav Lilienthal applied for a patent for a new blend. France and Austria granted the patent, but Germany withheld it at Richter's request, and a series of lawsuits ensued. The Lilienthals won the initial suit, confirming that their new patent was indeed for a different mixture than the previous one, and thus valid, but they lost a subsequent suit in which Richter claimed that the Lilienthals had given up the right to make similar blocks altogether in 1880. Otto and Gustav Lilienthal were ordered by the court to pay a large fine, surrender their newly designed mass-production equipment to Richter, and renounce forever the right to make stone block toys.

The brothers Lilienthal handed over the machinery, as ordered by the court, but before doing so they sabotaged it so that the machines would break down shortly after Richter began to use them. The innovative steam-driven presses designed to mass-produce the blocks never worked while in Richter's possession, nor did the entrepreneur ever try to reproduce them. During a time fraught with mistrust toward machine-made products, Richter chose to keep manufacturing the blocks by hand in order to preserve their appeal as handcrafted objects. He emphasized this fact continuously to potential customers in his advertisements. If, as architects and engineers, the Lilienthals may have seen their invention as means to advance the implementation of mass production and prefabrication in building, albeit on a miniature scale, then Richter, in his subsequent expansion of the toy, emphasized the handcrafted nature of the blocks themselves and the historical character of the structures they replicated. The construction booklets Richter enclosed with each set revealed a model of play that was highly prescribed, and lacking the invention promised by the blocks' innovative material composition and intended new means of production.

Max Born (1882–1970), the German physicist and Nobel Prize laureate, wrote in his autobiography about his late-nineteenth-century childhood and described a play session with the popular Anchor Stone Building Blocks. He explained that to follow the instructions for building one of the "horrible houses, castles, churches" was considered of great educational value, since if one made a single mistake in laying the bottom brick layers, one could not complete the depicted structures.[8] "I became fed up with this type of meticulousness very quickly and

Fig. 31. Large playhouse, Gustav Lilienthal, 1888.

began to follow my own imagination," he recalled, which led him to his first scientific discovery: using the bricks in an improvised manner and applying the arch principle, he managed to build bridges spanning almost one meter. "These bridges were so elegant and amazing that they even evoked an admiring comment from my critical Grandfather Kaufmann," Born wrote.[9] Encapsulated in the nature of these sets, which instructed one on how to build meticulously following plans and sections that replicated period architecture, was a language abstract enough to allow for invention.

By November 1887, the Lilienthals had abandoned the business of toy brick manufacturing. Gustav left Berlin for Paris in light of the litigation, and for two years he continued to design other construction toys, among them a playhouse made of wooden slats and panels, and large enough that it could easily shelter a child (fig. 31). The playhouse never became a commercial success, however, precisely because of its size: it was too large to amuse. The essence of the appeal of the Anchor Stone Building Block structures was, in contrast, their miniaturization.[10]

Different forces thus shaped the small stone blocks—initially called Patent-Baukasten—and led, in 1877, to their invention. Although contemporary architectonic and scientific thought, innovative materials, and new means of production may have informed their initial design by the brothers Lilienthal, commercial considerations shaped the blocks' subsequent production, systematization, and advertisement. In short, the building blocks exemplified times of change in the architectural culture of the 1870s, reflecting a tension between imitation and abstraction, and between the handmade historical object and other innovative artifacts, manufactured industrially and mass-produced, and which in architecture could be suggestive of mobility and prefabrication. That tension also reflected the contest between inventive pedagogy and the forces of consumerism. Through miniaturization, play became a testing ground for future, full-scale material implementations.

Anchor Stone Building Blocks became the trademark article among building blocks in Berlin, in Germany, and throughout the world. They were patented in numerous countries, and their accompanying instruction booklets were translated into twenty-one languages. Although the blocks were marginalized after the advent of Meccano and Erector Set in the 1930s, they were still popular enough to remain in production until 1963.[11] This early attempt at mass production in toy buildings prefigured later innovations: not only the twentieth-century invention of molded block toys and other small household objects involving new materials such as plastics, but also Gustav Lilienthal's own invention of prefabricated building parts, bricks, and wall panels. All these aspects constituted, during the last two decades of the nineteenth century in Germany and elsewhere, this building set's great attraction. As artifacts made by adults for children, invented by an architect and an engineer, and further developed by a businessman, Anchor Blocks bridged several different fields, including pedagogy and economics. The rest of this chapter traces the means by which architecture was related to other disciplines, through a toy that was intricately linked to the technology of the period.

The assemblies of blocks to form structures or parts of structures were evocative of tectonic parts and their combinations. Such tectonic combinations were depicted in Karl Friedrich Schinkel's *Architektonishes Lehrbuch* (1825), a textbook teaching to a systematic design method; in Karl Bötticher's *Tektonik der Hellenen* (1843, 1852), presenting an anatomy of classical forms; and in Gottfried Semper's *Der Stil in den technischen und tektonischen Künsten* (1860, 1863), proposing to establish the original formations that underlay all architecture. Relating Anchor Stone Building Blocks to these nineteenth-century definitions of the tectonic was not an explicit intention on the part of the inventors. Nevertheless, the sets appear to relate, visually and materially, to a similar category of pedagogical tools: blocks that provided object lessons and were intended to instruct their users in principles of stereometry or drawing (fig. 32). Single Anchor parts taught the essential components of building; assembled as structures, the blocks provided lessons in historical architectural composition, initiated an understanding of structural forces, and provided for easy comparison between different structures. Concurrently, by meticulously rearranging the stones in the box, one could acquire a sense of order and learn the grammar of decorative patterns.

Fig. 32. Stereometrie, oder, Gründliche Darstellungen der Körperlehre (Stereometry, or the art of measuring solid bodies). Blocks used to study stone cutting, manufacturer unknown, ca. 1820-40.

During the mid-nineteenth century, a decades-long debate raged in Germany in relation to the "tectonic" as part of a larger discourse questioning the style in which buildings should be built. The debate over tectonics epitomized the attempt to define the architectural discipline within a changing world—a world still bound materially and formally to historical foundations. This debate threatened to replace the long-standing faith in the classical orders with a body of architectural knowledge that would deal with structure, utility, and industrial developments but would also be conceived through contemporary notions of beauty and art, addressing issues of symbolism and representation.[12] Initially, the dictionary definition of "tectonic" pertained "to building or construction in general," but a shift in meaning occurred over time, and by the nineteenth century, "tectonic" had come to be understood as straddling two poles: ontology, on the one hand, and representation on the other.[13] What, architects asked, should become of the prevailing artistic symbolism given the introduction of new materials and construction technologies? What could architects retain of the familiar architectural language and still remain relevant within industrial culture? It seemed imperative at the time to look at the relation between architectural style and the technological aspects of building, and to question the position of classicism as architecture's definitive model. Thus, in order to take account of contemporary material and formal aspects in architecture, the definition of essential building units—tectonics—was needed.[14] Schinkel, Bötticher, and Semper identified the new building blocks, which became part of the vocabulary of options known to nineteenth-century German architects. Similarly, Anchor Stone Building Blocks seemed to provide primary building units—object lessons in tectonics.

For the greater part of his professional life, between 1810 and 1840, Karl Friedrich Schinkel (1781–1841) attempted to develop a methodical theory of architecture to form an *Architektonische Lehrbuch* (Architectural textbook). Although the project remained unfinished, his notes would have a strong impact on subsequent definitions of the tectonic put forward by Bötticher and Semper. Schinkel was critical of architecture's stylistic eclecticism—the apparently arbitrary replication of past styles—and wanted to originate new work that would equal in its structure and power of expression the classical art forms of the past. There was no correspondence in his epoch, he maintained, between the style of buildings and the culture, technology, and function they addressed.[15] A second concern Schinkel raised was the disconnect between ornament and building technology, which in the past had been intricately related. With the advent of industrialization, it became essential to find a valid new relation between construction and appropriate ornamentation. Copying classical precedent was at the heart of the problem: doing so circumvented the opportunity to form a new style and create a modern architectural practice. Schinkel's textbook sketches offered a new point of departure. Addressing only the constructive elements of building—walls, piers, vaults, and ceilings—he provided the basis for a new architectural method. His drawings of 1823 and 1825 present numerous stone walls and their openings as studies of mass and proportions, of the division of surfaces into solid and void. Constructed of basic geometric blocks and devoid of decoration, the walls demonstrated for him "the rational production of everything that remains hidden to the eye of the beholder in a completed piece of architecture."[16] He singled out the enclosing wall and its openings along with the ceiling and its requisite supporting devices as the two main tectonic elements capable of generating a vocabulary of forms that could rival the supremacy of the classical orders. Through the categorization of these basic structural concepts, Schinkel outlined new principles of architectural design.

An architecture based primarily in basic units of construction could be said to have materialized in the elements of Anchor Stone Building Blocks. However, Schinkel's vision of combining constructive reality and contemporary artistic language in an alternative model of building that could rise above the classical never materialized in practice. Nevertheless, in the *Lehrbuch* sketches, he provided the initial points of departure: basic, stripped-down architectonics that, like toy blocks, were ready to be played with.

Schinkel's fragmentary principles provided the basis for the thinking of Karl Bötticher (1806–1889), who first introduced the term "tectonic" and delineated his tectonic theory in his study of Greek structures, *Die Tektonik der Hellenen* (The tectonics of the Hellenes), two volumes published in 1844 and 1852.[17] Bötticher's theory of tectonics attempted to establish a connection between architecture's basic forms and a larger system of aesthetics. Following Schinkel, who had written that "architectonic relations are based on static laws,"[18] Bötticher believed that the correlation of utility, structure, and materials determined architecture's expression. Like Schinkel, Bötticher established the primacy of the ceiling, or roof, in the enclosure of space. For Bötticher, this was followed by the ground plan, which was defined by necessity and function. The enclosing wall— the mediating structure between the roof and the floor—was to determine the character of the space, while the specific assembly of the three elements—ceiling, ground floor, and enclosing walls—determined the tectonic relationship. Bötticher's tectonics were thus defined by an analysis of functional and social requirements, forming the plan, which in turn set the specifications for the vertical supports and enclosure. Historical models were not to be replicated; instead, an edifice was to be determined by its actual necessities.

Bötticher also analyzed the interdependence of structure (the necessary building elements) and ornament (the building's artistic expression). These two systems were mutually engaged. Building mass and structural form were identified as *Werkformen* (work-forms, or *Kernformen*—nuclei), while the symbolic expression of these static relations was labeled *Kunstformen* (art-forms). The latter could intensify a range of moments (the juncture of building elements or structural joints, for example) and act as an aesthetic illumination. Thus, *Werkformen* and *Kunstformen* constituted, according to Bötticher, the essence of architecture and its representational expression. The aesthetic dimension of architecture was to be derived from the amplification of its inner structural forces. Decorative form would become the external representation of internal static relations. By implying that ornament would follow the structure, Bötticher emphasized the importance of statics and of structural form.

Both Schinkel's *Architektonishes Lehrbuch* and Bötticher's *Tektonik der Hellenen* identified tectonic elements and rules of assembly as a starting point for new architectural combinations. Both questioned the age-old reliance upon the classical orders to constitute meaningful wholes. Stereometric solids devoid of ornamentation, Anchor Stone Building Blocks presented the common denominator of all built architecture. As object lessons, the blocks had the capacity to instruct in the same way as Schinkel's textbook or Bötticher's treatise. And like those writings, Anchor Blocks emphasized, first and foremost, statics and balance, followed by the formal qualities of their various assemblies. Devoid of ornament, the blocks acted as *Werkformen,* the geometric component used additively to assemble an architectural composition.

Elaborating on the concept of tectonics, Gottfried Semper (1803–1879) set out to write his own textbook aimed at defining the factors that condition architectural form. He proposed to find "original models" based in law, since he believed architecture to have "certain normal forms at its basis, that are governed by an original idea, by which a few forms reappear in endless variation, conditioned by special purposes or by local determining circumstances."[19] Any architect's work, Semper asserted, was subject to similar determinants of architectural form: symmetry, proportionality, and direction; concern with frame and enclosure; and laws of repetition. In order to define common tectonics, Semper proposed a comparative study of the most important original formations in architecture. By reviewing examples of monumental architecture, a "Comparative Theory of Buildings" would elucidate a logical method of inventing, which, Semper claimed, was lacking in architecture. In architecture, as in other sciences, "a chaos of facts and experiences without coherence or principles accumulated."[20] Thus, the task was "to reduce what is derivative and complex to its original and simple state . . . to group what is related into families."[21] Those families would reflect buildings' purposes: from dwellings, nursing institutions, and educational buildings, to religious buildings, judicial buildings, monuments, and more.[22] Through this comparative study of edifices, Semper hoped to understand architecture as an aesthetic organism whose analysis and classification of formal parts and inherent functional relations would lead to new physical combinations. This, he believed, would ultimately result in the invention of new typologies of built form.[23]

Anker-Steinbaukasten could be seen to materialize primary factors of architectural composition. Especially when assembled as structures, the blocks could draw out the primary concept of eurhythmy, which Semper defined as "stringing together uniform segments of space to form an enclosure."[24] They would generate effects of mass and gravity and would emphasize principles of stability. Altogether the practice of building with blocks could bring forth Semper's practical approach to aesthetics by identifying formal parts and combining them into new compositions—as if stringing them. Constituting parts of a system, the blocks could seem to reinforce the scientific aspect of the discipline; and by presenting distinct, constituent parts, they could exemplify a comparative method in architecture.

Schooled at institutions of higher education in Berlin during the 1860s, Otto and Gustav Lilienthal most likely knew of the contemporary discussion of tectonics and of the comparative theory in architecture. They were most certainly familiar with *Précis des leçons d'architecture* (*Précis of the Lectures on Architecture*) by Jean-Nicolas-Louis Durand (1760–1834), a famous pedagogical treatise for students of engineering and architecture, first published in Paris in 1802.[25] The comparative classification according to building types underscored the scientific nature of the discipline of architecture. The Lilienthals were probably also versed in comparative methods in science, such as the analysis and classification of constituent parts in zoology, chemistry, and ethnology. Baron Georges Cuvier (1769–1832), a French zoologist and statesman, had established a "so-called comparative form of science" in 1805, in order to restore order to anatomy and paleontology, disciplines in which vast amounts of information had accumulated (fig. 33).[26] Likewise, in 1869, the periodic table was established by the Russian chemist Dmitri Mendeleev (1834–1907), classifying

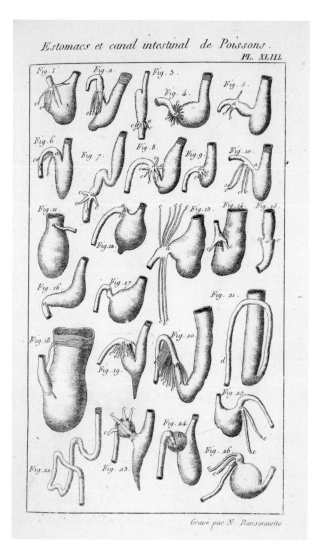

Fig. 33. *Estomacs de poissons* (Fish stomachs). From Baron Georges Cuvier, *Leçons d'anatomie comparée*, vol. 5, 1805.

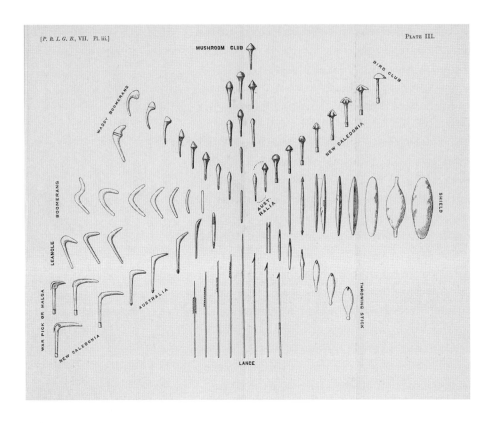

Fig. 34. Mushroom club. From Augustus Pitt-Rivers, *Evolutionary Relationships of Australian Weapons,* 1870.

chemical elements in order of increasing atomic number with abstract notation. In 1874 Augustus Pitt-Rivers (1827–1900), a British archaeologist influential in the development of evolutionary anthropology, mapped out graphically the "comparative evolution" of weaponry. Pitt-Rivers collected weapons from different geographical areas and organized them in tables, showing the transition from one tool to another, based on principles of classification that related space and time. He employed this graphic system to illustrate how, over time, the function of a tool evolved alongside its form (fig. 34).[27] In all of these studies, the belief prevailed that understanding an organism's parts and their interconnection would ultimately lead to invention, regardless of whether that organism belonged to the natural, scientific, or aesthetic realm. Inherent in the comparative method was

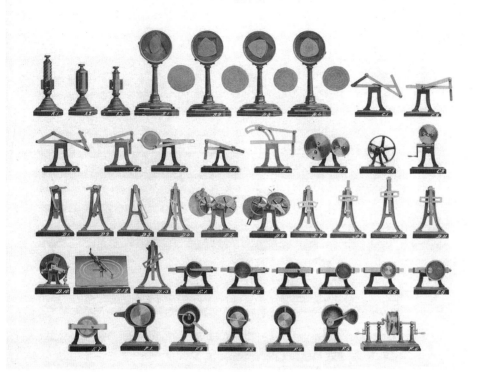

the belief that further development would emerge from within the discipline itself, and as a result, all of an organism's components were subject to study and observation.[28]

As for the brothers Lilienthal, having observed a great number of birds since childhood, and having constructed numerous wings with which they attempted to fly, it would be fair to assume that, in the vein of Cuvier's anatomical lessons, they had formed a comparative theory of their own. One comparative theory with which the Lilienthals were unquestionably familiar was the theory of kinematics, a pedagogical method in mechanical engineering invented by Franz Reuleaux (1829–1905). Reuleaux had been Otto Lilienthal's professor at the Berlin Gewerbe Akademie and was personally instrumental in getting a generous grant

Fig. 35. Kinematic models by Franz Reuleaux. Page from the catalogue of the manufacturer Gustav Voigt, 1907.

for Otto to remain in Berlin and pursue his studies (a grant that the brothers used instead, by Otto's account, to construct different flying devices). Living at the height of the Industrial Revolution, Reuleaux saw in the abundance of machines the exemplification of humanity's progress.[29] He tried to systematically analyze and classify the large number of machines that had proliferated, deconstructing them based on the manner in which they constrained motion and the way their different elements transmitted forces one to another. This "mechanical design theory" classified the machines based on the types of motion they embodied, which Reuleaux identified as the basic building blocks of mechanisms. The eight hundred models depicting different mechanical movements were to be used as tools of comparative analysis in schools of engineering (fig. 35). This abstract notation led to the creation of a dictionary of components—a vocabulary of machine movements. Combined and recombined, it would lead, Reuleaux hoped, to the systematic creation of new mechanisms and to mechanical engineering innovations.[30]

It is implausible to think that the pedagogical aims of the Lilienthals or of Richter were to teach children (or adults) comparative scientific methods or to inform them of the current debates within the architectural profession. Nevertheless, handling model building parts could lead one to question accepted architectural orders and forms of assembly, and would reinforce the nature of architecture as a discipline that, like science, could be examined through comparative analysis. On the one hand, these small blocks, which could be combined to form hundreds of different variations on one basic structure, reinforced the existence of an established language in architecture and mimicked established methods of building with stone. Thus they confirmed the persistence of existing building models and traditions. On the other hand, breaking a structure down into its constituent parts hinted at new rules of assembly, leading to a new and different theory of architecture. Anchor Stone Building Blocks could be construed as tools in this spatial experimentation and innovation—tools for progress, placed in the hands of the future generation.

It was in a climate permeated by Schinkel's influence that Gustav Lilienthal studied architecture at the Berliner Bauakademie from 1869 to 1871, a period during which many trade schools opened, as did the first arts and crafts museum in Germany—the Kunstgewerbe Museum in Berlin. After completing his architectural studies, Gustav became engaged in teaching handcrafts.[31] He simultane-

ously proceeded to illustrate the journal *Neuer Kindergarten* (New kindergarten), published by the educators Jan Daniel Georgens and Jeanne Marie von Gayette Georgens, which intended to disseminate Friedrich Froebel's practical pedagogy, Gifts and Occupations. Froebel's kindergartens had been closed by the Kindergarten Verbot in 1851, as their suspected underlying atheism was seen to run contrary to church teachings. They reopened during the 1870s, due in part to the success with which the Froebel system was received at the Centennial Exhibition in Philadelphia in 1876. More than twenty years after his death, Froebel's writings were explicated through numerous publications, such as *Neuer Kinder-*

Fig. 36. Gustav Lilienthal's quilting (*left*) and lace-making (*right*) designs from Daniel Georgens, *Die Schulen der weiblichen Handarbeit,* 1877.

Fig. 37. Gustav Lilienthal's needlework pattern design for
Gobelin (*left*) and Point d'Alençon (*right*).

garten, authored by educators and devoted followers. In 1877, following the Centennial Exhibition in Philadelphia, in which the German handicrafts presented had generally not fared well, Gustav Lilienthal collaborated with the Georgenses on a twelve-volume compendium on female handicrafts—*Die Schulen der weiblichen Handarbeit* (The disciplines of female handicrafts). Each volume provided typical techniques, precise instructions, and patterns for crochet, needlepoint, embroidery, sewing, knotting, braiding, and other popular occupations (fig. 36).[32] The traditions and techniques of various cultures were first described, followed by designs for use as ornaments in dress or interior design, part of an overall attempt to improve the taste of the middle class. Lilienthal's ornamental designs reflected his knowledge of tradition as well as his awareness of contemporary concerns. He, like Semper, shared the general enthusiasm surrounding the Orient brought about by the Vienna World's Fair in 1873, which endorsed handcrafts from India, Turkey, Greece, and Egypt.

It was Gustav Lilienthal's modern sensibility—his openness to various traditions and his knowledge of both contemporary handcrafts and technological advances—that led to his involvement with visionary social projects. He decided to contribute to the instruction of the arts and crafts by opening the "Continuing Education Institute for Women and Girls," where clothing design and techniques of textile handwork, as well as woodworking, would be taught (fig.

37).[33] Since at the time such craft schools were accessible only to male students, he considered opening his school to women alone as an opportunity for middle-class social reform.[34] It was during the same year—1877—that Gustav Lilienthal invented the stone building blocks, and although his career until then had been rooted in nineteenth-century techniques, his future occupations departed radically from these original interests. Rooted in social progressivism, his varied occupations could nevertheless all be seen as educational endeavors.

The blocks may have thus provided the architect's own period of practice, preparatory exercises that embodied a turning point. Through the miniaturization and manipulation of the built environment, a stable vision of the world was thus confronted, and a playful will for experimentation and change was entertained. The blocks could be seen as instigators of Lilienthal's future endeavors that reflected the nature of a changing era and intimated the modern. This turning point—a moment of change in Gustav Lilienthal's architecture—suggested not only an interest in formal change but an involvement with social causes and global displacement, including making architecture and building accessible to the middle classes.

Having returned to Berlin from Australia in 1890, and with two failed endeavors to break into the toy industry behind him, Gustav Lilienthal undertook the design of full-scale buildings. During the ensuing decade, he planned and built more than thirty houses in the Berlin suburb of Lichterfelde. Aimed at improving the living situation of the middle-income working family, they provided, according to Lilienthal, a viable alternative to the small rental apartment such a family would otherwise occupy in the congested city. The cost of land, construction, and the price of the commute had generally rendered the single-family home financially impractical, but Lilienthal had set out to reduce these costs in order to make this option more desirable and affordable.[35]

Pictorial elements appeared in all of Lilienthal's townhouses, earning them the title of "the castles of Lichterfelde" (fig. 38). The facades of the townhouses were punctuated by windows of various sizes, and the roofs were crenellated and punctuated by turrets. A "moat" was dug around each house, and a footbridge connected the garden to the entrance. The first house was Gustav's own, built in 1891. The plot was only 200 square meters, and the house was so small that it was, according to Anna Lilienthal's account, mocked by the neighbors.[36] It was soon supplemented by the neighboring plot to form a two-family house. Exterior stairs

Fig. 38. The Lilienthal family's townhouse and its adjoining neighbor, designed by Gustav Lilienthal, Marthastrasse 4–5, Berlin-Lichterfelde, ca. 1900.

led to the main floor, which comprised the living room and kitchen. The inner staircase, the only circulation element of the house, acted as a spine and connected all the rooms in a vertical procession. Below, in the half-sunken basement, the bedroom faced the street, and the bathroom and small servant space faced the back. The architectural historian and critic Julius Posener lauded the interior of Lilienthal's "row of gray castles." He found them superior to the "cranky houses of all kinds, castles, miniature pallazi, little Swiss houses, and brick castles . . . stuffed to the brim with all sorts of household items, with engravings and oil paintings,"[37] that one could find throughout Lichterfelde. Writing on the occasion of Lichterfelde's one-hundredth anniversary, Posener added:

> If one enters the house on Marthastrasse . . . one at once forgets the local color, even though it is not less "Lichterfeldisch" than other houses in the

area. . . . Almost against one's will, one discovers that the architect of the castles was a master. . . . What make the rooms remarkable are their furnishings, the wooden ceilings, the doors' hardware—details that recur in all the castles. The doors are a joy. All the fixtures relate to their medieval precedents in detail; they are formed more simply and solidly, like the best pieces that Philip Webb made for the house of his friend William Morris. . . . [H]e decorates his noble door with a door handle that is all about ornament, a German mask, as it doesn't even have a good grip.[38]

Yet, despite their handcrafted German ornament, the turrets, crenellations, and moats, Gustav Lilienthal's castles were also technologically advanced. In an 1890 article entitled "Das Vororthaus für eine Familie" (The suburban house for a family), published in *Prometheus,* an illustrated periodical of the mechanical and industrial arts, Lilienthal described his innovations (fig. 39). The design of his house would maximize the built area on a very small plot of land. According to him, "the roof and the foundation are those building parts, which make the construction of the single-family house most difficult";[39] thus, he sought to make their construction financially viable by transforming the attic and the basement into living spaces. The function of the "moat" that was dug around the house was to let light into the half-sunken basement. In order to make the space under the roof livable, Lilienthal invented the "wooden cement roof." Built at a 5-degree angle, it was used in all of his townhouses and led subsequently to his development of a prefabricated panel system.[40] This wooden formwork, Lilienthal wrote, would be covered "by rolling out . . . layers of paper which have been saturated with so-called wooden cement. In order to protect the paper from the wind, it is necessary to dump gravel, pebbles and sand over it. Such piling has such strength that grass and other small plants can grow roots."[41] He proved that this roofing system, durable and useful, could be installed at a minimal cost, and furthermore, he added, "By heaping on the roof even more ballast, the surface could be utilized as a small garden and thus, if the roof is accessible, one can build a small gazebo, which is particularly pleasant in the otherwise small lot."[42] This act anticipated the roof garden, which would be instituted years later as a significant attribute of modernist architecture.

Instead of a conventional coal stove, Lilienthal introduced forced-air heating in his houses: the picturesque turrets of his castles constituted the exhaust vents

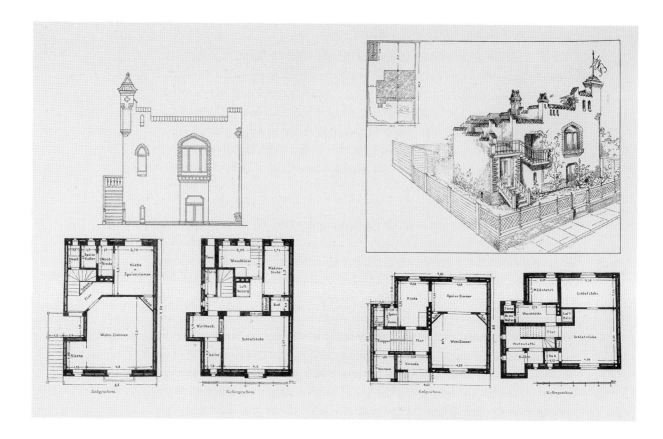

Fig. 39. Designs for "The Suburban House for a Family," Gustav Lilienthal, *Prometheus,* no. 54 (1890–91).

for the central ventilating system. As picturesque as they seemed, Gustav Lilienthal's townhouses incorporated technological innovations that were instigated by social concerns: the creation of aerated and comfortable, affordable homes for the middle-class family outside of the congested city.[43] These interests were part and parcel of Gustav Lilienthal's exploration of the possibilities of architecture that started with the building blocks and continued with his development of prefabricated building panels, which would become a hallmark of technological progress in the twentieth century.

Along with Gustav, Otto Lilienthal became involved in contemporary movements of social reform.[44] Both brothers took part in the "Freilandbewegung" (Freeland movement) founded by the Viennese economist Theodor Hertzka (1845–1924). In his influential book *Freiland: Ein sociales Zukunftsbild (Freeland: A Social Anticipation)*, Hertzka advocated for an agrarian social utopia,

Freeland, in the form of "a cooperative commonwealth in which the State could act as an interested party in the production and distribution of goods."[45] Hertzka described Freeland as a land of experiments—a community living together on a commonly owned piece of land in which every individual was free to work in his field of expertise, yet all shared their earned profits.[46] Inspired by Hertzka, the Lilienthals enthusiastically embraced the development of cooperative systems, *Genossenschaftswesen,* which they put into practice by founding, in the early 1890s, the orchard cooperative Eden. Named after Edendale, Freeland's imaginary capital, Eden constituted an urban attempt at an agrarian cooperative society. It was followed in 1895 by Gustav Lilienthal's founding of the cooperative colony Freie Scholle, or "free piece of land," meant to free the lower middle class from capitalist exploitation and profit-seeking landlords and provide a healthier lifestyle outside the congested city.[47]

Freie Scholle was erected in the outskirts of Berlin. It was officially founded on September 17, 1899, with Lilienthal as the architect of the community and the chairman of the board of the fourteen founding members. The construction of the houses took place according to Lilienthal's original plans, although the communal parts were never built. It was on sandy ground, which inspired Gustav to design molds with which cement blocks, much like the Anchor Stone Building Blocks, could be fabricated on-site. The members of the cooperative, many of whom were unemployed, became actively involved in the construction of their own homes (fig. 40). By engaging members in block making and construction, Lilienthal also saved on the high costs of labor and transportation of building materials.[48] The small, free-standing one-bedroom houses built by teamwork remained part of the common property and were occupied by the members only, who received in addition a shed and 400 square meters of land. Garden plots and crafts workshops were to provide employment and support for some, as well as income for the entire community.[49] It could seem as if Lilienthal's experiences with the mass production of building blocks for young players was reiterated on a larger scale, through the instigation of a construction system—a kind of "build-it-yourself architecture"—to be assembled and later inhabited by unskilled laborers.

The prefabricated cement blocks of Freie Scholle and the cement roofs of the castles in Lichterfelde led Lilienthal to develop another kind of prefabricated system—armed-cement wall and floor panels, Terrast-Decke—which could be assembled on-site. The development of standardized systems and prefabricated

Fig. 40. The first houses built on Egidystrasse, Freie Scholle, designed by Gustav Lilienthal, ca. 1900.

parts answered the need of building quickly, as well as employing unskilled labor, for the construction of light-, middle- and heavy-weight building units to accommodate a variety of functions. An early version of gypsum board consisted of a "stone mass combined with waterproof cellulose" that covered vertical supports on both sides. Light or heavy wall panels—5 or 10 centimeters thick—could be used to accommodate the different programs, and were adaptable to different kinds of weather.[50] By 1901 Lilienthal instituted the Terrast Baugesellschaft m.b.H. (Terrast Building Corporation) and expanded the line of original prefabricated elements, which he presented as applicable to a variety of circumstances:

The possibility of fabricating comfortable buildings that could be dismantled provides completely new opportunities for the use of rural land. It is now possible to erect a house—on a leased land and for a specific time frame—whose costs would be much smaller than those of a wood frame structure. These prefabricated buildings would have the advantage of being dismantled and reconstructed somewhere else, without losing comfort or destroying any part. In the mountains or on the coast one always has access to infertile or otherwise unusable land. Now, one can easily construct a building here in a few days. One train car can easily transport a house of approximately 50 square meters in area. Transportation costs are therefore very low, and in those cases, in which we cannot do the construction work ourselves, we give explicit instructions according to which every worker or laborer can do the construction by himself instead.[51]

The catalogue displayed numerous plans and elevations showing the possible combinations of "demountable Terrast houses," which allowed for a broad range of building types including housing, laboratories, industrial sheds, and social clubs (fig. 41). Lilienthal himself implemented the system by designing large barracks for agrarian cooperatives for the homeless. The system, which became famous in its capacity for insulation, received numerous prizes.[52] The cement-covered, wire-mesh panels and the insulated foundations were resilient against humidity and rodents, since Terrast building panels were "without joints nor gaps, making it impossible for insects to nest[,] . . . easily disassembled without destructing the individual pieces[,] . . . insulated against earth vapors in rising dampness, and guaranteed to be mold proof" (fig. 42).[53] Since the structures were found to be termite-proof as well as capable of withstanding the tropical climate, Gustav Lilienthal was invited to implement the prefabricated system in Brazil. He left Berlin for Rio de Janeiro in 1912, where, for two years, he struggled to put the method into practice. Success eluded him once again, and he constructed only few private residences near Rio and a large railroad hangar in Ribeirão Vermelho, in the inner part of the country. Gustav gave up his dream of reforming building through prefabrication. Reflecting back on his decision, Anna Lilienthal wrote in 1930:

> So Gustav Lilienthal came back home in 1913. The introduction of the new system of construction for housing was not yet successful in those days. . . . [T]he appreciation for small unpretentious living spaces, in which the good spirits of comfort could dwell—despite the savings in cost and space or maybe specifically because of that—was not yet in existence. Building departments balked at the new methods and did not support small-scale housing construction at all. Getting a construction permit always meant a battle.[54]

Anna Lilienthal reported that, demoralized upon his return from Brazil, Gustav "went back to that occupation which he had always cherished most during his youth—drawing, designing and building models to experiment with flight,

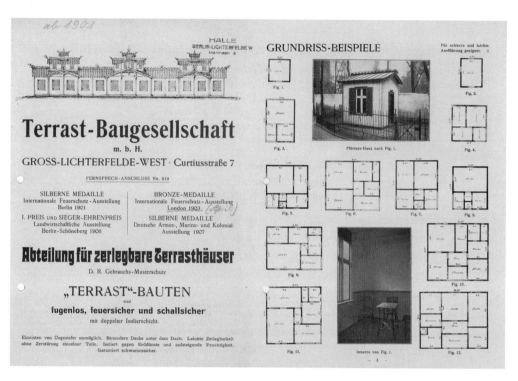

Fig. 41. Terrast-
Baugesellschaft
building catalogue
with examples of
possible floor plans.

Fig. 42. Townhouses
built with the Terrast
building elements
in Berlin, 1910.

and his flight workshop once again became the place of his untiring efforts."[55] In time, Gustav Lilienthal's architectural endeavors would be overshadowed in the history books by his involvement with the development of flight. Yet, since flying machines occupied both the imaginations of Gustav and his brother Otto from an early age, it is difficult to believe that, on some elemental level, the dream of flight did not permeate each and every one of their activities.

The late nineteenth century was a time of expanding travel, when aerial loco-motion became a major focus of investigation. Spurred on by the desire to fly, the intense interest in the bird's physiology united disciplines as diverse as engi-neering and aeronautics, with zoology and photography. The research of Éti-enne-Jules Marey (1830–1904) best encapsulated this pursuit. In 1873, the French zoologist, doctor, and inventor wrote *Animal Mechanism: A Treatise of Terres-trial and Aerial Locomotion,* in which he analyzed motion in general and animal locomotion in particular, and used comparative anatomy to study the movement of a variety of animals, including insects and birds.[56] He developed numerous precision instruments for the measurement of bodily movements (as well as blood circulation). The ramifications of these inventions and discoveries, further aided by Marey's development of chronophotography—recording on one sur-face several phases of movement—were far-reaching and allowed for advances in medicine, cinematography, and aviation.[57] "The reproduction of the mechanism of flight preoccupies many researchers today," Marey explained. "We do not hesi-tate to admit that what has sustained us in this laborious analysis of the different acts of the bird's flight is the firm hope to succeed in imitating, in an increasingly perfect manner, this admirable type of aerial locomotion."[58]

Approximately ten years before the publication of Marey's book, during the early 1860s, the teenagers Otto and Gustav Lilienthal had become obsessed with flight. Growing up in the small northern German city of Anklam, they were probably not aware of the scientific discoveries Marey was making in Paris. In the preface to Otto Lilienthal's book *Birdflight as the Basis for Aviation,* published in 1889, Gustav Lilienthal wrote about the fervent pursuit that consumed his and his brother's attention: "An important work monopolizes a man and, besides many other sacrifices, claims the whole personality. It fires the imagination of the child, and softly approaches its elected disciple in an alluring, toying way, appro-priate to the serenity of child life. But gradually it draws the soul more firmly into

Fig. 43. Gustav Lilienthal with the wing of an albatross from his voyage to Brazil, standing in the garden of his house, Marthastrasse 5.

Fig. 44. Otto Lilienthal (*standing*) and Gustav Lilienthal, ca. 1860.

its golden nets. It fascinates the youth and never relaxes its hold on the adult" (fig. 43).[59] Watching the storks fly in the skies of their native city, the brothers Lilienthal began to analyze the aeronautical principles of the birds' movements and to transform those principles into a built form. What would seem at first to be an act of play became a lifelong, passionate, and consuming endeavor.

Gustav and Otto Lilienthal constructed their first wings at the ages of thirteen and fourteen, respectively, and tried to fly (fig. 44). These wings, Otto recounted, "measured 2 metres by 1 metre, and consisted of thin beech veneer with straps at the undersides, through which we pushed our arms. It was our intention to run down a hill and to rise against the wind like a stork."[60] That first attempt was followed by numerous others, as the brothers relentlessly continued their trials throughout their adolescence. They invented various types of contraptions, gradually replacing wood with willow canes, feather with fabric, and attempting to achieve lift through the use of stepping mechanisms, bicycle motion, and more.[61] The brothers attached an apparatus to the outside wall of their uncle's house, and with stepping motions in place attempted to study its lift. They then concluded, in 1868, that flight would be impossible without forward motion and a proper positioning of the center of gravity (fig. 45). Thus they proceeded to experiment with smaller bird-like models, the best of which, spring-loaded, could flap its wings twenty times.

The War of 1870 and the boys' schooling delayed additional, larger-scale experiments for a time. When they resumed, however, the new devices were enhanced by Otto's study of motors and kinematics. The next flying

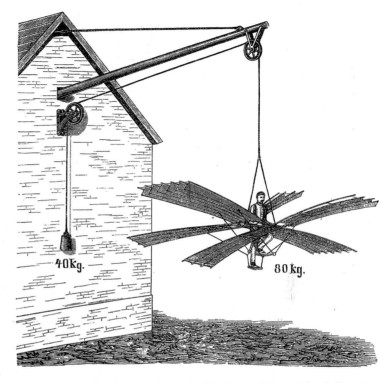

Fig. 45. Device with stepping mechanism built by Otto and Gustav Lilienthal in 1868.

machine the Lilienthal brothers built was an exact replica of a bird; it was the size of a stork, made with willow canes and feathers, and propelled by a light motor. The system of tubular boilers with high and low pressure cylinders proved too powerful for the wings, however, which broke during the first trial. The more successful experiments that ensued tested wind resistance and the properties of curved and flat wings, and provided the Lilienthals with the experience necessary for gliding.[62] The brothers had been very young when making their discoveries—they were still engaged in childhood play—yet their work was so significant that Otto Lilienthal was subsequently accused of withholding groundbreaking information from the scientific community when, in 1889, he finally published his then-fifteen-year-old findings in *Birdflight as the Basis of Aviation*.[63]

The brothers constructed a "hill" in Groß-Lichterfelde from which they could take off and glide. In 1891, after repeated attempts, Otto Lilienthal became the first man ever to fly and land a glider—a nonpowered, heavier-than-air craft capable of sustaining flight. His famous first flight took him only a few feet into the air, but gradually, with more sophisticated machines and higher jumping grounds, he flew a distance of 270 feet in 1892, and 1,150 feet by 1896 (fig. 46). Otto Lilienthal was visited by flight enthusiasts from around the world, and the brothers' findings provided invaluable information for the Wright brothers and other aviators more than a decade later.[64] The Lilienthals had five years of gliding experience, had built eighteen models, and had taken more than two thousand glider flights when, in 1896, Otto crashed and died during a test flight, atypically without Gustav at his side.[65]

After Otto's death, Gustav left flight experimentation behind. Only upon his return from Brazil in 1913, following the failure of his own prefabrication business, did he resume Otto's unfinished research on the ornithopter. A flying machine that uses the flapping of wings to imitate the flight of birds, the ornithopter was first designed by Leonardo da Vinci (1452–1519) in the late 1400s and had continued to fascinate aviators throughout the ages. Otto Lilienthal strove continually to design a successful ornithopter, believing that a winged apparatus powered by a small motor would fly. He built two models, in 1893 and 1896, but neither was successful. In 1913, Gustav decided to pursue his brother's dream and undertook the design and construction of a huge mechanical bird (fig. 47). There was no sound reason or significant technical application for ornithopters at that time, yet Gustav Lilienthal was convinced of their relevance for the future of flight. He shared this belief with other flight enthusiasts prior to World War I, and from 1924 continued with great persistence to develop a giant model of a bird with flapping wings.[66] With a 15-meter wingspan and weighing 450 kilograms, the bird occupied a hall at the Berlin Tempelhof Airport assigned especially for the task (fig. 48). A small motor activated the wings of the large ornithopter, which never managed to leave the ground. After a hurricane destroyed the motorized bird in 1928, Gustav Lilienthal spent the last five years of his life reconstructing it. He died alongside the winged apparatus on February 1, 1933.

Ornithopters attempted to advance flight technology through the imitation of a familiar winged structure. In a similar manner, Gustav Lilienthal's different designs incorporated an inventive vision and innovative technologies on the one hand, while remaining tied to traditional techniques and modes of fabrication on the other. Likewise, Anchor Stone Building Blocks, developed during a lull in the brothers' flight experiments, related to mass production—Otto Lilienthal had designed machines for the blocks' manufacture—while still using known

Fig. 46. Otto Lilienthal taking off from "Fliegeberg," the hill especially constructed for that purpose in Groß-Lichterfelde, Berlin, 1894-95, and in flight.

spatial models. Concurrently, the small, heavy blocks intimated mobility and prefabrication, if only by suggesting disassembly and reconstruction. This divergence, exemplifying the conflicts embodied in nineteenth-century culture, was clearly seen in Gustav Lilienthal's various works. Julius Posener wrote:

> If one stands in front of the castles and thinks of the flying, the Anchor Building Blocks, and the cooperative housing developments—there is no end to the wonder: because flight appeared then as a "castle in the air" and the castles, on the ground, seemed to embody, among other things, technical experiments since as early as 1890, they incorporated forced air heating. One knows that Lewis Mumford, the American urban theoretician, related the cooperative housing developments to flight: the year 1903 showed the two big inventions—manned flight and the garden suburb. The airplane of the Wright Brothers and the Garden City Letchworth proved themselves to be more effective than the hang-glider and Neue Scholle; . . . but surely the latter, more effective inventions were influenced by the romantic progressive spirit which lay within the brothers Lilienthal.[67]

Fig. 48. Gustav Lilienthal
constructing the
ornithopter, ca. 1928.

A reciprocal exchange between play and scientific achievement fueled the quest toward the defiance of gravity and the emulation of the bird's flight: with its slow success came the realization of the possibility of displacement, of transplanting oneself to distant lands. Advances in flight occasioning radical changes in human motion implied a breakdown of the accepted certainties about the nature of space and resonated throughout the stable, gravity-bound world of architecture. Years before Le Corbusier's Plan Voisin shed light on the potential impact of the airplane on urban planning, the Lilienthals related these two seemingly disparate areas of design. Their activities provide a glimpse of their time and, as Posener wrote, enabled us "to imagine the optimism at the turn of the century for the changes to come": "Looking backward to history and to the past, and forward to the future, a complicated mind emerges, but one that is not as disconnected from reality as it seems: Lilienthal anticipated things before their time, and important realizations were granted to him."[68] While advances in technology and means of production had an impact on Gustav Lilienthal's building block designs, notions of play prevalent during the second half of the nineteenth century may have also contributed to their formation. As Gustav Lilienthal wrote and illustrated textbooks and educational journals based on Friedrich Froebel's teachings, and Richter published those same manuals, both were certainly aware of the contemporary pedagogical theories of play. At that time, the understanding of play followed the scientific tradition and was based in the evolutionary theories of Darwin. By the 1870s, the concept of play had evolved from the position of Kant and Schiller, which helped shape Froebel's Gifts.[69] The motivation for play had previously been understood to be internal: it involved understanding the natural play of inner thought and following it through a creative act. With the evolutionary perspective, play became less about inciting the mind to follow the principles of a natural form and more about adapting and adjusting to given conditions. Both Herbert Spencer (1820–1903) and Karl Groos (1861–1946)—influential biologists and psychologists of the period—conceived of play as an essential act for the practice of skills promoting growth. Play was seen as the necessary means for success in a game of survival, involving external activities and socializing functions. Play meant partaking in the world and adapting to it.

Herbert Spencer emphasized the utility of play, and whereas Kant and Schiller presented play as a creative act of the mind, Spencer claimed that the forces that stimulated experience were continuously provoked by reality, as the world imposed external restrictions and limitations upon man. In his *Principles of Psychology* (1855), Spencer wrote that play was meant to expend surplus energy when the body was not at work, so as to keep the organs in shape in order to succeed in "the struggle for life."[70] As a necessary means for success in a game for survival, and as a struggle with existing conditions, play was actually presented by Spencer as agonistic rather than cooperative and nonviolent. Nevertheless, it is precisely through the juxtaposition of the two sides of man—the competitive, animal side and the civilized side—that Spencer acknowledged the educational function of play.

Karl Groos, the Swiss zoologist, psychologist, and professor of philosophy at the University of Basel, wrote two seminal works: *Die Spiele der Tiere* (*The Play of Animals,* 1896) and *Die Spiele der Menschen* (*The Play of Man,* 1899).[71] Groos, too, argued that play was an activity necessary for survival, yet one carried out chiefly to practice skills, since play, Groos claimed, was not always prompted by a need to expend surplus energy, as Spencer had proposed. Rather, there was a period in childhood, a necessary time of growth, intended specifically to be spent in play. Play was an activity for practicing future adult acts, meant to strengthen the acquisition of skills, which explained play's imitative aspects. Play, Groos explained, would train the young child in adult behavior through imitation, which would replace instruction: "Imitation is the connecting link between instinctive and intelligent conduct. Thanks to it we can add much to our accomplishments without other instruction, and in a manner agreeable to ourselves, for enjoyment of its exercise is natural."[72] As imitation, such play served as preparation to partake in society, as preparation for work, and thus acquired an important educational and civilizing function.[73] Since the definitions of play by Spencer and Groos elevated the social utility of play, solitary play was seen negatively and was to be avoided. Groos warned that solitary play would lead to excessive imagination: "When a child becomes absorbed in solitary musing . . . he should be aroused by application to useful occupation or by social stimuli which bring him in every possible way in contact with the external world. Even the noble gift of the imagination may from overindulgence degenerate into a deadly poison."[74]

Play with Anchor Stone Building Blocks seemed to follow these premises. The adaptation to the environment was practiced through play, by building small, realistic structures and simulating well-known building methods. It was a kind of play that affirmed social patterns without challenging their conventions, play that acknowledged the city's typical formations rather than investigating imaginary realms or building "castles in the air."

The dream of flight, on the other hand, presented an act of play that did involve imagination. In 1889, the year Lilienthal published *Birdflight as the Basis of Aviation,* the French philosopher Paul Souriau (1852–1926) published *L'ésthetique du mouvement* (*The Aesthetics of Movement*). Aligned with the general interest in flight and global displacement that also underpinned Marey's work, Souriau analyzed the perceptual, psychological, and aesthetic ramifications of movement, including its expressive qualities and the pleasure it engendered. The physical instinct at the root of any movement, and the pleasure derived from it, Souriau claimed, associated movement with play. In the chapter entitled "The Pleasure of Movement," he wrote more specifically about play's relation to airborne movement and to flight, two years before Lilienthal's first successful glide:

> One can . . . observe in any physical activity a particular kind of pride, naive and childish perhaps, yet all the deeper and more instinctive, in overcoming the forces of nature. Let nature but invite me to do something and I will refuse. Let it seem to forbid me and I will go ahead, from a spirit of contradiction or even rebellion. Thence the pleasure of climbing a slope, of pushing aside an obstacle, of walking against a strong wind. . . . But of all the forces of nature that we consider hostile and take pleasure in overcoming, gravity is the one that offers the most challenge and the one that we will fight in all our activities with the greatest obstinacy.[75]

By establishing a relation between play and the defeat of gravity, Souriau emphasized the ludic aspect as well as the competitive nature of flight. Rather than adapting to reality—to given conditions and forces—this airborne type of play incited the imagination to rise, literally, above ground level and transcend existing circumstances. The dream of flight thus embodied the fantasy of overcoming gravitation and rising above reality and day-to-day life.

In *The Play of Man,* Groos further elaborated on the pleasure derived from airborne movement, making the relevance of the Lilienthals' gliding experiments explicit:

Fig. 49. Santos Dumont encircling the Eiffel Tower in his dirigible on October 18, 1901, by Eugene Grasset.

Perhaps it is the exemption from friction, from the slight hindrances and detentions which commonly attend our movements, which accounts for our pleasure. . . . It is to be hoped that among the sports of the future, flying either in balloons or with flying machines will be included. [Otto] Lilienthal, in recounting his experiences in these arts, assures us that gliding through the air in a slanting direction affords a new and delightful sensation.[76]

Could play as flight and play with Anchor Stone Building Blocks be in fact related? Although flight started as an act of play, its technological achievements had far-reaching impact. The perception of space changed, and new visual experiences emerged. With its high vantage point, the all-encompassing bird's-eye view obscured details and allowed for a comparative outlook focused on essential features: size, color, mass, and height. It accentuated the form and relative disposition of structures, and the relationship between structures.[77] This generalized view reduced and abstracted an increasingly noisy space—and life—to its essential, quieter, and simpler components, as if they were simple building blocks.

The privilege of viewing the coherence and order of things was afforded by viewing them from above. Detachment from the ground, and its attendant sense of escaping gravity and eliminating all friction, were embodied by the Eiffel Tower in 1889, the year in which both Otto Lilienthal's and Souriau's books were published. Built for the Paris International Exhibition at the height of global interest in flight, the tower encapsulated an adventure in vision, the desire to overcome gravity, and the dream of flight. It quickly became a datum to be matched or surpassed by flight enthusiasts intent on conquering the sky (fig. 49).[78]

This built dream of conquering the sky was reiterated in small by the alternative construction set Gustav Lilienthal developed and attempted to manufacture while in Paris in 1888, just as the Eiffel Tower's silhouette was rising above the skyline. The wooden slats of Modellbaukasten simulated thin iron girders by allowing the construction of tall, airy structures—a prefiguring of the steel Meccano and Erector Set yet to come (fig. 50).[79] Anchor Stone Building Blocks, the stone building blocks invented by the Lilienthals in 1877, twelve years before the construction of the Eiffel Tower and twenty six years before the Wright brothers' first flight, allowed for miniature fictions to be constructed: constructions that in scale and detail seemed to be viewed from above. It was a perception of the built environment that was new: a parallel to the bird's-eye view, simulating low, airborne flight. According to Roland Barthes, writing years later in 1953 about the Eiffel Tower, this new perception caused the structures of the city to become "intelligible objects, yet without—and this is what is new—losing anything of their materiality," a new category of objects embodying "concrete abstraction."[80] It is an understanding of this kind of abstraction in the city's structures that Anchor Stone Building Blocks attempted to impart. Not limited in their use to the construction of individual buildings like a city hall, a cathedral, or a castle, the building blocks, rather, were meant to provide "the bliss of altitude," presented by the "continuous [albeit complex] image," since, according to Barthes, "no 'accident' managed to interrupt this great layer of mineral and vegetal strata, perceived in the distance."[81]

The "bliss of altitude" and the "happy lofty outlook" afforded by the Eiffel Tower were sensations similar to those Walter Benjamin (1892–1940) mentioned

OTTO LILIENTHAL in GROSS-LICHTERFELDE.

Herstellung von Modellbauten aus Leisten verschiedener Länge.

PHOTOGR. DRUCK DER REICHSDRUCKEREI.

Zu der Patentschrift

№ 46312.

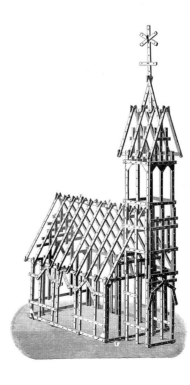

Fig. 50. Designs for the construction set Modellbaukasten, Gustav Lilienthal, designed in Paris in 1888, and patented by Otto Lilienthal.

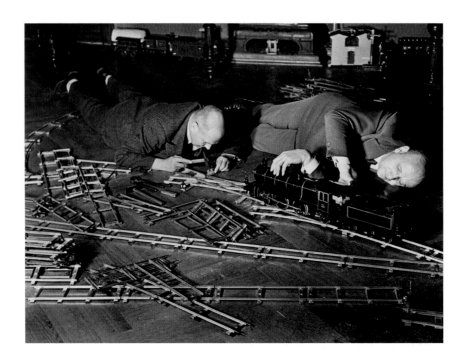

when describing the experience of handling miniature objects, such as toys. He wrote of the liberating effect that playing with toys had for the adult. "When the urge to play overcomes an adult, this is not simply a regression to childhood. To be sure, play is always liberating," he wrote. "The adult, who finds himself threatened by the real world and can find no escape, removes its sting by playing with its image in reduced form."[82] Playing with miniature, realistic-looking toys—a kind of play that was more meaningful to the adult than to the child—could provide such relief, according to Benjamin, who recalled a scene that must have happened often with Anchor Blocks: "We all know the picture of the family gathered beneath the Christmas tree, the father engrossed in playing with the toy train that he has given his son, the latter standing next to him in tears" (fig. 51).[83]

The feeling of relief afforded by play provided freedom from the weight of reality. Groos wrote: "As soon as the individual has progressed far enough to realize the seriousness of life . . . the liberty of play signifies to him relief from this pressure. The more earnest is a man's life, the more will he enjoy the refuge afforded by play when he can engage in sham occupations chosen at will, and

ARCHITECTURE IN PLAY

unencumbered by serious aims. There he is released from the bondage of his work and from all the anxieties of life."[84] Play with altitude provided a way to detach oneself from the weight of daily tasks, and if one could not yet physically reach great heights, the building toy shrank the world, distancing it by reducing its scale (fig. 52). Thus, playing with Anchor Blocks presented an apprenticeship with given structures and hence adaptation to reality. Simultaneously, construction with the blocks presented an image of play that was gravity-free, simulating a view from above. "Why does one envy the bird its wings?" Souriau once asked.[85] The blocks provided the means to access a controlled view of the world, a hands-on bird's-eye view. Like the triumph of the bird over weightiness, the blocks would seem to provide, at least visually, what Souriau described as one's "own spontaneous and personal gravitation."[86]

Fig. 52. Play with altitude: Alberto Santos-Dumont having a meal at his aerial, elevated dining table in "Santos-Dumont Gives an Aerial Banquet," *Chicago Tribune,* April 21, 1903.

Fig. 53. One of Erector Set's first ads, *Saturday Evening Post,* October 18, 1913.

Meccano, 1901, and Erector Set, 1911

In his autobiography, *The Man Who Lives in Paradise,* Alfred Carlton Gilbert proclaimed that, in the fall of 1913, he became the first toy manufacturer to buy "big" advertising space in national magazines.[1] His ads—in the *Saturday Evening Post, Cosmopolitan, Popular Mechanics,* and the *American Boy*—were promoting the Erector Set he had just invented and produced, and addressed readers in large, bold letters: "Hello Boys! Make lots of Toys!" Some ads were directed to the parents, others to the boys: "You can build big things—steel buildings just like contractors erect, with square steel girders that look like structural steel."[2] One ad featured a bridge made with Erector girders; another showed a tall steel-frame building with an elevator inside. "Mysto Electric Motor runs elevators in this building,"[3] the caption said (fig. 53).

Contrary to Gilbert's claim, however, the "big" Erector ads were actually quite small, measuring 2 by 3 inches at most. In the same magazines, that same fall, another company was featuring a comparable toy (fig. 54). In a similar tone, the full-page ad directly addressed the readers—"if you have a boy, if you are a boy or if you are a friend of a boy"—to let them know that "the successful men of tomorrow are getting their training today."[4] The images showed similar constructions: cranes and bridges made with metal strips perforated throughout their lengths with holes. The ads asserted that "the boy who builds toy bridges, towers or derricks with MECCANO in play—is learning the principles of engineering, steel construction, and the co-ordination of hand, eye and brain that will help him in his life work."[5]

Fig. 54. Meccano's full-page ad, *Saturday Evening Post,* October 4, 1913.

Here, toy historians or avid collectors of Erector Set or Meccano might step in and claim the priority of one toy over the other. The advocates of Meccano would say that it was invented by Frank Hornby in London years earlier, while the fans of Erector Set may assert that its offering of "structural steel girders" from the start made Erector Set a totally different kind of toy. A. C. Gilbert was a well-known American personality—an Olympic champion in pole-vaulting, an industrialist and entrepreneur, and the founder of the Toy Association of America. He was the Henry Ford of toys. Although Gilbert may have liked to present Erector Set as the predecessor of all structural-mechanical playthings, the larger Meccano ads, costly already in 1913, testified to the other company's commercial success well before. By the same token, European histories of toys mention only Hornby and the British Meccano, making no reference at all to Gilbert or Erector Set.[6]

Throughout their lives, both Gilbert and Hornby extensively fictionalized the tales of Erector Set's and Meccano's invention. In doing so, they have inspired the liberty I take in this chapter in drawing different connections and piecing together the parts—ideas, influences, and images—that contributed, at the beginning of the twentieth century, to the invention and manufacture of the structural-mechanical toy. I am not concerned with the priority of either invention, but rather with their simultaneity: I attempt to uncover the formal and spatial foundations of these toys and to analyze the manner in which they construct space. I also explore the meanings invested in replicating iron and steel structures with small girders and trusses, inquiring how play with technology's parts provided an education and promised success in the encounter with modern life.

It was in 1911, while riding the train back and forth between New York and New Haven, that Alfred Carlton Gilbert (1884–1961) had the revelation that playing with miniature steel girders could provide boys with lots of fun. In his autobiography written years later, in 1954, he recounted staring idly out the train window for months, watching the steel girder posts being erected alongside the tracks to carry the power line, as that section of the tracks was being electrified (fig. 55). But the realization of possible play hit him, as he recalled, "all of a sudden in the fall of 1911. I went right home, and got some cardboard to cut out girders. I fiddled with the cardboard until I had several different lengths and shapes out of which many things could be built."[7] Then, in the machine shop of his plant, he noticed

Fig. 55. Electrification of the New York, New Haven and Hartford Railroad, 1911.

Fig. 56. An Erector
girder, from a 1916 set.

a set of pieces made out of steel. "When I saw that sample," he said, "I knew I had something."[8] At the time, Gilbert was the director of the Mysto Manufacturing Company, producing magic trick boxes and "sleight of hand" equipment for magicians. After only two years it had become a successful company, manufacturing professional equipment for both amateurs and professionals.[9] The business thrived, having hardly any competition, and was expanding very fast. Thus when—at the age of twenty-seven and considering himself to be an expert in entertainment and fun—Gilbert saw the miniature steel girders, he was certain of their success. "Anyway, that's where the idea for Erector came from," he said. "Sometime when you are riding on the New York, New Haven & Hartford [Railroad], you can see that the girders supporting the wires look a good deal like Erector girders" (fig. 56).[10]

Similarly, while riding the train from London to Liverpool ten years earlier, in 1901, Frank Hornby (1863–1936) realized that playing with a miniature steel crane could provide a lot of pleasure to his boys. Hornby was a bookkeeper in a meat importing business in Liverpool. On the side, in a shop set up at home, he had tried for more than twenty years to invent all sorts of mechanical devices.[11] Unlike his previous inventions, however, the idea of a mechanical toy came, according to him, with no premeditated intention. In the biography of his life, *The Boy Who Made $1,000,000 with a Toy,* written in 1915 and addressed to children, Hornby recalled his traveling on the train before Christmas, gazing out the window as the train "rumbled over the bridges." Outside he saw "the great derricks and cranes at work in building operations and saw the wagons, and the various machines and the factories along the way." He then recalled how, as a boy, "he had wanted to build a bridge that he could run his cars over and O Joy!" And he had dreamed of building "a crane which could lift things and swing them around and put them down somewhere else."[12] He started sketching while still on the train, and as "he thought, and thought, and thought, . . . at last an inspiration came to him. It flashed into his mind that if he could make metal strips of varying lengths and with some kind of a fastening to hold them together, these strips could be held in position to form the crane he was trying to build."[13] Back in his shop, he punched holes through ½-inch-wide strips of copper. Since "he knew that to interest boys his new invention should be fastened together as nearly like a real crane as he could make it. . . . He decided to use real little nuts and bolts for this purpose."[14] He fabricated all the necessary parts and then set "to build the strips in accordance with the little sketches he had made on the train."[15] "When this first model was finally finished," he recalled, "just think what joy came into that household" (fig. 57).[16]

Following a visit to an exhibition of toys in 1928, Walter Benjamin wrote: "The perceptual world of the child is influenced at every point by traces of the older generation and has to take issue with them."[17] The technological and structural developments of the latter part of the nineteenth century indeed manifested themselves in miniature on the living-room floor of the early twentieth century. Since the 1860s, structural engineering feats have communicated overwhelming technological progress on a civic scale, with monuments such as the Eiffel Tower (1889) and monumental structures such as the Firth of Forth Bridge (1890) and, later, the Marseille Transporter Bridge (1905). With the American System of Manufactures, the standardization of machine parts, and mass production, steel also transformed personal means of transportation with the bicycle and the

Fig. 57. Frank Hornby's first model, 1901. An original print found in Meccano's factory.

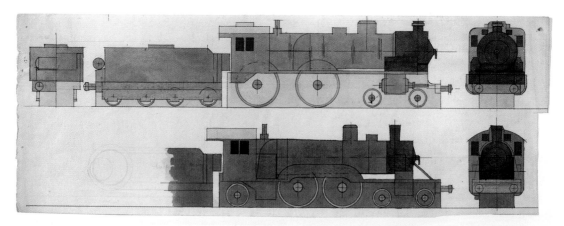

Fig. 58. Design (*top*) and prototypes (*bottom*) for toy locomotives, Lyonel Feininger, 1913-14, ink and watercolor on paper; carved and painted wood.

car. Introduced in the development of tools and appliances, steel simultaneously affected life at home. At a time when these technological innovations—cars and planes, elevators, skyscrapers, suspension bridges, cantilever bridges, and more—invaded the landscape of daily life, Erector Set and Meccano quickly became very popular.[18] Compared with late-nineteenth-century toys, both Meccano and Erector were very innovative. The most prevalent construction toy until then, Anchor Stone Building Blocks, assembled to make stone structures simply by stacking, without a system of connections or joints. By contrast, the automata and tin replicas that flooded the market of playthings moved by spring-wired motors or flywheels that could make them leap forward a few feet and as such were considered "mechanical." Thanks to new manufacturing techniques such as die-casting, these toys replicated in great detail mechanical objects such as cars and boats; nevertheless, they could not be disassembled. Other contemporary toys were inspired by the railroad as well, as could be seen by Lyonel Feininger's toy train of 1913 (fig. 58).[19] Yet Erector Set and Meccano transcended the literalness of the train car and presented an imagery of industry and construction, decomposing the surrounding structures into repetitive steel parts. The two inventors were neither architects nor engineers, yet they represented their surroundings as an innovative play material in the form of steel girders and trusses. Idealizing the sites of construction as well as the machines involved in construction labor, "the constructional toys such as Meccano or the Erector Set," wrote Dan Fleming in *Powerplay: Toys as Popular Culture,* "have come to seem the archetypal toys of the early 20th century. Linking the plaything to the replica (play as the building of a replica), they evoked an expansive capitalism and growth in production, including predominantly the mass production."[20]

The first crane conceived by Hornby and shown on the patent application he filed in England in 1906 was made entirely with perforated strips, to which were added a set of wheels, a rod, and a crank. With similar parts and additional angle pieces, the first Mechanics Made Easy (Meccano's original name) allowed one to make a lattice bridge, a traveling jib crane, and a replica of the Eiffel Tower. Hornby's patent—"Improvements in Toy or Educational Devices for Children and Young People"—relied primarily on "flat strips of strong material perforated with a series of holes arranged trans-

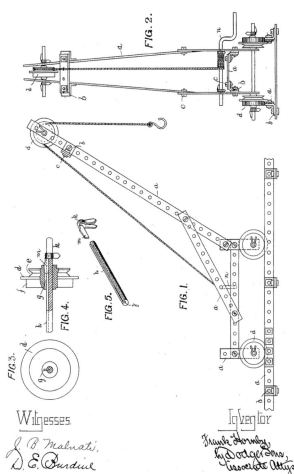

No. 810,148. PATENTED JAN. 16, 1906.

F. HORNBY.
TOY OR EDUCATIONAL DEVICE.
APPLICATION FILED JULY 22, 1901.

Fig. 59. Meccano patent granted to Frank Hornby in the United States for "Toy or Educational Device," January 16, 1906.

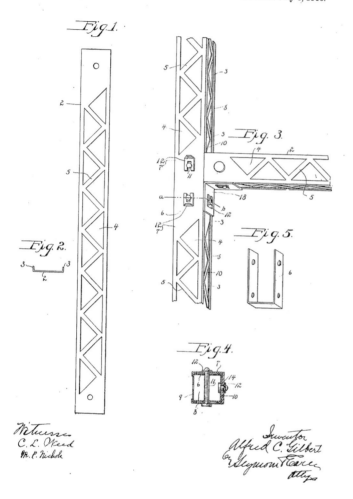

A. C. GILBERT.
TOY CONSTRUCTION BLOCKS.
APPLICATION FILED JAN. 20, 1913.

1,066,809.

Patented July 8, 1913.

Fig 1.

Fig 2.

Fig. 3.

Fig. 5.

Fig 4.

C. L. Weed
M. P. Nichole

Inventor
Alfred C. Gilbert
by Seymour Nave
attys

Fig. 60. Erector Set patent granted to A. C. Gilbert for "Toy Construction Blocks," July 8, 1913.

versely along the center line therein at equidistant intervals apart" (fig. 59).[21] The machine-made, standardized strips provided uniform measurements, enabling the child to arrive at the correct placement of fasteners simply by counting the number of holes rather than by measuring. Nuts and bolts created strong static connections, while washers allowed for swerving and rotation. Additional building elements, such as perforated plates and bent strips, were added to Meccano in the decade following the toy's introduction. In all of the models, though, the narrow lines of metal delineated each structure's silhouette. The perforated metal strip—the defining characteristic of the Meccano system—constituted the decisive advance of the metal construction set and was key to the success of this toy.[22]

Although Erector Set also included perforated strips and was comprised of many different steel pieces, one would most likely erect structures with 3-inch, 6-inch, and 12-inch girders—Erector's quintessential building parts.[23] "This invention," the original patent of 1913 stated, "relates to an improvement in toy construction blocks, the object being to provide blocks by which toy structures of various kinds may be erected, the blocks simulating what is known as steel construction" (fig. 60).[24] In its description of the girder, the patent included all possible forms of a beam or truss: "Preferably

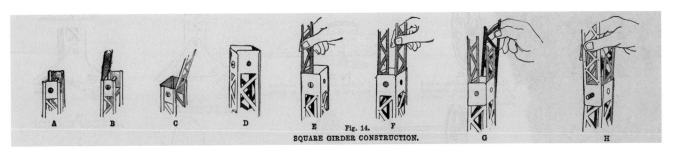

Fig. 61. "Square Girder Construction," page 1 of instruction manual for The Mysto Erector: The Toy Whose Girders Resemble Structural Steel, 1914.

portions of the central portion of the strip will be cut out forming openings [4] leaving diagonal sections [5] simulating the appearance of steel beams, though it is apparent that the character of the stamping may be varied at will, or the strips may be left uncut."[25] Whereas Meccano's perforated metal strips allowed connection and rotation every half inch, Erector Set's girders could only connect at the ends, emphasizing expansion in length or height. Meccano's elements seemed to delineate a structure's general outline, while Erector Set's elements, configured to form the same structure, appeared bulkier and more stable, creating a model more faithful to that structure's appearance in real life.[26]

The more complex Erector Set structures could be formed with square girders, which consisted of four trusses assembled with screws at each end.[27] Their design was based on the first cardboard pieces Gilbert had conceived of during his train ride. He recalled manipulating the first steel sample: "I got a box of bolts and nuts and started putting my pieces together. When I tried to put four girders together to make a square girder like those on the railroad, I found it wouldn't work until I made a kind of lip along the edge of each piece. . . . With the groove along the edge of the Erector girder, I could fit four pieces together with two small bolts and I had a square girder. The groove also helped keep single pieces steady and firm when bolted together."[28] In this manner, with only two bolts, a "square girder" could be formed; according to Gilbert, "this little invention was probably the most important single factor in the success of Erector."[29]

The manual emphasized the square girder construct with extensive instructions and stressed the importance of assembling the parts over and over (fig. 61).[30] Similar warnings appeared in many Erector ads: "Caution: We strongly advise performing these operations a great number of times. This is the foundation of the finer construction work that is not accomplished with any other form of building material."[31] The player was further warned: "Do not build models until you have built all these Standard Details several times. You will thank us for so warning you because when you get to building the large models you will be so familiar with the connections that it will be very easy to solve the new problems which will arise."[32]

In 1914, and for years afterward, Erector Set's box cover showed two boys building a colossal bridge of square girders, an elevator housed in one of its towers and a train crossing its broad span (fig. 62). "Hello Boys! What are you building?" asks the father with bewilderment. "Come Daddy! See what we've built!" says one of the proud lads. In the toy's instruction manual, more such structures appeared—bridges, elevator towers, and skyscraper frames, along with models representing other technological advances of the time such as the Zeppelin, the Ferris wheel, and the Wright biplane (fig. 63). Versatility became the decisive factor in the success of the metal construction set, confirming Gilbert's rule that "every new part must maintain the principles of inter-change-ability,"[33] and reiterating in the toy world the modern use of standardized, interchangeable parts, some fifty years after standardization was instituted with the American System of Manufactures.[34] According to Gilbert, Erector Set exemplified versatility. When he exhibited the toy "in all its glory" for the first time at the 1913 Toy Fair in New York, he proclaimed that children "could build scores of models with it."[35] Play with Erector Set, requiring "far fewer parts to build the greatest number of different things," posed challenges for the child, but ones that ensured learning "absolutely correct mechanical principles"[36] based on the interchangeability of parts and mass production—the fundamental tenets of modern technological progress.

Similarly, Hornby advertised the "inter-change-ability feature" of Meccano. The versatility of Mechanics Made Easy became apparent to its creator once he took his first crane apart. The holes being regularly spaced on the metal parts and allowing any two pieces to connect made the invention even more potent, as the crane could become a wheelbarrow, a little wagon, or a four-wheel truck. "Do you now see how easy it is for any boy to build one thing, then take it apart and build something else, then take that apart and build still more things?" Hornby asked.[37] Both Meccano and Erector Set promised boys, and their parents, hours of occupation as they incorporated one hundred toys in one.

Fig. 62. The Mysto
Erector, manufactured
by Mysto Manufacturing
Company, New Haven,
Conn., 1914, steel.

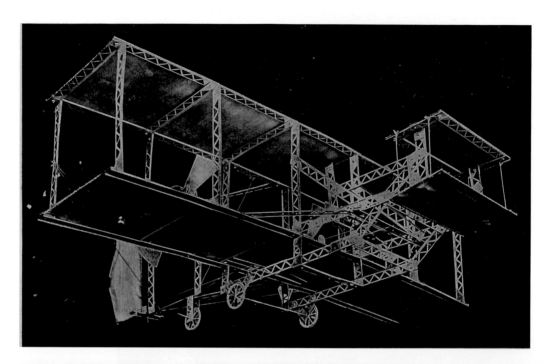

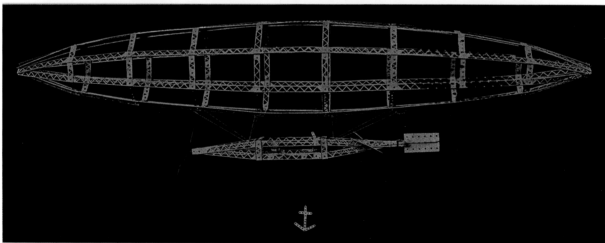

Fig. 63. Models of Wright biplane (*top*) and dirigible balloon (*bottom*) from Erector Set's first instruction manual. All models in this manual were built and photographed by A. C. Gilbert himself.

The pages of Erector Set's instruction manual were filled with models of different structures: single-girder bridges, multistory steel frames, elevator towers, revolving derricks, signal towers, and more—the sum total of the structural and mechanical advances of the early twentieth century.[38] All models were shown from the same oblique angle, from slightly above. No elevations or plans were provided, and no detailed instructions outlined a sequence of assembly (fig. 64). The builder was thus forced to guess at how the structure was to be assembled, a fact that emphasized that only through trial and error, perseverance, and daring could a child accomplish the challenging task. An instruction manual for construction toys such as Erector Set or Meccano might logically be organized by the increasing complexity of assembling the models it illustrates. Models might be arranged by category or by increasing scale (fig. 65). Instead, Erector's manual presented a jumble of dissimilar objects on a page, its appearance more closely resembling a department stores catalogue than an organized instruction booklet. Also, starting with the simplest models and progressing to those with the greatest number of parts, the manual juxtaposed models without thematic relation. The progression from the revolving crane to the portable crane, from the traveling crane to the rotary crane, was unclear, since among the models of technological artifacts that had invaded all areas of early-twentieth-century life were interspersed furniture and appliances—domestic objects of the home. An easel and a coat hanger were featured next to a small crane and mortar and field cannons. A picture frame, a fancy table, and a chair were shown next to the revolving derrick, the single-girder bridge, and the amusement slide.[39] All models reflected an admiration for technological progress: some by presenting actual innovations of the time, while others (such as the picture frame, table, or bench) by merely borrowing a technological appearance in utilizing the truss. Elevator structures may have been constructed with girders, but period tables and chairs definitely were not. By suggesting the erection of a boat, then a sewing machine, and later a car—a variety of objects at different scales and with different degrees of association with progress all built with common, interchangeable parts—the manual concealed the pedagogical aim behind the constructive task.

Play with interchangeable parts mimicked the act of constructing with contemporary technology while simultaneously attempting to invent a new usage for this technology. This kind of play positioned technology as both its model and its aim. Through repetition it forced the builder to find a common denominator between the car, the crane, the picture frame, and the table. That common

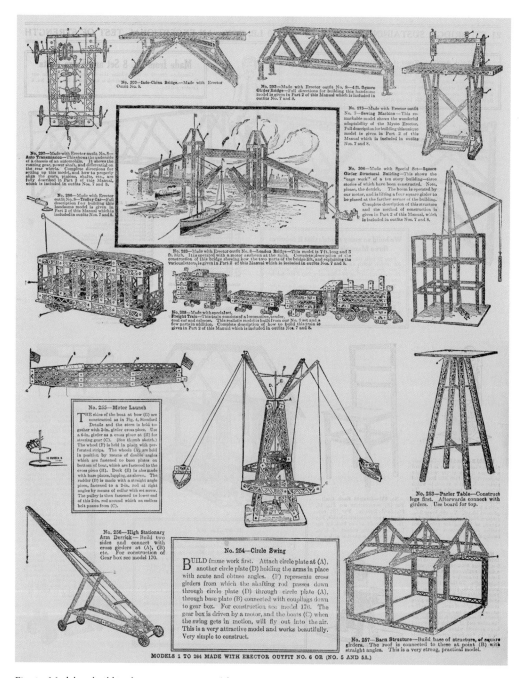

Fig. 64. Models to build in the instruction manual for Erector No. 7: The Builder with Real Structural Steel Girders, 1915.

Fig. 65. Chairs and tables made with Erector square girders from the instruction manual for The Mysto Erector: The Toy Whose Girders Resemble Structural Steel, 1914.

denominator was the steel truss. By emphasizing the overwhelming presence of the truss in the daily landscape, the different models suggested that familiarity with engineered structures and engineering principles was the educational aim of the toy. Why, then, if engineering principles were indeed the instructional goals, did the manual suggest building simple household objects with the same elements? What additional objectives were at play in the manipulation, at home, of small steel parts?

The claim that Erector and Meccano provided an education in engineering was used over the years to promote the toys. With a smile denying any difficulty, A. C. Gilbert appeared to shout from the pages of Erector's numerous ads: "Hello Boys! Become an Erector Master Engineer!" Many boys, it would seem, followed his advice. Henry Petroski, an engineer and historian of engineering, recalled that he, "like so many young engineers-in-the-making[,] was drawn to Erector set," which he called the "toy that builds engineers."[40] Like him, the Princeton

Fig. 66. Cover of a brochure, *How to Become an ERECTOR Master Engineer,*
featuring A. C. Gilbert with an Erector Toy Engineering Diploma, ca. 1916.

engineering professor David Billington recalled, "As a boy, Erector sets were my favorite toy, so there must have been some predestination towards engineering."[41] Sir Harry Kroto attributed his 1996 Nobel Prize in chemistry to his play with Meccano. His childhood experiments with the toy led, he maintained, to his work mapping the complex structure of the C60 cage molecule. Meccano gave him the idea that there must be an engineering explanation for why the molecule was so strong. "With Meccano you learn how structures stay together," he said. "You make shapes and some are rigid and some aren't. . . . You have to tighten a screw enough to stop things from falling apart but not so tightly you destroy the thread. . . . [Y]ou imagine building molecules as if they were bits of Meccano."[42]

In the massive number of ads published after 1913, Gilbert always addressed boys exclusively. His bias in associating play with steel parts to the male child reflected the norms of a society in which technology and engineering were inscribed in a fraternal, overtly masculine culture. Although the number of women in the engineering profession increased consistently during the first half of the twentieth century, women accounted for only 3 percent of the engineer-

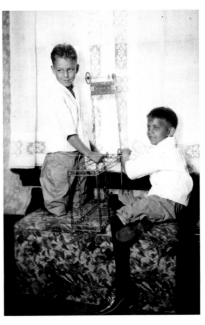

Fig. 67. Proud builders with their models built with Erector Set. Photographs sent to A. C. Gilbert, possibly to earn a Toy Engineering Diploma, dates unknown.

ing workforce until the end of World War II.[43] The cultural infrastructure that permeated production floors, construction sites, and machine shops and found expression in professional newsletters as well as the autobiographies of engineers meant to incite youth to enter the field, was addressed to men and contributed to maintaining engineering as a male occupation. John Waddell (1854–1938), a leading American bridge engineer, delineated the boundaries of the vocation in front of a professional circle in 1903: "We have the man who fires the boiler and pulls the throttle dubbed a locomotive or stationary engineer; [and] we have the woman who fires the stove and cooks the dinner dubbed the domestic engineer."[44]

Visual artists reinforced with symbolic imagery the cultural norm of the male engineer. The poster of the Panama-Pacific International Exposition in 1915, for example, featured a muscular Hercules—standing in for the prowess of the engineer—who seemed to be parting the rock and creating the Panama Canal by his sheer physical strength. Similarly, in literature at the turn of the century, writers such as Rudyard Kipling, Anna Chapin Ray, and Willa Cather constructed their plots around male engineers, whose masculinity and integrity were inseparably linked to their choice of profession.[45] A. C. Gilbert followed suit. During the early years of operation, his company manufactured a series of toys for girls—the future domestic engineers—that included a nurse's outfit, a sewing kit, and a laundress set, but their production did not last long. And if Gilbert's marketing of Erector Set exclusively to boys perhaps reflected a personal prejudice, his acts were not questioned in a society with a predilection toward categorizing technology and engineering as male pursuits. On the contrary, Gilbert followed the example of existing professional associations, which promoted camaraderie and incited leadership among engineers, to create his very own.

By 1916, Gilbert had created the Gilbert Institute of Erector Engineering (fig. 66). The institute operated like a professional society. It published a newsletter, *Erector Tips* (circulation: 750,000), and held meetings, some of which drew more than 600 members, all boys. The institute conferred three degrees through correspondence: Erector Engineer, Erector Expert Engineer, and Erector Master Engineer. Boys would send photographs of models made with Erector Set, preferably of their own design, and achieve higher ranking based not only on their "construction effort" but also on their "originality and inventive skill."[46] Each Erector Engineer received a gold-enameled lapel button and a diploma, while the highest-ranking "professional," the Master Engineer, was awarded a gold fraternity pin, a gold watch, and a personal recommendation from A. C. Gilbert to any employer (presumably for a summer job), testifying to his superior abilities. "At this point," Gilbert congratulated the boy, he was "honestly able to predict a real future for the lad" (fig. 67).[47]

Simultaneously, and possibly as an advertising ploy, Gilbert presented the pedagogical aims of Erector Set differently: "Don't *'educate'* them!" he proclaimed. "You can take the joy out of anything a boy does by telling him he is being 'educated.' A boy has no great interest in the future. He lives in the present."[48] Gilbert refused to sell Erector Sets to schools and educational institutions, explaining: "For years, our schools seemed to be conducted on the theory that real learning was painful, and anything enjoyable couldn't possibly be instructive. We were afraid that if kids saw our things in schools, they . . . would have nothing to do with them."[49]

A *Forbes Magazine* article on A. C. Gilbert and his achievements published in 1920 also cited criticism of institutions of higher education, stating that "too large a percentage of their product have scorned occupations, which entail the soiling of fingers and the discarding of collars and cuffs."[50] The article's author, B. C. Forbes, was concerned that, increasingly among American graduates, "the office is preferred to the factory, the 'road' is preferred to the machine-shop, the bank stool is preferred to the railroad yard."[51] Forbes asserted, however, that the ideal education should teach "how to accomplish things and at the same time derive genuine joy from the effort."[52] The "upbuilders of America," Forbes maintained, "have been and still are men who began work that demanded the soiling of their fingers, work in the theater of practical operations rather than in the office."[53] Most notable among them was Henry Ford, who "would never have produced his now famous car had he been able to manipulate only a pencil and a drawing board; he succeeded because he was able to conduct his own mechanical experiments and to build his own machine."[54] "Production experts" like Ford knew about all operations in their various plants. They knew how to increase output, reduce labor, and conserve materials. As a result, they commanded the highest salaries in America. "The demand today," Forbes wrote, "is for men who know how to do things, for men who can produce things, for men who are practical masters of their business, for men who are as much at home in the plant as in the office."[55]

Play with Erector claimed to create such men, by encouraging the training of mechanical engineers in the machine shops. The historian Monte Calvert, in *The Mechanical Engineer in America, 1830–1910,* described that training. This machine shop, Calvert explained, "might have been on an ocean-going steamship, at the central yards of a railroad, a theoretical one conducted on the pages of a technical journal. . . . Wherever it was located it offered the element of shop culture, a sharing of ideas and practical techniques."[56] The machine shop allowed "complete upward mobility from the lowliest apprentice to the engineers who ran the shops and the entrepreneurs who owned them . . . and the routine of rising up the ladder step by step from apprenticeship had the air of ritual about it."[57] The shop was the storehouse of all mechanical knowledge, emphasizing the solving of practical problems over theorizing solutions. It functioned as an experimental laboratory where processes would be perfected through the sharing of information. The function of the shop was thus of "a pre-professional institution performing many of the functions taken over by the professional association and the school later in the twentieth century."[58] Its role was both technical and social, encompassing the exchange of knowledge and ideas as well as the fostering of camaraderie. Early mechanical engineering periodicals extended the reach of the shop in sections called "shop kinks" or "shop hints." There, new techniques, ideas, and skills developed in one shop were shared with all others. In a similar manner, Gilbert's newsletter, *Toy Tips,* encouraged the exchange of information with other Erector engineers by asking boys to write in for advice and by publishing their letters and models. *Meccano Magazine* likewise echoed shop publications in its tone and focus, providing tips for building and publishing daring designs by the young players. In this manner, both toy publications instilled the sense of "shop culture" that playing with Erector and Meccano provided. And with the honors bestowed upon prolific builders, Erector Set in particular also simulated the social hierarchy existing within the machine shop. Gilbert's educational efforts were lauded by Forbes, who concluded: "Surely, any plan which inculcates into thousands and thousands of young Americans a love for the practical, the mechanical, the scientific, is of incalculable value, since it directs the mind to actualities and trains the hand to create. It stimulates interest in, love for, and knowledge of work calling for skillful use of other tools, apparatus and appliances than the pen, the typewriter, the adding machine or other adjunct of the office and counting house."[59]

Gilbert used two pedagogical practices—the "formal" university-style conferment of degrees and the collegial exchange imitating machine-shop training—to advertise Erector Set. Still, for those to whom neither diplomas nor machine-shop skills appealed, Gilbert used yet another "educational" argument. "Construction," as used in Gilbert's promotions, did not refer to the constructive capabilities of the girders to create strong, stable structures but rather to the "constructiveness" of the toy—that is, its capability to build the character of the boy. Similarly, in his biography, Hornby is quoted as saying that he'd seen the destructive side of boys; he knew "the pleasure all boys get out of taking something to pieces."[60] And although he saw this urge to take things apart as a natural desire of every boy, to Hornby's way of thinking it "seemed to be a negative or backwards training." "So he thought how much better it would be," his biographer explained, "if he could invent something that would make the boys think how to construct it, instead of how to tear it apart."[61]

Advertisements of Erector Set described boys' nature as both constructive and destructive. The first ad of this kind appeared in the *Christian Herald* in December 1915. A boy's face, smiling mischievously, was halved: one side was rendered in dark print; the other side, in light (fig. 68). The dark, "destructive" side showed the boy throwing a stone at a building, breaking a window. The light, "constructive" side showed the boy and a friend building a huge bridge with square girders, familiar from Erector Set box covers. "Every Boy Has Two Sides," the ad pronounced, "Every mother knows that a boy overflows with vigor and vim. His untiring energy can take two directions—the one destructive, the other constructive. Which one it will be depends largely upon circumstances. Develop His Constructive Side. . . . Give him something to do which is not only constructive and useful but also has the essential element of fun—then you'll see how easy it is to suppress his destructive side."[62] In the *Literary Digest,* December 7, 1918, an ad urged mothers to buy Erector Sets; otherwise, the ad implied, they would be cheating their boys on Christmas (fig. 69). In the *Ladies' Home Journal* of December 1918, a two-page ad made to look like an article written by A. C. Gilbert again addressed mothers. It told the story of a mother who once complained, "I don't know what I'm going to do with my boy, he's getting so *destructive!*" She went on to explain: "His destructiveness I found, consisted of an unquenchable desire to take things to pieces—the clocks, the phonograph, the washing machine and so on. He always planned on putting them together again but generally they were too much for him." Gilbert elucidated the boy's motives: "What he wanted— what *every* real boy wants—is to see things take shape under his hands—to grow, to assume new forms. It is the dominant instinct of life, just coming to the surface in a boy. . . . So to satisfy his creative instinct he had literally to destroy. He 'took things to pieces' partly because, in doing so, they assumed new shapes for him, partly in the hope of putting them together—*building* them, again!"[63] Thus, "constructiveness" was mainly intended in Gilbert's advertising language to mean the "character building" of a boy. "Use of the models will guide the boys' thoughts and action in play along constructive lines,"[64] said the superintendent of a boys' home who bought six Erector Sets for the boys. Parents wrote to Gilbert that until their boy had played with Erector Set, "his conduct and his habits and his associations gave them grievous concern, but that since becoming interested in designing and constructing things . . . the boy had completely changed, acquiring habits of industry and study and manifesting the most laudable ambitions."[65] One letter, among the thousands Gilbert claimed to receive every day, said, "I like my Erector Set because it changes boys into men."[66]

Every Boy Has Two Sides

Every mother knows that a boy overflows with vigor and vim. His untiring energy must have an outlet of some kind.

Now this energy can take two directions—the one destructive, the other constructive. Which one it will be depends largely upon circumstances.

Develop His Constructive Side

A boy is likely to be destructive and engage in mischievous pranks simply because he hasn't anything else to do.

Give him something to do which is not only constructive and useful but also has the essential element of fun—then you'll see how easy it is to suppress his destructive side and develop his constructive side.

Solving The Boy Problem

That was my aim in inventing Erector. I knew that it would solve the boy problem for mothers. I knew that it would appeal to a boy's idea of fun and at the same time develop his constructive side.

Your boy starts to build with a definite picture in his mind of some model. He begins with the foundation and fits the steel girders to their proper places.

Erector Holds His Interest

Thus he is getting an unconscious lesson in practical construction and engineering. His interest and enthusiasm increase as the structure grows.

When it's finished, he proudly shows it to you. To him it is a great achievement. It is a miniature success— the forerunner of greater things in later life.

Big, Strong Models

Boys can build over 500 *big*, *strong*, lifelike models with Erector. The models look identically like the real steel structures themselves. Erector is the *only* construction toy with girders that exactly resemble the structural material used in the big steel skyscrapers.

The electric motor, free in most sets, adds wonderfully to his interest. He can run scores of models with this powerful motor.

$3000 Prize Offer

To make your boy's interest still keener, and to stimulate his ingenuity, I offer $3000 in prizes to the boys who build the best models. There are 307 of these prizes – automobile, motorcycles, bicycles, tents, canoes, etc.

The Toy Like Structural Steel

The prizes are illustrated and described in my boys' magazine, *Erector Tips*. I want to give every boy, absolutely free, a three months' subscription to *Tips*, including the big holiday issue in colors, brimful of stories and photographs.

Be sure to get this interesting magazine so that your boy can read the absorbing story, "How I Invented Erector," and the special articles telling my experiences as a World's Champion Athlete.

Write today for the three months' subscription— also a free copy of my new 24-page Book, telling all about construction toys. Don't send any money or postage; just give your dealer's name.

Buy Erector for Christmas. Dealers everywhere sell it, $1 to $25; a good set for your boy is No. 4, which costs $5, has 571 parts and motor, builds 250 models and is packed in handsome oak cabinet.

A. C. GILBERT, President
The Mysto Manufacturing Company
109 Fox St., New Haven, Conn.

No. 4 Set

Send for my Free Book and Boys' Magazine "Tips"

Coupon

Mr. A. C. Gilbert
The Mysto Manufacturing Co.
109 Fox St., New Haven, Conn.

Please send me, without charge, your book and a three months' subscription to Erector Tips.

Name ....

Address ....

My dealer's name is ....

Fig. 68. Erector Set's "destructive-constructive" ad, *Christian Herald,* December 1915.

Fig. 69. "Don't Cheat Your Boy on Christmas Morning," Erector ad, *Literary Digest,* December 7, 1918.

The "destructive-constructive" advertising campaign started in 1915 and continued until the end of 1918. Presenting construction as counteracting the destructive instinct of boys was part of a nationwide effort during World War I. During that time, the Erector Set factory was partially converted to produce components for machine guns and Colt .45 handguns, since it was capable of manufacturing precision steel parts. Following Gilbert's convincing argument to the Council of National Defense that educational toy manufacturing was an industry vital to the country's social soundness in times of war, he was allowed to continue producing Erector Sets alongside the guns.[67]

Before Erector Set, Gilbert contended, playthings "were baubles, constructed as cheaply as possible from papier-mâché and such material, meant to please the eye, and then be forgotten. It was all a purely make-believe world."[68] Therefore, from the early days of Erector Set and Meccano, the word "real" consistently appeared in the advertisements and descriptions of the toys. "I know what boys like," proclaimed Gilbert in Erector's inaugural ad, "so I made this to imitate real square steel girders like you see in bridges and buildings."[69] "To make Erector I studied the steel-work of real life, and designed the parts of Erector to be just like the genuine,"[70] he said in another ad. The large, strong models "will be exactly like real steel construction,"[71] and the boys will get a "real engineering thrill."[72] Other construction sets of the time, such as Ives's Strukturiron or Bill Deezy (build easy), used thin steel rods, but neither achieved the success of Erector or Meccano, perhaps because they did not simulate "real" steel construction at all. Erector and Meccano deconstructed the contemporary landscape into constituent pieces. The miniature steel parts followed "real" constructs, from the single truss to the entire structure. Their manipulation faithfully mimicked "real" processes of assembly, disassembly, and collapse—processes integral to the technological experience of the early twentieth century. Thus, the real-world context in which the toys came to be is the basis of the formal and spatial organization of the toy. Simulating building process by repeating, over and over, the acts of connecting and taking apart interchangeable parts was believed to provide a solid ground for a young boy's future success in life.

The formal parent of the Erector Set's square girder was the Town lattice truss (fig. 70). Considered the first "true truss," it was designed in New Haven in 1820 by the architect Ithiel Town (1784–1844), and was built as a bridge—100 feet

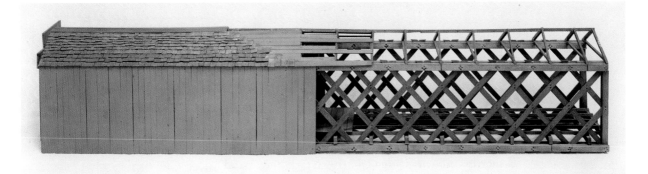

Fig. 70. Town truss bridge model, Ithiel Town, ca. 1820.

long, 14 feet wide, and 12 feet high—for the New Haven Turnpike Company over Mill River, two miles north of the center of New Haven.[73] Based on its design, the architect was granted a U.S. patent on January 28, 1820, for the Town truss, intended to improve the design of bridges, for which there was no uniform model. "It has been too much the custom for architects and builders," Town wrote, "to pile together materials, each according to his own ideas of the principles and practice of bridge building and the result has been that nearly as many models of construction have been adopted as there have been bridges built."[74] The purpose of the new system, he described, was "to establish a general mode of constructing bridges of wood as well as iron, which shall be the most simple, permanent and economical, both in erecting and repairing."[75] Town's invention consisted of creating a lattice-like web made of multiple intersecting diagonals. These were pinned together at the crossings and tied to string pieces, top and bottom. Three such lattices formed the sides and bottom; a fourth formed the top and enclosed the bridge. For the first time, in Town's project, a bridge acted structurally as a single beam, as a large square girder. All previous trusses had been composites, combining a truss with an arch—a structural element, which until then had always been considered necessary to provide stability.[76]

The ability to replace any two-by-four piece of timber with another was praised by Eli Whitney, the inventor of the cotton gin, who greatly promoted the practice of interchangeable parts through his manufacture of muskets. In 1823, he built a Town truss on his grounds in New Haven, and subsequently gave a letter of recommendation to Town, who used it in the endorsements of his bridge system.[77] Whitney wrote: "It appears to me to be much lighter in proportions to its strength than any other wooden bridge that I have seen. . . . The construction is such as to afford great facility in taking out any piece of timber and replacing it with another. On the whole, its simplicity, lightness, strength, cheapness and durability are in my opinion such as to render it highly worthy of attention."[78] The practicality of the Town truss was in its use of wood. Unlike other trusses and bridges requiring massive pieces of timber and connected with mortise-and-tenon joints, the Town truss was assembled with standard two-by-fours, treenails, and bolts (fig. 71). It required neither skilled labor nor specialized equipment in its construction. The many intersections of the web created a rational system that allowed the truss to be used in any length, over piers or between two shores. The system was easily adaptable to any given terrain and thus reproducible on any site. Since there was no need to redesign the bridge each time one was constructed, Town charged by the foot for the use of his invention: one dollar per foot for the bridge to be erected; two dollars per foot, as a fine, for the bridge erected without Town's consent.[79] Town personally supervised the construction of approximately fifty such bridges during his lifetime, and dozens of other bridges utilized his invention. Town's design was thus easily "shipped" anywhere across the continent and could be easily assembled with readily available materials by anyone, like a simple "kit of parts." Like the Town truss, Erector Set educated to construction with a rational and interchangeable system of parts. Exemplifying the strength of the square-girder construct and reproducible in any model type, both life-size model and toy made play with technology more accessible and familiar.

Because of its practicality, the Town truss was adopted widely and has been credited with the rapid spread of railroads.[80] Gradually, iron and steel bridges following a similar design replaced the original wooden bridges, and their numbers grew with the increased need for rail routes. Yet, at the end of the nineteenth century and during the early twentieth century, as construction with the truss became more prevalent, images of steel piles and collapsed girders circulated widely. The fame of these bridges became tightly linked to disaster and collapse, as "bridge and train, the 2 symbols of an era, lay wrecked in shambles" (fig. 72).[81] Conflicting attitudes toward these early engineering feats—awe and fear or "untamed euphoria and paralyzing horror"—became intricately tied.[82]

Erector manuals emphasized practice with square girder construction, but

Fig. 71. Jordan River Town truss bridge, Salt Lake City, Utah.

Fig. 72. Fake bridge collapse and train wreck, made with Erector girders in Hollywood, California, and used as "flash shot" in a motion picture. Date unspecified, sent to A. C. Gilbert Company.

assembly was not always easy. Play often culminated in piles of metal on the floor. Some players recalled clumsily manipulating the small nuts and bolts in the awkward, tight spaces between the steel girders. "I couldn't have been the only boy to send my Revolving Dock Hoist flying across the room in a fit," confessed an adult of his early play. "My Windmill looked like a steel magnolia," he added, and "Unloading Crane—more like the feathered cranes found fishing in rivers than denizens of a construction site."[83]

A series of famous collapses propagated fear but also paved the way to engineering masterpieces. Such was the case of the famous Firth of Forth Bridge between Edinburgh and Fife, Scotland, whose successful design was tied to the earlier collapse of its neighbor, the Firth of Tay Bridge, which was said to copy in iron the wooden Town truss. The 1879 collapse of the Tay Bridge is considered a turning point in the history of engineering design—the end of an era of optimism and faith in developing technology and the beginning of anxiety, fear, and doubt.[84] Constructed in Dundee, Scotland, between 1871 and 1877, the bridge—a regular sequence of piers and girders—was considered at the time to be a world wonder (fig. 73). The central section of the Tay Bridge consisted of a regular sequence of large lattice girders supported on cast-iron tubular piers that created a long, monotonous structure undulating through the bay. The large girders—giant box-trusses the size of a train car—took four weeks to assemble, weighed 190 tons, and used eighteen thousand rivets each. They were built on shore, transported to the site on floating barges, and set on the piers with the rising tide before the piers themselves were raised (fig. 74). Possibly referring to its timber predecessor, the Town truss, the Tay's "style" was then labeled "early-American."[85] All of Town's bridges had been made of timber, but because he had defined the system as applicable to iron bridges, the Town truss was considered the precursor of the metal truss, anticipating steel-girder construction by almost seventy-five years. When, at the beginning of the twentieth century, the wooden lattice bridges gave way, they were almost immediately replaced by steel bridges of a similar design.[86]

During the short life of the Tay Bridge, its ties and girders perpetually rattled as trains passed. Bolts and pieces of iron constantly fell off. According to records, the caretaker regularly replaced the bolts, screws, and rivets, and had noticed, repeatedly, the loosening of the wind ties.[87] Then, in December 1879, the bridge collapsed as a train entered the center span (fig. 75). On a dark, stormy night,

Fig. 73. The first Tay Bridge (1871-77) as seen from the north.

Fig. 74. A girder being floated out during construction of the first Tay Bridge (1871-77).

Fig. 75. The collapse
of the Tay Bridge,
December 1879.

with no electricity, no one saw the crash, but train personnel surmised what had taken place when the train failed to arrive on the other side. It was perceived that the accident, killing all seventy-five passengers onboard, "was almost unprecedented in the annals of earthly disasters."[88] The Wreck Commission found fault with the bridge's design, which could not adequately withstand the effects of wind pressure combined with the oscillations of the structure. Furthermore, the commission uncovered faults with the structure's execution, as the iron parts were full of air holes. These findings destroyed the career, and indeed the life, of the bridge's engineer, Sir Thomas Bouch (1822–1880), who died shortly after the devastating collapse.

That failure of the Firth of Tay Bridge led to an incredible feat of engineering—The Firth of Forth Bridge, which already in 1904 was featured as a model to be assembled with one of the earliest Meccano sets (figs. 76, 77). It was a requirement that the stability should be visible during the different stages of construction. This condition could have not been achieved with a suspension bridge, which was the reason why that structural option was immediately abandoned and a cantilever system was chosen instead.[89] Sir John Fowler (1817–1898) and Sir Benjamin Baker (1840–1907), then known as the best engineers in Britain, had their plans approved in two hours. "The most important stipulation," the construction permit stated, "was that the bridge should become known among the public not merely as the largest and strongest, but also as the stiffest bridge in the world."[90] The complexity of the construction required the building of cranes, derrick cranes, and even houses to be anchored within the bridge's own structure. Fowler, who had apprenticed as a hydraulic engineer, and Baker experimented on a large scale every step of the way. Men were working inside and out of the tubes and girders, traveling upon them in cages and hydraulic "travelers." During construction the bridge appeared as a mix of permanent structures and invented machinery, as thousands of people were building it up in different directions simultaneously. A contemporary account related: "Every piece of work done becomes the basis of another advance, and the Forth Bridge men labour much in the same way as the Esquimaux who ascend the ice-cliff by cutting steps, one after the other in its face."[91] Even the final girder pieces connecting between the cantilevers, rather than being first assembled on shore, were built up and fastened from the cantilever piece by piece, therefore using the cantilever principle. Perhaps because of fear and the extra caution used, the result was a bridge that was designed to be twice as stable as was deemed necessary.[92] The Forth Bridge became the climax of the cast-iron age. Through the bridge's design,

Fig. 76. South cantilever of the Forth Bridge, in W. Westhofen, "The Forth Bridge," *Engineering*, February 28, 1890.

Fig. No. 61. Forth Bridge
(MADE WITH MECCANO OUTFIT No. 6 OR No. 5 AND No. 5A)

	Parts required in addition to Outfits.				
PARTS REQUIRED.	No. 1	No. 2	No. 3	No. 4	No. 5
164 12½" Perforated Strips.	158	154	152	144	116
264 5½" " "	254	246	243	236	224
122 3½" " "	121	120	116	116	98
112 2½" " "	100	96	88	84	24
248 Angle Brackets.	230	230	203	194	138
850 Nuts and Bolts.	820	800	773	728	600

Fig. 77. Model of the Forth Bridge made with Meccano Outfit no. 6, as shown in Meccano instruction manual, 1904.

Fig. 78. The south
arm of the Quebec
Bridge immediately
before the collapse
on August 29, 1907.

its tremendous size, and the extraordinary stresses to which it was subjected during construction, trust in steel was conveyed.

Nevertheless, the confidence acquired in the cantilever bridge and conveyed by the stability of the Forth's cantilevers led to another famous collapse. Like the Forth that became famous following the Tay's collapse, the second-most famous bridge of the era was also shaped by disaster. At 1,800 feet, the cantilever span of the Quebec Bridge was to be the largest constructed in North America.[93] The lines of the bridge were reminiscent of its Scottish predecessor, but in contrast with it, its sections were minimal (fig. 78). Compared in scale, Quebec's bottom structural members could fit inside the massive Forth's. Nevertheless, because the Forth used tubular hollow steel, its weight per linear foot was considerably less than that of the Quebec. Construction at Quebec was proceeding from both shores. The cantilever arm and the two halves of the suspended span were erected toward each other by means of cranes, traveling along the built parts. By the sum-

Fig. 79. The wreckage of
the Quebec Bridge, 1907.

mer of 1907, the south arm was completed, as well as a third of the suspended arm, when a deflection in the bottom chord was noticed. On the afternoon of August 29, 1907, "work was going on as usual, the men being employed in placing the immense girders in position," although the situation worsened. Then, with no warning, "the bridge fell at exactly twenty-three minutes to six . . . just as many of the workmen were preparing to leave. It was . . . so horribly effective in wiping out the lives of the men employed on it that very little is known as to how it happened." Killing eighty-four men, it was considered the worst disaster in the history of bridge construction in North America (fig. 79).[94]

It was discovered that an error had been made in assuming the dead load, and the bridge collapsed when one of the main compression members in the south arm failed under approximately half the load it was supposed to later sustain. *Scientific American* reported that "the tremendous significance of this disaster lies in the suspicion, which is staring every engineer coldly in the face, that there is something wrong with our theories of bridge design, at least as applied to a structure the size of the Quebec Bridge."[95] The men responsible included superintendents on the site, who had allowed construction to continue, as well as the bridge's designer, Theodore Cooper (1839–1919).[96] Still, twenty years after the collapse of the Tay, "a bridge represented more than the triumph of an engineer; it was tangible evidence of the power of the nation that built it. . . . This being the case, any failure was doubly catastrophic. . . . The greatest bridge in North America lay, a crumpled heap of steel, on the banks of the St. Lawrence. . . . In the eyes of the world, the reputation of the American engineering profession sank with the bridge."[97] Construction started on a new Quebec Bridge in 1912. It was to be a cantilever also, with a 1,800-foot span, much heavier than the original and the first major truss bridge in North America to finally abandon pin connections in favor of rivets. Erector Set reflected this development in 1914, as Gilbert introduced the appearance of rivets on the small Erector girders.[98]

Toward the end of construction, in 1916, the cantilever arms on both shores were ready to receive the suspended span. Built off-site, the span was floated into place, with a large assembly of people watching. It was to be lifted to its place 150 feet above the water, but as soon as the operation began, a jack on the bridge failed, causing the span to buckle and fold, in front of the riveted audience, eventually plunging deep into the river. Again, the accident cost numerous lives, and it caused a year's delay in the bridge's completion.[99]

The collapses of the Tay and Quebec Bridges were the most famous, but they were far from being the only ones. *Engineering News* in April 1890 reported a total of 286 bridge failures since 1879, 43 of which were bridges made of iron.[100] The numbers of failures continued to rise as bridge construction grew. In 1895, there were 37 failures of railroad bridges, and by January 1896, *Engineering News* reported, 104 bridge failures were recorded in the United States and Canada, including 37 railroad bridges and 16 bridges made of iron.[101] According to the engineer J. A. L. Waddell, writing on bridge failures in *Bridge Engineering* in 1916, "very little publicity was given in the technical press to these accidents at the times of their occurrence."[102] But since the number of casualties was not minimal, the public could not ignore the collapses, and fear of the bridge and of railroad travel increased. *Engineering News* recorded the "external" causes of failure. Most railroad bridges were knocked down by derailed cars. Some highway bridges fell because of sudden increases in load, it was reported, such as a

ARCHITECTURE IN PLAY

Fig. 80. Wreck of Zeppelin LZ4 after Echterdingen disaster, August 1908.

crowd watching a fire, a political parade, or simply a horse and a carriage. Smaller bridges were destroyed by water currents. Wooden bridges burned. Some failures, however, were recorded as "square falls," where the bridge simply collapsed without a load or other obvious cause. In other catastrophes, girder structures, such as Zeppelins, would also collapse, further demonstrating the perils of technology at the time (fig. 80).

In the face of these ominous threats of failure, the press felt a need to emphasize stability and balance. For example, in order to convey the stability of the Forth Bridge despite its scale and daring design, the supervisor of the cantilever's construction, Wilhelm Westhofen, superimposed two horizontal Eiffel Towers upon the Forth's cantilever span in an 1889 article celebrating the structure's opening (fig. 81). The famous tower, duplicated and leaned on its side, was meant to convey the strength and rigidity of the Forth's span; at the same time, the juxtaposition of imagery also meant to suggest that the thrill of crossing the bridge equaled the experience of reaching great heights.

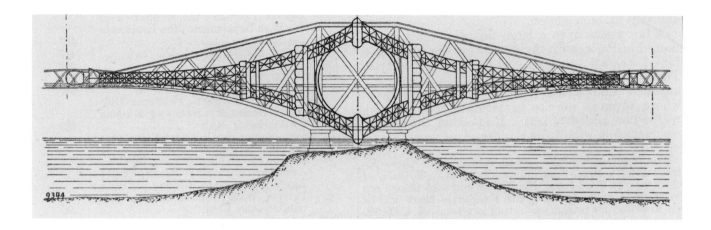

Fig. 81. "Diagram
Showing Relative Sizes
of Two Eiffel Towers and
Two Half-Spans of Forth
Bridge," W. Westhofen,
Engineering, May 3, 1889.

Westhofen also used what he called the "Living Model" to demonstrate the stability of the structure. The much-publicized illustration of the structural principle of the Forth's cantilever span was first shown in 1887, during a lecture at the Royal Institution in London (fig. 82). Chairs represented the large granite piers, a third of a mile apart; the men's arms represented the huge lattice of steel girders; and sticks at the bottom represented the 12-foot-diameter tubes at the base of the bridge. This human model attempted to convey the trust that man should have, not only with steel construction but also with the principles of the bridge's design.[103] All in all, as people were surrounded by airplanes, bridges, and towers made with girders and trusses, their fear had to be counterbalanced with reassurance and understanding. People needed help coping with the challenges of a complex technological life (fig. 83).

Since Meccano and Erector Set duplicated real, full-scale engineering structures, play with the small steel parts may have contributed to people's comfort with the technological environment and the new challenges it presented in everyday life. Three possible understandings of play with the structural-mechanical toys could thus arise. Meccano and Erector Set could be understood as "self-help" toys; as toys presenting play in the image of work; and also as toys allowing children to play with the urge to destroy.

Images of metal piles, of destruction and collapse, were ingrained in people's minds. The ability to construct and assemble the parts, to put together familiar structures with "real" steel pieces, may have helped restore the confidence one needed to confront the challenges presented by technology. Frank Hornby described in his biography the strong impact one book had on his life. This was

Fig. 82. "Living Model," illustrating the cantilever principle of the Forth Bridge, in W. Westhofen, "The Forth Bridge," *Engineering,* February 28, 1890.

Fig. 83. Wright biplane encircling the Eiffel Tower, 1909.

Self-Help by Samuel Smiles (1812–1904), first published in 1859, which by the end of the nineteenth century had been translated into twenty-two languages and had attained phenomenal success worldwide.[104] Hornby claimed that the invention of Meccano was directly inspired by *Self-Help.* The book was based on a series of lectures Smiles had given to a group of approximately one hundred workmen who had set up the first school for adult education in Leeds. As a journalist in Leeds, Smiles became acquainted with the poverty and lack of education of the masses and the impossibility of their collective advancement, and turned to ideas of self-help as means for the workers to achieve "self-culture" and success.

His lectures, a blend of practical advice and biographical anecdotes, became very popular in Leeds. Smiles borrowed the anecdotes from another book he had written, *The Lives of the Engineers* (1862), a four-volume compilation of the numerous trials, hardships, and failures on the road to success of many inventors and engineers.[105] The self-help principles he illustrated with these examples conveyed that success could be achieved by anyone who tried—regardless of background, education, or wealth—if only one applied oneself to a task with relentless perseverance.

All of the examples Smiles offered in *Self-Help* demonstrated the benefits of mechanical manipulation, as the author emphasized that manual skills were the surest means to achieve self-culture. "The training of young men in the use of tools would," he asserted, "impart to them the ability of being useful, and implant in them the habit of persevering physical effort."[106] Smiles presented this as an "advantage which the working classes, strictly so called, certainly possess over the leisure classes,—that they are in early life under the necessity of applying themselves laboriously to some mechanical pursuit or other,—thus acquiring manual dexterity and the use of their physical powers."[107] He gave as example the great scientist Sir Isaac Newton and the innovator and railway engineer George Stephenson, who were among the many successful inventors to have used their hands during their youth, "knocking and hammering . . . making models of windmills, carriages and machines of all sorts."[108] James Watt, the inventor of the steam engine, acquired his dexterous skills when, as a child, he manipulated the geometrical quadrants lying around in his father's carpenter shop. "Even when a boy," Smiles wrote, "Watt found science in his toys."[109] The ingenuity of great inventors and engineers, he concluded, was caused by the "constant use of their hands in early life."[110] Later in life, the men also shared three significant experiences. At first, they encountered seemingly insurmountable difficulty; then they experienced failure, which Smiles's examples indicate happened more than once. Eventually, with arduous work, tenacity, and relentless perseverance, the engineer or inventor overcame failure and arrived at a successful resolution. Throughout the book, Smiles repeated tirelessly the lesson "that it is not men of genius who move the world and take the lead in it, so much as men of steadfastness, purpose, and indefatigable industry."[111] Thus, *Self-Help*'s motto was to work through problems and overcome failure to achieve true success in life.

It was thus Samuel Smiles who inspired Frank Hornby, not only to persevere in his inventions and relentless aspirations for success, but to invent Meccano, which Hornby said, "you might nick name . . . the 'Self Help' toy."[112] Besides teaching fundamental principles of mechanical and structural engineering, this "self-help toy" was meant to teach how to "be helpful" and to "build on sound principles."[113] "Building right," in Meccano's language, meant not only doing what "the gang of men who are working like a swarm of busy bees on the big skyscrapers in the city are doing,"[114] but also taking one's fate into one's own hands, constructing one's own life and future. "Build right now, with Meccano," Hornby said, "and Meccano will teach you how to build right in the future."[115]

A similar kind of "self-help" literature existed in the United States at the time of Erector Set's invention. Although there is no mention of Gilbert having read any of the success and self-help literature that was so popular at the time, it could not have gone unnoticed. Gilbert himself was the subject of articles in the related press, as for example, in *Efficiency Magazine*.[116] Orison Swett Marden (1848–1924), the founder of the Success Movement, was the American counterpart of Smiles. Marden, who had read Smiles and considered him to be the greatest influence on his life, wrote more than thirty inspirational books chronicling his own struggles and offering advice on how to become a successful, "self-made" man. *Pushing to the Front, or Success under Difficulties,* published in 1894, was Marden's first popular self-help book.[117] The names of its chapters were imbued with engineering-related vocabulary. The chapter "An Iron Will" showed that with resolution there is no limit to a boy's career, while the chapter "Round Boys in Square Holes" taught how to shake disappointment, leave behind one's weaknesses, and live by one's strengths. Aspiring "to encourage and stimulate to higher resolve those who are setting out to make their own way,"[118] Marden published *Rising in the World; or, Architects of Fate* in 1895. In a chapter called "Self-Help," Marden reiterated Smiles's teachings and demonstrated that men were either "self-made or never made."[119] Marden also founded *Success* magazine,

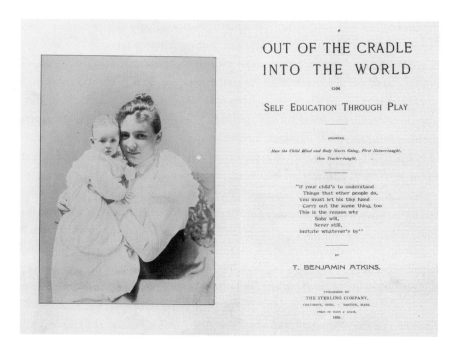

Fig. 84. T. Benjamin
Atkins, *Out of the
Cradle into the World
or Self-Education
through Play,* 1895.

which reached its peak circulation at the beginning of the twentieth century. *Success* followed the model of the self-help books and related the stories of individuals who fulfilled their aspirations through hard work.

Other contemporary books echoed similar concerns and related more specifically to education and to play. *Out of the Cradle into the World, or Self Education through Play* was written by T. Benjamin Atkins in 1895 (fig. 84).[120] "There are two schools," Atkins stated, "the play school and the book school. In the book school the child is taught by the aid of teachers; in the play school he is self-taught."[121] Atkins set a child's early play as self-education toward his vocation in later life. The chapter "Play, A Self-Education in the Industrial Arts"[122] emphasized that play was a training school, "indispensably necessary to the work of manhood and womanhood. Without this 'play work' children would never become working men and women."[123] The chapter "The Use of Toys as Self-Education in the Use of Tools" conveyed that repetition was necessary to acquire skill, as "dexterity is not natural to the child. On the contrary, what a flabby, awkward, ridiculous thing the child is in his first efforts at self-help."[124] This book and others convey the proliferation of ideas surrounding the concept of self-help. Although there exists no trace of Gilbert's library, it is likely that he came across self-help and success publications that were popular throughout the United States and England at the time of Erector Set's inception.

Principles of self-help, as defined by Smiles and Marden, could be practiced by manipulating the small parts of the steel toy. The difficulty in handling the pieces exasperated most children, as well as adults. Could the constant presence of the parent next to the boy—in advertisements and box covers—suggest that the structural-mechanical education was in fact directed also to the older generation, to the adult? Were Erector Set and Meccano meant to provide an adult education? *Self-Help* presented a sort of hands-on manual on how to get on in a world that was increasingly competitive, industrialized, and urban. Similarly, by demonstrating the lessons of hardship, failure, and perseverance—the lessons of self-help—both Meccano and Erector Set could be defined as self-help toys, promising success in life through play with engineering.

Another understanding of play with structural-mechanical toys relates to their embodiment of work and labor. In late-nineteenth-century and early-twentieth-century industrial America, work was understood to be the core of moral life. "The factory system represented, in one sense, the triumph of the work ethic," wrote the historian Daniel Rodgers in *The Work Ethic in Industrial America, 1850–1920,* as "the elevation of work over leisure involved not an isolated choice, but an ethos that permeated life and manners."[125] This work ethic called for intense production, reflecting a belief in the virtue of activity and a scorn for idleness. It was especially felt in the Northeast, where, until 1919, 70 percent of U.S. goods were manufactured. Notions of success and self-help were part of this ideology, elevating work to high moral ground. Self-help manuals and success writings formed part of a larger body of literature produced to sustain the argument that work would lead to independence and that diligence and perseverance would result in wealth and greater social status. The "ingredients of the mid-nineteenth-century work ethic," Rodgers wrote, were "the dream of success and a faith in work as a creative act. . . . In the fluid American economy, hard work, self-control, and dogged persistence were the certain escalators of success."[126] With the growth of manufacturing and industry, this work ethic intensified: it was all about work, work, work. At the turn of the century, the typical steel worker labored twelve hours a day, seven days week; in 1910, although an eight-hour day was established, workers still reported seven days a week.[127]

Alongside the growth of enterprise, strenuous factory work, and the elevation of work ideals, a shift occurred that gave rise to new notions of recreation and play. As Rodgers explained, the end of the century represented "the years in which middle-class Northerners learned to take holidays, to play, and with some effort, to relax—all in growing confidence that the world could afford their vacations from labor."[128] Excess work was rejected in favor of play and recreation, words that slowly entered the "success vocabulary" as well. "Fun is a necessity," proclaimed Marden in *Success* magazine,[129] while another success writer wrote, "The boy of success is always busy—busy studying, busy working, busy playing, busy resting."[130] Also during that time, the Playground Association of America was founded, and the new profession of recreation and playground specialist was created. Joseph Lee, the head of the Playground Association, was one of the main protagonists in the shift from relentless discipline to spontaneous play. Kindergartens and playgrounds proliferated across the United States, as well as literature praising play and celebrating man's physical instincts (fig. 85). There was an explosion of leisure activities, offered by sporting events such as football and baseball, and amusement parks such as Coney Island. Nevertheless, play consisted mostly of activities that were as energy consuming as work—muscle building and athletics—and emphasized competition, which was considered an essential initiation into manhood. "Action was a central preoccupation of the age," and "the cult of strenuosity and the recreation movement grew together, minimizing the distinctions between usefulness and sport, toil and recreation, the work ethic and the spirit of play."[131] In 1907, in a survey of play and games, George Johnson, a sociologist, noticed the shift toward more strenuous activities and the evaluation of play based on its usefulness, concluding: "The child should not be led to expect a life of toil. Rather he should be taught that a life of play-work is the ideal, and that it is his privilege to seek it."[132]

The difficulty, then, during the second half of the nineteenth century, became how to strike a balance between the value of work and the utility of leisure. Relaxation was still a new concept that was inflected with opposing nuances. As Rodgers explained: "All recreation writers advertised play as an intensely serious endeavor. Play was not idleness, nor leisure loafing."[133] In the beginning, there was no ambiguity about play: play needed to be just as strenuous and difficult as work. So as not to upset the familiar certitudes of perseverance and self-discipline, even new playgrounds were designed to encourage vigorous physical exercise. To accept that play was as necessary and productive as work was unsettling; hence play was tolerated only if it was shown to be as intensely serious an endeavor as work—difficult, productive, and necessary. In this cultural context, Meccano and Erector Sets could be seen as "work toys," providing play in the image of work.

A further appreciation and understanding of the toys is gained by contemporary definitions of play. In 1911, the year of Erector Set's invention, John Dewey (1859–1952) was a professor of philosophy at Columbia University and wrote extensively about the philosophy of education. He contributed the definition of "play" to the *Cyclopedia of Education,* first published during that same year. Play, Dewey wrote, is "a name given to those activities which are not consciously performed for the sake of any result beyond themselves; activities which are enjoyable in their own execution without reference to ulterior purpose."[134] For a long time, Dewey explained, the theory of play was based on the definition provided by Herbert Spencer in his 1855 *Principles of Psychology.* Play was believed to arise from the overflow of surplus energy not expended in the daily activities necessary for maintaining one's health and survival. For this reason, children (who were mostly spared from providing their own sustenance) had more surplus energy at their disposal and thus played more than adults. Nevertheless, the channels for the discharge of a child's energy followed channels similar to those of adult acts motivated by necessity, and consequently, play often took the form of practical activities. Karl Groos, a psychologist who wrote *The Play of Animals* and *The Play of Man* at the turn of the cen-

CHICAGO MUNICIPAL OUTDOOR GYMNASIUM

We furnished twenty outfits, like the above, to the City of Chicago in 1906, the largest order for Playground Apparatus ever awarded.

Playground Apparatus
Public or Private
Swings, Rings, Ladders, See-Saws
Teeters, etc.

Gymnastic Apparatus
Sargent, Swedish, German
Running Tracks, Mats
Everything for the Gymnasium

Lockers
Wood or Metal
Standard Sizes Carried in Stock

Write for Catalogs | **NARRAGANSETT MACHINE CO.** PROVIDENCE, R. I., U. S. A.

Fig. 85. Ad for playground apparatus featuring the Chicago Municipal Outdoor Gymnasium, 1906, by the Narragansett Machine Co. Providence, R.I. From *Playground,* no. 1, April 1907.

tury, provided yet another definition.[135] He noted that play took the form of acts that proved to be useful later in life. His explanation differed from Spencer's by emphasizing the value of the act of play—play as the practice of future deeds—rather than its motivating force. Albeit in different ways, play served an ulterior purpose in the thinking of Groos and Spencer.

In contrast, Dewey's definition of play, encompassing activities performed for the sake of immediate gratification without reference to an ulterior purpose, stemmed from the belief that the organism was in constant motion and hence did not require surplus energy to lead to action. His definition related, yet differentiated, the acts of play and work. Both play and work started in a similar manner: a stimulus causes an activity, the result of which is pleasurable. There is then a desire to repeat the activity in order to maintain the pleasure: "Seeing a thing in a certain way evokes responses that make further seeings enjoyable."[136] Such enjoyable repetition may be called play. If, however, following such repetition, "the idea of the result operates as a stimulus to renew the otherwise flagging activity, and if, in addition, the accomplishing of the result involves a certain selection and arrangement of acts antecedent to it, we get a type of activity sufficiently contrasted to be termed work."[137] Thus, according to Dewey, work "is inevitably preceded by play and grows insensibly out of it."[138] "The chief point of difference," he added, "is not the agreeableness of one and the disagreeableness of the other, but that in the case of work the idea of an end enforces reflection on the relations of means to end, and stimulates a corresponding readjustment of activities originally spontaneous."[139] When the ends and means are barely differentiated, the activity engaged in can clearly be called play.

Play, Dewey thus concluded, had an important place in culture and an invaluable role in education. Since most adult activity was a result of the activity of an earlier period in life, there existed

> the necessity that the earlier plays be of such a sort as to grow naturally and helpfully into the later more reflective and productive modes of behavior. This means that play should pass insensibly into work . . . and that earlier play and work alike be of the kinds which afford exercise in the occupations that are socially useful. . . . In other words, the natural transition of play into work is the means and the only means of reconciling the development of social efficiency with that of individual fullness of life.[140]

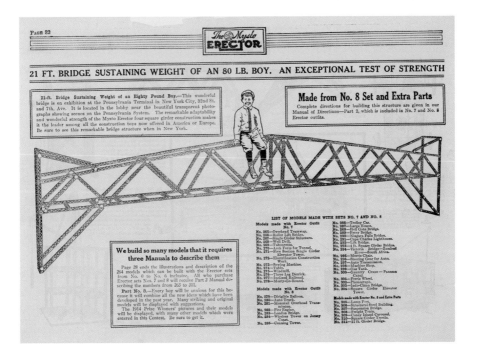

Education, then, played an important role, especially, Dewey wrote, in an era marked by increasing specialization and industrialization:

> It is a part of the business of education to fortify and enrich the imagination so that the mechanical phases of industry shall not leave an unformed mind at the mercy of sense, appetite and trivial fancy. It is a part of its business to come into sufficiently close contact with the conditions of industry so that those who go from school into industry shall be trained to understand the whole of which their work is a small fraction, and thus to see a meaning in their work which they could not otherwise perceive.[141]

Erector Set and Meccano presented the "bridge" that Dewey described between the early stages of education, necessitating imagination and play, and the later stages of work, which at the beginning of the twentieth century were daunting in their requirements for technological know-how, specialized menial skills, and repetition. These toys provided a natural transition from play to work—a transition Dewey posited as requisite for a person's sense of fulfillment in life (fig. 86).

Fig. 86. "21 ft. Bridge Sustaining Weight of an 80 lb. Boy. An Exceptional Test of Strength." From instruction manual for The Mysto Erector: The Toy Whose Girders Resemble Structural Steel.

Spencer's earlier definition of play emphasized an additional component that was not sustained in Dewey's formulation. "Play," Spencer wrote, "is equally an artificial exercise of powers which, in default of their natural exercise, become so ready to discharge that they relieve themselves by simulated actions instead of real actions."[142] Referring to the surplus energy ready to discharge, the simulated acts of play could very well be, according to Spencer, the embodiment of acts of a destructive nature that were not usually allowed free expression in life. "For dogs and other predatory creatures," he explained, "show us unmistakably that their play consists of mimic chase and mimic fighting—they pursue one another, they try to overthrow one another, they bite one another as much as they dare . . . an ideal satisfaction for the destructive instincts in the absence of real satisfaction for them. It is the same for human beings."[143] "The sports of boys, chasing one another, wrestling, making prisoners, obviously gratify in a partial way the predatory instincts."[144] The bodily powers, Spencer added, "the destructive instincts, and those emotions related to them that dominate in life because they are directly concerned in the struggle by which life is maintained,"[145] mark a path for all other faculties, looking first for instant gratification, with no reference to ulterior motives or benefits:

Gratifications that accompany actions performed without reference to ends, will mostly be those which accompany actions predominating in the creature's life. And hence this first form of them called play, is shown in the superfluous activity of the *sensori-motor* apparatus and of those destructive instincts which habitually guide its actions. When they are established, the higher orders of co-ordinating powers also come to have their superfluous activities and corresponding pleasures, in games and other exercises somewhat more remote from the destructive activities.[146]

Thus, according to Spencer, the destructive instinct is one of the first faculties to be expressed in play. Erector and Meccano taught various uses of the girder—from engineering structures to domestic applications. With these toys, one exercised, at an early age, dexterity, construction skills, resourcefulness, and the coordination of hand and eye. But simultaneously, Erector and Meccano also allowed for the performing of acts not tolerated later in life. In play, they allowed one to exercise the primal urge to destroy.

Playing with Erector Set and Meccano could be an act of "self-help": building trust in a complex technological world, building reassurance that world would not collapse. Play was also conducted in the image of work, at a time when play was accepted only if it was made to be as difficult and strenuous as work. Lastly, play with the steel toys could implicitly mean "to destroy": play as the practice of that urge to break down and take apart.

Meccano Magazine, like Erector Set's pamphlets, circulated the latest engineering news to its players. In 1926, *Meccano Magazine* announced the construction of the "Largest Arch Bridge in the World" and showed renderings of the 50,000-ton steel arch bridge intended to span Sydney Harbour in Australia (fig. 87). The accompanying caption read: "Already Meccano enthusiasts are building models of the Sydney Harbour Bridge. This one, built by Everard J. Earl of Sydney, is strong enough to bear the weight of its builder, his sister and his father, showing that the model is constructed on correct engineering principles."[147]

Looking at the family—father, daughter, and son—standing on the bridge that the eight-year-old Everard had constructed with Meccano parts, its center span slightly buckling, one is compelled to ask: Are they practicing their destructive-play impulse by trying to break the bridge? Or are they testing their faith in technology, trying to reassure themselves—and the world—that the bridge will not collapse?

Fig. 87. Sydney Harbour Bridge built with Meccano parts by Everard J. Earl, eight years old (*left*), who is standing on the bridge with his father and sister. From *Meccano Magazine* 11, no. 12, December 1926.

Fig. 88. A sketch illustrating the significance of a child's space, Gyorgy and Juliet
Kepes, in "The Most Important Room," *Interiors,* January 1949.

The Toy, 1951, and House of Cards, 1952

As World War II drew to a close, interest in design for children began to rise. Toys and furniture became the subject of numerous articles and exhibitions that appeared in art- and design-related venues. The June 1948 issue of *Everyday Art Quarterly*—a journal published by the Walker Art Institute that aimed to present design as a bridge between everyday life and modern art—featured objects for children, some of which were designed by architects, including a hobbyhorse by Anne Tyng and a magnetic toy by Arthur Carrara. Other journals followed suit. In January 1949, *Interiors* magazine printed an article by György and Juliet Kepes entitled "The Most Important Room" that presented sketch proposals for toys, furniture, and sculpture intended for children (fig. 88). *Arts and Architecture* of December 1952 featured an exhibition organized for children at the Pasadena Art Institute entitled *The Little Craftsman* that encouraged the Lilliputian museumgoer to experience with tools and materials directly.[1] As the Kepeses' article suggests, the interest in designing objects, exhibitions, and environments for children reflected a growing consensus that "the first years [of a child's life] are a time of concentrated learning and development. They should also be a time of wonder and delight. They should be spent in a room that . . . should contain materials with which to color, mold and make things."[2]

It was within the context of this general interest that in September 1951, in an article entitled "Another Toy to Tinker With," *Interiors* magazine introduced The Toy. Designed by Charles and Ray Eames, The Toy was presented as a "happy change from the intricate, puzzling, super-mechanical constructor set which has been the standard building toy since little Gilbert wore knickers."[3] Designed a year later, House of Cards was introduced by *Interiors* in July 1953 as another one of the Eameses' "unusual construction toys [with which] hundreds of different constructions can be made . . . without the attendant frustration of cards building." "Fresh new forms," it proclaimed, "can be assembled and reassembled."[4] In addition, the Eameses' toys were presented as being of particular interest to adults: "When the old folks discover that The Toy is handy for party decorations, backdrops, floats, or other fruits of their rusty imaginations, they may be persuaded to keep a couple of boxes of The Toy kicking around the house like Band-Aids or Kleenex, just in case,"[5] suggested the editors; House of Cards was portrayed as "a boon to bored shut-in adults who have tired of cheating themselves at solitaire."[6] This notion foreshadowed what one of the Eameses' grandchildren would maintain in a 1959 *Vogue* article: "Toys are not for children, they are for grandparents."[7]

Designing toys was very serious play for Charles Eames (1907–1978) and Ray Kaiser Eames (1912–1988). Their architectural office had designed children's furniture in laminated birch since 1945. They had also designed molded plywood animals—horses, bears, frogs, and elephants—upon which children could sit or with which they could play. What started as an offshoot of their work with wood laminates evolved during a fifteen-year period to include a series of objects relating to children: furniture, masks, costumes, and toys. The couple also produced films, the main protagonists of which were puppets, toy buildings, and mechanical toys. Some of the projects were intended specifically for children, while others—such as the films—were addressed to audiences of all ages: they conveyed the beauty and color, as well as the great sense of order, found in everyday acts of play.[8]

Of the numerous objects and toys that Charles and Ray Eames designed for children, The Toy (1951) and House of Cards (1952) were the only two construction sets that were manufactured. Both sets presented open-ended play: a multiplicity of combinations could be formed using a single-joint system that established a set language of forms. The focus of these two manufactured toys follows a well-known diagram that Charles Eames drew in 1969, on the occasion of an exhibition at the Louvre Museum entitled *Qu'est ce que le design?* (What is design?). Three overlapping areas represented the design process of the Eames

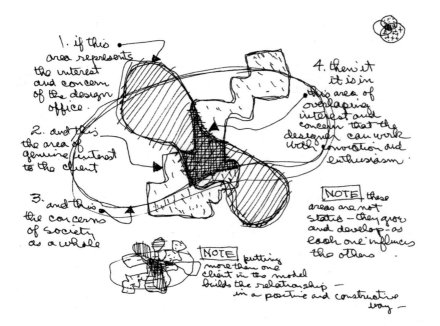

1. if this area represents the interest and concern of the design office.

2. and this the area of genuine interest to the client

3. and this the concerns of society as a whole

4. then it it is in this area of overlapping interest and concern that the designer can work with conviction and enthusiasm.

NOTE these areas are not static — they grow and develop — as each one influences the others

NOTE putting more than one client in this model builds the relationship — in a positive and constructive way —

Office (fig. 89). One area shows the demands of society; the second, the general interests of the design office; and the third, the requirements of the client. It was in the area common to all three zones—the area of overlapping interests—that, according to Eames, the designer could "work with conviction and enthusiasm." Although the diagram was intended to situate the entire creative output of the Eames Office within its contemporary context, it can be seen as applying to their design of toys more specifically. The Toy and House of Cards, manufactured for years after their initial design, can be seen as "residing" in that overlapping zone, connecting societal demands with the requirements of the clients and being of significance to the design office. The cards convey the Eameses' obsessive collecting—some could pass for photographs of carefully choreographed corners at the Eames House—and force the player to partake actively in their celebration of everyday life.[9]

The Eameses' toys stood out among contemporary construction sets. Other building toys reflected the recent changes in the American landscape: the supremacy of the automobile and the development of the suburban home. Fox Blox, for example, a toy manufactured in California in 1950, presented a system

Fig. 89. Charles Eames, diagram of the design process, 1969.

147

Fig. 90. Charles Eames with The Toy, as shown in *Life,* July 16, 1951.

of slotted wooden panels that assembled to form a ranch-type house, much like a prefabricated home. Another popular construction toy, Plasticville, U.S.A., also first manufactured in 1950, allowed for the speedy erection of an entire town. Miniature façades of a motel, a gas station, and an airport, as well as highly detailed homes, all made of the innovative material plastic, would snap together quickly to form suburban sprawl, which could then be populated with Plasticville citizens designed to scale. The Eameses' toys, by contrast, were more abstract. Made of paper, they did not refer overtly to the environment, reflecting what Charles Eames said in the opening of the firm's film *Toccata for Toy Trains:* "In a good old toy there is apt to be nothing self-conscious about the use of materials. What is wood is wood; what is tin is tin; and what is cast is beautifully cast." "It is possible," continued the narrator, "that somewhere in all this is a clue to what sets the creative climate of any time, including our own."[10] The Toy and House of Cards were both "good old toys" in Charles Eames's description: they were reminiscent of earlier playthings, yet they had advanced beyond those toys, too. By directing players towards novel assemblies, methods of construction, and consequently new spatial environments, the toys became suggestive of the creative architectural climate of their time.

On July 16, 1951, amid a plethora of political writings on world news and U.S. domestic problems, *Life* magazine published the article "Building Toy" featuring the first toy that Charles and Ray Eames designed that was actually manufactured. The article boldly displayed full-page photographs of Charles Eames constructing a tall structure with The Toy and of children playing inside different environments created with its triangular panels (figs. 90, 91). The Toy was described as "one of the most imaginative playthings of the year," intended "to intrigue young men (5–10) who have an engineering or architectural bent and young ladies (same ages) with a homing instinct."[11] Unlike in the advertisements for earlier construction sets such as Meccano or Erector, girls were now acknowledged as having a possible interest in building, although their play constructions,

Fig. 91. The Toy, designed by Charles and Ray Eames as it appeared in *Life,* July 16, 1951.

Fig. 92. The Toy,
instruction sheet, Tigrett
Enterprises, Jackson,
Tennessee, 1951.

it was suggested, would relate to their future domestic role, unlike the professionally inspired constructions of the boys.

Designed and manufactured in 1950, The Toy consisted of brightly colored triangular and square panels measuring 30 inches on a side. Wooden dowels with pierced ends slid through sleeves on the panels' edges, and pliable connectors (pipe cleaners) joined the stiffened forms to create a series of prisms that—as the instruction sheet illustrated—could become a tent, a tower, or a theater set (fig. 92). The instruction sheet proclaimed, "*The TOY* gives each one the means with which to express himself in big structures and brilliant color." Charles Eames

Fig. 93. Ray Eames outside her home and studio in Pacific Palisades, California, constructing with The Toy in August 1950.

added that it was made "for teenagers to decorate their rooms, and for parents to make sets for plays, pageants, ballets and parties."[12] The panels were made of a recently developed, plastic-coated, moisture-proof paper that was flexible enough to be rolled into a hexagonal cardboard tube. The writing on the tube proclaimed: "Large, Colorful, Easy to Assemble, For Creating a Light Bright Expandable World." "In a jiffy any child can have a real play-in size house . . . or an airplane," a publicity leaflet promised.[13]

Charles and Ray Eames and their office staff built many structures with The Toy. Versatile and adaptable, it deployed quickly to form large, three-dimensional prismatic forms. When configured as a two-dimensional form hung from the ceiling or spread out flat on the wall, The Toy became a decoration for the home. Canopies, tents, and theater backdrops mixed with the Eameses' furniture to create colorful interiors, and airy, open structures filled the grounds outside their office, conveying the impression of a light, collapsible, temporary world. In one photograph, Ray lies on the grass among crystal-like space-frames and towers; in another, she constructs a totem pole (fig. 93). Unlike other construction toys, which referred overtly to the built environment, The Toy, expandable and foldable, with light materials, bright colors, and geometric forms, resembled a different kind of object: the kite.

Fig. 94. Box kite used in the Gibson Girl survival kit during World War II.

The flying deployable toy, constructed, like the Eameses' product, out of color-ful, lightweight materials, could also be found in stores in the early 1950s, rolled up in a long hexagonal cardboard tube.[14] Kite flying, which had been a common recreational pastime for centuries, experienced a resurgence in popularity in the postwar era. Just prior, the kite had proven valuable to the war effort: the Gibson Girl Kite was part of a rescue kit used during World War II (fig. 94). The kit contained a radio with a wire antenna that could be attached to the kite and then flown above the rescue boat to emit a distress signal. Another kite, invented in 1943 by a curator of aviation at the Smithsonian Institution, also aided in the war effort. The image of an airplane was drawn on the top side of a large kite of the Eddy type, designed in the shape of a lozenge. The kite could be made to move in a controlled manner—banking right or left, climbing, or nose-diving—like a plane. It was used by the U.S. Air Force to train aircraft gunners to shoot at moving enemy targets.

Charles and Ray Eames, whose work always combined aspects of play with efficiency in design, embraced the kite as an object exemplifying these same qual-ities. Their enthusiasm for kites dated back to the beginning of their practice in 1941, when they included kites in the interior decoration of various projects including the Herman Miller Showroom in Los Angeles of 1949 (fig. 95). Kites

Fig. 95. Kite used as interior decoration in the Herman Miller Showroom, Los Angeles, California, 1949.

were also incorporated in graphic design projects, such as the cover of *Portfolio* magazine in July 1950, which showed a large pastel-colored flying toy. The designers were avid kite collectors whose collection was comprised mainly of rare kites brought back from the couple's extensive travels throughout Asia. Among the designs were Chinese kites representing fish, owls, butterflies, and dragons; Japanese kites depicting Kabuki faces, human forms, and painted landscapes; and multicolored Indian kites. The Eameses were consistently solicited to participate in kite-flying festivals and to submit material from their collection for publication.[15] By the end of the 1960s, they were loaning as many as one hundred kites to exhibitions across the United States.[16] In 1978 the pair would produce *Kites,* a short film about the making and flying of a kite, as part of the longer film *Polavision,* which demonstrated Polaroid's instant movie camera.[17] *Kites* attested to the fact that even in the last year of their joint practice, the Eameses thought the colorful toy a splendid object to behold.

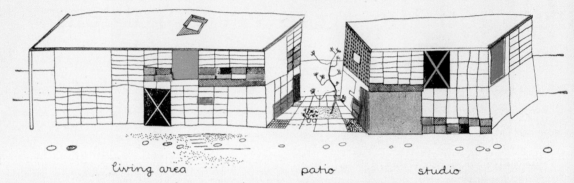

LIFE IN A CHINESE KITE

Standard industrial products assembled in a spacious wonderland

living area   patio   studio

Diagram by Eames shows flexibility of frame, many ways of rearranging facade of patterns

Fig. 96. Eames House, featured in "Life in a Chinese Kite," *Architectural Forum,* September 1950.

The kite also became a model for the Eameses' architectural projects. "Life in a Chinese Kite," an article that appeared in *Architectural Forum* in September 1950, depicted Case Study House #8, the living and working spaces designed in 1949 by Charles and Ray Eames in Pacific Palisades, California (fig. 96). The home and studio would later become known as the Eames House.[18] The article described an architecture that made efficient use of light building materials yet presented a colorful and playful construction, just like a kite. The house was pictured as "light and airy as a suspension bridge—as skeletal as an airplane fuselage."[19] Although resting firmly on the ground, it was made of kite-like "standard industrial products assembled in a spacious wonderland."[20] The illustration accompanying the article featured the now-famous sketch of the house, drawn freehand, in which two boxes—accommodating the living room and the studio—stand side by side. With its thin, gridded skin enclosing airy volumes, the house resembled a Hargrave box kite, the first scientific kite structure, which consisted of two rectangular cells connected by straight, rigid rods.[21] Hargrave's was a stable kite whose lifting ability broke previous records and provided the basis for later aviation experiments.

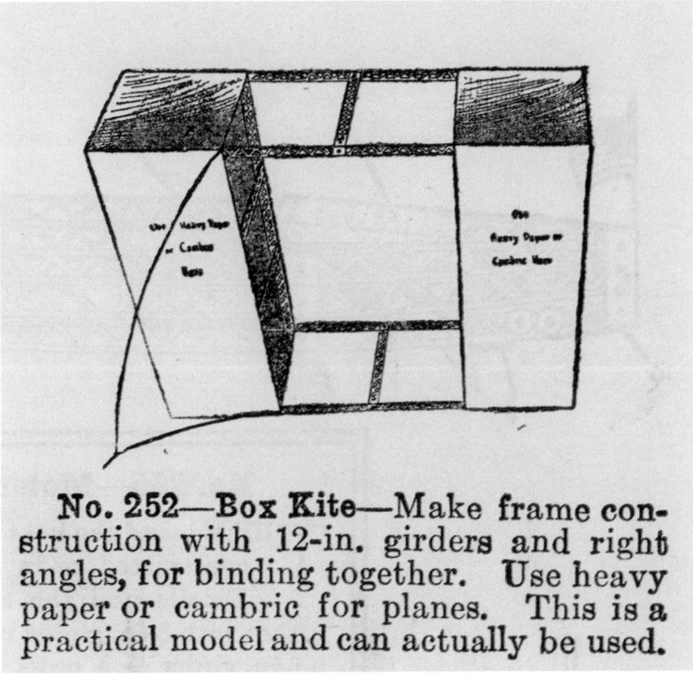

Underscoring the playful nature of the Eameses' creative acts, the article explained that the "ready-fabricated parts" chosen from a catalogue of factory-made steel products were "bolted together like a Meccano set" to construct the house (fig. 97).[22] "Using this gigantic, clean-cut toy," the editors explained, "Eames carved himself some 30,000 cu. ft. of space out of the air of the Pacific coastline. . . . Into the frame of his steel box kite he fitted sheets of glass, wire glass . . . asbestos, [and] plywood or plaster in varying colors. . . . All combined to create an ever-changing play of light and shadow, a series of surprise vistas, of sudden planes of color suspended in mid-air."[23] In the spaciousness, colorfulness, and playfulness of its architecture, the Eames House

No. 252—Box Kite—Make frame construction with 12-in. girders and right angles, for binding together. Use heavy paper or cambric for planes. This is a practical model and can actually be used.

Fig. 97. Instructions for assembling a box kite. From instruction manual for The Mysto Erector: The Toy Whose Girders Resemble Structural Steel, 1914.

resembled a kite. But a material stronger than wooden dowels was needed to erect the structure. "How light is steel?" the *Architectural Forum* article asked. In response, Charles Eames recounted his effort to create a spacious steel-frame structure. He discovered the strength of steel: a 12-inch-deep truss could span more than 20 feet, a bent sheet could bridge 7 feet, and a 4-inch steel column could stand 17 feet tall. Turnbuckles and crossed wires held together the bolted frame. The architect's interest in aviation and marine equipment was reflected in his choice of materials. Referring to his use of "light steel"[24] in the house, he declared, "This is a material inspired by the daring of aviation engineers, rather than by the more timid techniques of traditional building."[25]

The spaciousness of the house, the seeming weightlessness of its building elements, and the modularity of its different, industrial parts all related the home to the light structure of the kite. And like a kite, the Eames House was conceived as a kit of parts, which could be assembled and taken apart. As Beatriz Colomina has pointed out, the fixed set of factory-made elements that made up the home and studio could be combined and recombined to form alternative constructions; and furthermore, all of the Eameses' designs consisted of the arrangement and rearrangement of parts.[26] In a similar manner, when constructing with the geometric panels of The Toy, different modular prisms could be assembled, arranged, and rearranged in endless variations, all of which presented open, colorful, flexible spaces. Thus, when playing with The Toy, one practiced building with a kit of parts, forming spacious enclosures with lightweight industrial elements, just at a time when architects were experimenting with the modular parts of the factory-made house. However, The Toy did not present a domestic agenda: unlike play with other contemporary construction toys, play with The Toy's parts did not necessarily result in the modeling of a suburban home—not even a small avant-garde Eames House. Play was open-ended and involved combining elements, assembling interconnected webs and then taking them apart. The Toy provided tools for experimentation. Its basic elements, when formed into prismatic building blocks akin to structural particles, forced the player to conceptualize new spatial configurations.

The Eameses' exploration of novel structures—large and small—was echoed by the inventive research of their friends and colleagues, such as R. Buckminster Fuller and Konrad Wachsmann. Years before Charles and Ray Eames designed The Toy, Fuller (1895–1983) was already playing with geometric elements, with the aim of developing the most efficient dwelling structure (fig. 98). While serving in the U.S. Navy during World War I, Fuller had become familiar with the processes used in shipbuilding and aircraft manufacturing. He witnessed how very large economic resources were poured into the research and development of efficient wartime machines. It suggested to him the possibility of channeling similar scientific and economic resources into the design of the human environment in times other than war. During World War II, Fuller worked as technical advisor for the editors of *Fortune* magazine (1938–40) and served as head engineer on the Board of Economic Warfare (1943). From the vantage points provided by these posts, he observed the ineffective distribution of world resources. He had started work on the Dymaxion House already in 1927; nevertheless, his observations and experiences during times of war led him to an unwavering involvement with researching light, transportable construction and its possible application for dwelling structures. Scientific research, he hoped, could be applied to the design of housing; by doing so, making architecture could become a calculated endeavor, similar to the fabrication of a boat or an airplane.

From 1944 to 1946, while Charles and Ray Eames were establishing their practice in California, Fuller found a supportive environment for his research at the Beech Aircraft Company in Wichita, Kansas. In a climate dominated by highly advanced technology and systems of production, Fuller and his team developed a circular metal housing structure that could enclose a large space very rapidly and that was so rigid it could withstand large environmental stresses such as tornadoes, hurricanes, and earthquakes. Dynamic forces—wind flow, heat loss, and changes in atmospheric pressure—were identified as the factors affecting the design of the house, encouraging the creation of a structure that, like an aircraft, could adjust to an ever-changing, unstable environment. Hovering above the ground to allow air to flow beneath the floor, and with a ventilator revolving on the rooftop, the shiny prototype appeared, once completed, like an aerodynamic craft. An example of calculated research applied to dwelling, the Wichita House aroused great interest among both the professional community and the population at large. It remained, however, a prototype.[27] Nevertheless, Fuller continued to pursue his dream of revolutionizing the building industry, by attempting to design transportable dwellings that would adapt to different surroundings. Such a design, he believed, would provide a worldwide solution for housing shortage.

Fig. 98. Buckminster Fuller experimenting with the tetrahedron.

After completing the Wichita House, Fuller published, in 1946, *Designing a New Industry*.[28] The "new industry" he described would entail a novel approach to architecture: one that would not replicate known forms but—through the handling of new, significant elements—would adjust to an unstable set of circumstances. The booklet contained a compilation of statements directed toward engineers who had come to see the prototype. Fuller sent to his friends the Eameses a copy of the publication with the personal dedication, "To Charles and

Ray Eames, Number one colleagues in the building of this all important industry."[29] The building industry, according to Fuller, was lagging behind other trades in the amount of scientific and economic resources invested in its development. A renewed involvement with science, Fuller suggested, would inform and change design.

Fuller maintained that man, in responding to emergency situations and survival strategies, had always designed his housing with inefficient technologies and materials that were merely readily available, rather than well suited for the job. As a result, houses resembled fortresses but could not perform as protective shelters. One of the critical features requiring change involved the weight of buildings. Although weight was the main factor in the design of boats and planes, it did not come into play in the design of houses. "Architects are ignorant of the weight of their own buildings," Fuller wrote, "though weight is the key to all industrialization."[30] According to Fuller, failure to consider weight as a major factor left the house outside the forefront of industry. Housing should be thought of in terms of mobility and industrialization, and should be valued on its "performance per pound."[31] As a consequence, Fuller advised that the house should be lightweight, designed aerodynamically to resist the stresses created by wind, and easily transported. In the attempt to find a structure that matched these criteria, the inventor-engineer developed his notion of "energetic-synergetic geometry." Working under the assumption that nature operated in the most efficient manner within a rationally determined coordinate system, Fuller devised a series of building blocks based on "nature's geometry."[32] Using such blocks in architecture, Fuller strove to achieve what John McHale defined as the "maximal advantage in environmental control structures through effective energy accounting."[33]

Fuller looked for the minimal arrangement of vectors that would best represent the energy system of the universe. Packing small spheres around a central nucleus, he arrived at a fourteen-faced geometrical polyhedron that he called "Vector Equilibrium," as all its vectors were equal in length and also equal in the distance of each vertex to the center (fig. 99). This complex form was composed of octahedral and tetrahedral parts and through a series of phases could contract to become smaller polyhedrons, culminating in the octahedron, which in turn could be split into two tetrahedrons. The tetrahedron—a solid formed by four equal triangles—could not be split any further; Fuller labeled it "the minimum prime divisor of the omni-directional universe."[34] It was an indivisible unit and,

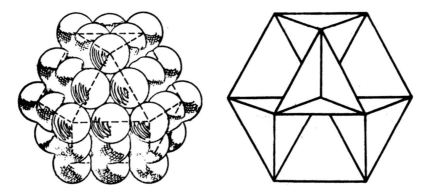

Fig. 99. Buckminster Fuller, The Closest Packing of Spheres (*left*) and Vector Equilibrium (*right*).

therefore, a basic structural element: all other structures were a complex of tetrahedral transformations.[35]

According to Fuller, building with the tetrahedron as the elementary cell would lead to "maximum performance per pound of material invested."[36] He claimed that energy or force would always strive to push through the shortest distance—through the diagonals of a rectangle or a square. In light of this, triangular webs represented the most economical energy networks.[37] Thus, the engineer constructed systems or networks that derived from triangles. The projection of symmetrical, equilateral triangular systems composed of tetrahedra, octahedra, and icosahedra onto a sphere generated a structural system of great economy and provided maximum resistance to both external and internal forces.[38] This was the geodesic structure. By using networks of spherical triangles, Fuller formed the geodesic dome.

Fuller suggested experimenting with the tetrahedron and was keen on teaching tetrahedral principles, even to the very young. He wrote *Tetrascroll: Goldilocks and the Three Bears, A Cosmic Fairy Tale* for children (and adults), in which the main protagonists were Goldy, the three bears, and a tetrahedron (fig. 100).[39] The book, published in 1975, was based on the bedtime stories he had told his daughter years earlier, when she was a child. These stories revolved around a series of conversations in which the bears asked questions and Goldy provided answers. By relaying his thoughts to his young daughter in this engaging format—and thereby defying previous construction-toy manuals that addressed solely boys—Fuller believed that "it would be possible to effectively induce that child's discovery of the most complex and profound phenomena."[40] The Toy, designed and

Fig. 100. Illustrations (called Stones) from R. Buckminster Fuller's *Tetrascroll: Goldilocks and the Three Bears, A Cosmic Fairy Tale,* 1975.

[*Left*] Stone 1: "Here is Goldy having a sky party with her three friends, the Polar Bear family . . . .
Goldy has a tetrahedron beside her on the beach. Its four vertexes . . . are oriented as are Goldy and
the Three Bears, with Mommy . . . at A, Daddy at B, Wee Bear at C, and Goldy at D."

[*Right*] Stone 2: "Goldy takes three triangles and brings them together edge-to-edge around a single corner and
inadvertently produces the fourth base triangle. Thus she discovers that one-plus-one-plus-one equals four."

manufactured twenty-four years before the publication of *Tetrascroll,* provided hands-on object lessons with the tetrahedron.

While Buckminster Fuller was developing his energetic-synergetic geometrical system, the German-born architect Konrad Wachsmann (1901–1980) was carrying out his own experiments with modular construction techniques. In 1948, Wachsmann moved to California to attempt to manufacture the Packaged House a prefabricated system he had developed with Walter Gropius (1883–1969).[41] He was soon thereafter captured on film wearing a mask and clowning around with Ray Eames (fig. 101). In 1955, the U.S. Air Force commissioned Wachsmann to develop a structural system for a very large airplane hangar. "The problem," Wachsmann later wrote, "was to develop a building system which, based on standardized elements, would permit every possible combination of construction, geometrical system, building type and span, expressed in a flexi-

Fig. 101. Ray Eames and Konrad Wachsmann wearing masks and dancing for the camera, possibly at the Eames studio, 1950.

ble anonymous design."[42] Furthermore, the hangar had to cover a very large area with no spatial impediments and be as light as possible, since the entire structure was to be made of collapsible parts that could be shipped in a compact (and thus economical) volume. Untrained construction professionals (i.e., soldiers) had to be able to assemble the structure, again very fast, into any desired arrangement.

The requirements for the airplane hangar led to the design of a space-frame that, according to Wachsmann, necessitated the use of a basic cell—the tetrahedron (fig. 102). The choice of the tetrahedral cell was decisive: like crystals, each tetrahedron possessed rigidity along its three different axes, and like crystalline growth, the aggregation of many cells provided the larger truss with greater rigidity. The nodes of the tetrahedron used in the hangar's design were 10 feet apart, and a joint at the node was designed so that it could accommodate connections with up to twenty members. Based on this joint, different layers of the structure were built up to create a system capable of spanning approximately 500 feet, with

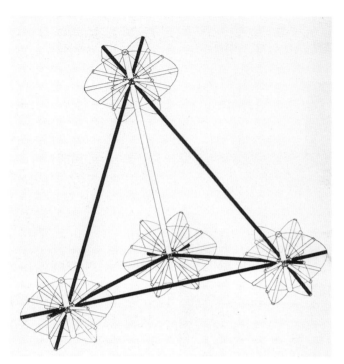

Fig. 102. Three-dimensional structural principle developed for use in constructing an aircraft hangar, Konrad Wachsmann, 1954. From Konrad Wachsmann, *The Turning Point of Building: Structure and Design,* 1961.

120 feet between supports. The space-frame—a tetrahedral truss—could be shipped, assembled in the shape of a huge roof and substructure on columnar supports, and subsequently disassembled, quickly and easily (fig. 103).

In his book *The Turning Point of Building: Structure and Design,* Wachsmann wrote: "Building, which in the last analysis is a material struggle against the destructive forces of nature, obliges us to face the consequences of advances in science and the discoveries and inventions of technology, in order to identify, with every available aid and technique, the new laws of harmony between mass and space."[43] Wachsmann stated that "in discarding many of our old ideas about building, we have reached a turning point." "A new understanding of space," he asserted, "can only be achieved indirectly, by mastering materials, techniques and functions, by realizing creative decisions."[44] In this new project, he wrote, "all preconceived opinion and notions of design are avoided and the best available resources and scientific knowledge freely applied. Quite indirectly, almost like a by-product, there emerged, at last, a structure capable of communicating a perfectly new spatial experience by technological means, while simultaneously expressing ideas of the conquest of mass and free dynamic spaces on a scale previously unknown."[45] The turning point of building, then, implied building with light yet strong parts, allowing for modularity, transportability, and rapid adaptability to different circumstances. It entailed conquering space through lightness and rigidity rather than mass and weight. It also involved a system of building so universal that it would be easily communicated to nonprofessionals.

All these aspects of construction would be enabled through the use of a repetitive unit, or cell. Manipulating such a module constituted a novel approach to design. Robert Le Ricolais, a French engineer and contemporary of Wachsmann, commented in an article on the architect's work that, "contrary to an ancient doctrine, in which the plan was divided into structural elements, the

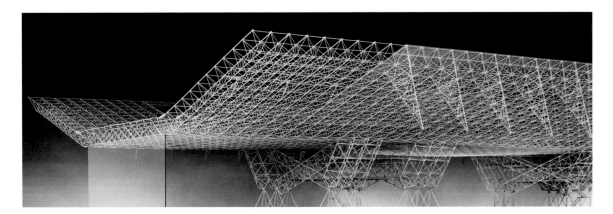

inverse procedure is being developed actually: the elementary cell is integrated, by proliferation in the construction."[46] Furthermore, despite their geometrical appearance, the triangulated space-frames that Wachsmann produced were immune to immediate mathematization; the calculations for an asymmetrical space-frame structure, for example, were inextricable to the extent that they could only be undertaken by specialists, he said.[47] Such structures in the early 1950s—an age preceding easy access to the computer—could be best developed through models.[48] This process emphasized an architecture evolving from a tentative and additive procedure: a process of experimentation. Intimating these procedures, handling The Toy, suggested that through play and experimentation anyone could build and enclose space in a novel manner, with lightweight yet rigid members.

Over a half century before Wachsmann developed his tetrahedral space-frame, Alexander Graham Bell (1847–1922) had played with the tetrahedron (fig. 104). Indeed, the architect identified the construction of Bell's lightweight tetrahedral cell structures as an influential moment in the development of structural design, along with the creation of monuments such as the Eiffel Tower (1889) and the Firth of Forth Bridge (1890).[49]

Fig. 103. Prototype for an aircraft hangar designed for the U.S. Air Force, Konrad Wachsmann, 1955.

Fig. 104. Alexander Graham Bell with tetrahedral cell structures, ca. 1906.

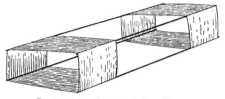

DIAGRAM 1. HARGRAVE BOX KITE.

DIAGRAM 2. TRIANGULAR CELLS.

DIAGRAM 3. REGULAR TETRAHEDRAL WINGED CELL.

Fig. 105. Diagrams of a box kite (*left*), triangular box kite (*center*), and tetrahedral cell kite (*right*).

Bell, who invented the telephone in 1875, started to experiment with kites in the late 1890s. Initially undertaken for his own pleasure and amusement, his research grew into a serious affair when he realized it could have bearing on the contemporary "flying machine problem."[50] "The word 'kite' unfortunately is suggestive to most minds of a toy,"[51] Bell wrote, "just as the telephone at first was thought to be a toy." Bell's large flying toy, like his telephone, was developed as a mode of communication—"an aerial vehicle large enough and strong enough to support a man and engine in the air, and yet light enough to be flown as a kite in a moderate breeze with the man and engine and all on board."[52] The idea of perfecting the kite came from the desire to reduce the velocity of the flying machine, so as to eliminate fatal accidents. A large, lightweight apparatus providing a small ratio of weight to surface area would be more subject to the forces of the wind and thus would be flown as a kite. In case of an accident in midair, the lighter machine would continue to glide with the wind until gently reaching the ground.[53] The thinking went that a heavier machine would be unaffected by the wind and thus would need to travel at a higher velocity in order to stay in the air, causing more accidents to occur.

In Bell's day, scientific kite-flying primarily involved Hargrave's cellular box kite (fig. 105, diagram 1). Lawrence Hargrave (1850–1915) had proven that two rectangular cells separated by a large space but connected by a framework provided stability that surpassed that of all previous kites. By 1894, the U.S. Weather Bureau was using Hargrave's box kites to lift meteorological equipment to great heights. Bell began his own experiments with the Hargrave construction while attempting to create a kite of greater cell size. He discovered that the kite lost its lifting power as the larger rectangles became structurally weak, and as the additional diagonal bracing needed to reinforce them made the kite heavier. During his test flights, Bell found that the horizontal surface of the kite resisted descent, while the vertical one steadied the construction and prevented it from tipping over in the air. Bell concluded that diagonal planes might replace the horizontal and vertical ones of the rectangular box kite, creating a triangular kite of larger dimensions that could retain flying capabilities similar to the smaller, rectangular box kite. Such a kite had less lifting power (having only one horizontal plane) but had more strength and stability and was lighter, because one diagonal plane took the place of the two used in the rectilinear model (fig. 105, diagram 2).

The sides of the triangular kite were initially formed by rectangular panes that required additional diagonal bracing when built at a large size. This again added to the weight of the kite and drastically reduced its ability to rise. In an attempt to improve the lifting ability of the kite, Bell converted the rectangular faces into stronger, triangular ones. Thus, six rods of equal length joined to form four adjoining equilateral triangles: the skeleton of a tetrahedron (fig. 105, diagram 3). The regular tetrahedron, he realized, modeled with equilateral triangles on every side, was a self-bracing form. This tetrahedral cell possessed extraordinary strength, even when made of lightweight elements, providing the maximum rigidity with the minimum amount of material. Bell wrote: "[The tetrahedron] is not simply braced in two directions in space like a triangle, but in three directions like a solid. If I may coin a word, it possesses 'three-dimensional' strength; not 'two-dimensional' strength like a triangle, or 'one-dimensional' strength like a rod. It is the skeleton of a solid, not of a surface or a line."[54] Covering two adjoining triangles with silk or another light material transformed the skeleton into a tetrahedral kite, or "winged cell." "The whole arrangement," the inventor maintained, "is strongly suggestive of a pair of birds' wings raised at an angle and connected together tip to tip by a cross-bar."[55]

Bell found that when a kite was enlarged while keeping its exact proportions, the ratio of weight to surface area increased; the heavier kite could not sustain its own weight, let alone carry an engine and a man.[56] He then speculated that a large kite could keep its lifting power if made by combining a series of small structures side by side. Bell formed a four-celled structure by connecting four tetrahedral unit cells at their corners, the entire structure taking the form of a tetrahedron. These four cells multiplied by four formed a sixteen-celled structure, and

Fig. 106. Alexander Graham Bell conducting tetrahedral kite experiments in Baddeck, Nova Scotia, in 1907.

so forth (fig. 106). The ratio of weight to surface area remained equal regardless of how many tetrahedral cells were combined together to form a compound kite. Furthermore, Bell found that "when these tetrahedral frames or cells are connected together by their corners they compose a structure of remarkable rigidity, even when made of light and fragile material, the whole structure possessing the same properties of strength and lightness inherent in the individual cells themselves."[57] After conducting numerous experiments, he observed that the equilibrium of the flying structure actually increased with the compound cell structure. A sudden gust of wind acting on one large surface could cause the structure to lose its balance, whereas a kite made of numerous cells would only sway slightly. He built kites of all forms based on the tetrahedral cell principle, and all had very good lifting power, were very stable, and, when released, returned very steadily to the ground.

Bell's kites were actually "enormous flying structures . . . really aerial vehicles rather than kites, for they were capable of lifting men and heavy weights into the air."[58] These kites could not be held by a single person by hand but, rather, needed to be anchored to the ground with ropes wrapped around cleats, like a boat. He presumed there was a limit to the number of cells he could add before a detrimental effect would be observed, but it was a limit he never reached. In his laboratory he put together 1,300 winged cells to form the 20-foot-wide Frost King, which, in field tests conducted in 1905, carried its own weight plus that of several hundred feet of heavy rope, and supported a man 40 feet in the air (fig. 107). The success of the Frost King convinced Bell that a large-scale tetrahedral construct was not impractical.[59] In December 1905, he proceeded to apply this knowledge of the tetrahedral cell directly and explicitly to enhance the safety and stability of the flying machine.[60]

As strength and stability were desirable attributes for most earthbound—as well as airborne—structures, Bell recognized the broad applicability of the tetrahedral cell: "Just as we can build houses of all kinds out of bricks, so we can build structures of all sorts out of tetrahedral frames, and the structures can be so formed as to possess the same qualities of strength and lightness which are characteristic of the individual cells."[61] Using tetrahedral cells, Bell constructed three boats, windbreakers used to shield large kites on an open field, and an observation hut used during his kite-flying trials (fig. 108). The largest structure he built with cells was a giant tower, located at the top of his experiment grounds at Beinn Bhreagh in Nova Scotia. The tower itself was a tetrahedron, its legs formed by a 72-foot equilateral triangle (fig. 109). Each leg was constructed of tetrahedral cells made of wrought-iron pipes joined with cast-iron connectors. The whole structure weighed less than 5 tons. Assembly of the structure was comparatively simple and was carried out in 1907 without the aid of cranes, scaffolding, or skilled labor.[62]

Bell's use of the tetrahedral truss some forty years before the advent of space-frames attested to his realization of the advantages of cellular structure—in terms of rigidity, weight, and ease of assembly, even by unskilled labor. In 1961 Wachsmann wrote of Bell: "Continuing his studies of the tetrahedral construction used in his air frames, in which weight was of decisive importance, he developed space-systems in the form of combinations of compression members,

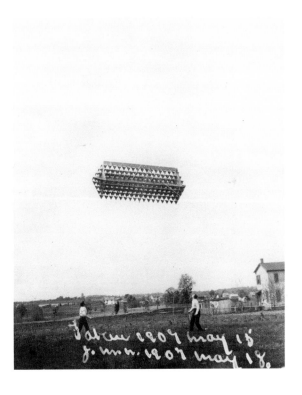

Fig. 107. Two of Alexander Graham Bell's assistants flying Frost King (built in 1905) at Baddeck, Nova Scotia, in 1907.

Fig. 108. Bell (*left*) and his father sitting inside the tetrahedral observation hut watching experiments with kites in Baddeck, Nova Scotia, in August 1902. Here, Bell dictates his observations to a secretary.

Fig. 109. Tetrahedral cell tower designed by Alexander Graham Bell, Beinn Bhreagh, Nova Scotia, August 1907.

tie wires and stressed surfaces. All these were investigations which have become important in building research only recently."[63] At the turn of the century, Bell arrived at this recognition through a process of experimentation. His was not a theoretical enterprise; only through trial and error did he determine the supremacy, in terms of strength and stability, of the tetrahedral cell structures. In a similar manner, the work of architects like Wachsmann and Fuller advanced through experimentation. Similar to scientists in a laboratory, they manipulated different materials over and over until a pleasing result was achieved, thus blurring the distinction between invention and play.

The Eameses also treated their practice like a laboratory and their studio as the place for experimentation. Examining numerous options for every design, closely comparing performance and form, they used their workshop as a testing ground for furniture, film, architecture, and toys. Playing with The Toy—combining one tetrahedron with another, adding, subtracting, measuring, and trying different configurations—circumvented the usual strategies of design. It required making objects rather than planning them in drawn form. As educators, they wished to extend to others their design approach, and The Toy could thus be seen as providing the elements necessary to lead a successful experiment, anywhere. Such experimentation would not yield a determinate building structure, such as a house or a school; instead, the combination of parts might lead through playful endeavor to unexpected and innovative results.

The individual components of this experimentation were light, transportable, modular, and easily assembled, which, when combined, formed rigid, airy, inhabitable structures. Like molecular particles, the tetrahedral cells bonded to one another to make a larger, stronger system. Throughout the 1950s and 1960s, other architects began to experiment with similar triangular networks in the design of buildings. Louis Kahn combined the tetrahedron, which he referred to as a "hollow stone," vertically, in his project with Anne Tyng, Tomorrow's Town Hall of 1952–58. Eckhard Schultze-Fielitz designed his Space City Project in 1960, while Kenzo Tange developed his triangulated space-frame projects throughout the 1960s.[64] Toying with tetrahedrons in open-ended play proved to have a useful role in the development of architectural form at midcentury.

Fig. 110. *The House of Cards,* Jean-Baptiste Simeon Chardin, ca. 1740.

Charles and Ray Eames, still at play, undertook a different kind of spatial experiment in 1952, when they designed their "good old-fashioned toy" House of Cards. Houses of cards had been popular for ages, ever since children and adults tried to tackle the seemingly impossible task of precariously balancing playing cards on their sides. Such construction posed a difficult challenge that required great patience and presence of mind.

In 1735, Jean-Baptiste Chardin (1699–1779) painted *The House of Cards,* which depicted the intense concentration of the son of his friend Jean-Jacques Le Noir, a cabinetmaker, at work on a house of cards. In the painting, an air of stability and calm prevails, as if to maintain the fragile stability of the structure.[65] Around 1740, Chardin painted another work entitled *The House of Cards.* In this one, another builder, a housekeeper still wearing an apron, is immersed in creating

Fig. 111. Card Houses: Upon a Novel Plan, Alphabetical & Zoological, Suitable for Children, manufactured by J. Wisbey & Co. (London), before 1891, chromolithographed cardboard.

the delicate construction (fig. 110). In both paintings, the players have taken time out from their daily activity to focus on building a frail cardboard house. They seem to hold their breath. Peacefulness and permanence reign as they become absorbed in the mastery of this ephemeral pastime. Is it all under control? Are they mastering a skill? Or is there room here, as with games of cards, for chance?

Decks of cards that were intentionally designed for building appeared during the nineteenth century. Card Houses: Upon a Novel Plan, Alphabetical and Zoological, Suitable for Children was produced in London by J. Wisbey and Co. circa 1890. It featured a tab-and-slot assembly system that provided stability to the emerging structure—an equilibrium that freed a young player's mind to focus on, and thus learn, the alphabet and names of animals (fig. 111). The connections enabled the "conventional" stacking techniques of card construction—leaning one card against another, balancing cards into triangular trestles, creating scaffold structures—that we have come to associate with card castles. Paper toy theaters were very popular as well. Cut-out figurines could be made to perform on a cardboard stage, complete with paper stage sets creating the illusion

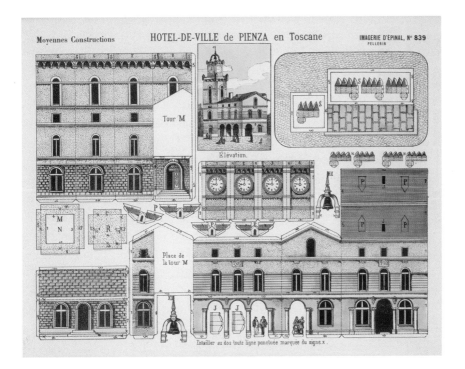

of depth. Other paper construction toys of the nineteenth century relied on the printed image to construct a three-dimensional object (fig. 112).[66] Playing card–sized panels depicting building materials such as roof tiles, bricks, or corrugated metal were meant to act as wall panels and were assembled through the use of additional parts (such as wooden sticks, for example, in the case of Gustav Lilienthal's 1886 Modellbaukasten). These paper toys reflected play in an age of growing consumption. Rather than painstakingly assembling a structure, the flat, cut-out cardboard pieces always embodied a façade, and the printed card, a wall; and in an instant a two-dimensional image was transformed into a three-dimensional monument.

The constructions made with the Eameses' House of Cards in 1952 did not resemble a house; nor did they mimic building materials or present a "pedagogical" lesson. The Pattern Deck was comprised of fifty-four cards, each unique, "reproduced from book papers, cut-outs, fabrics and wrappings from England, France, Switzerland, Germany, China, Japan and America . . . [that] enable you to make buildings, bridges, cities—a miniature world." The Picture Deck

Fig. 112. Hotel-de-Ville de Pienza en Toscane, Le Petit Architecte, published by Imagerie d'Épinal, ca. 1900, cut-and-fold paper, colored lithograph on heavy woven paper.

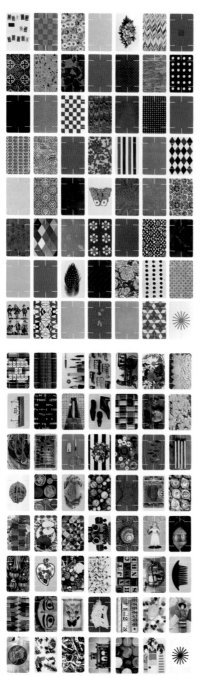

contained fifty-four cards as well, and presented a variety of objects from the home: an apple, a plate, miniature boats, marbles and little toy trains (fig. 113). Play started, for example, by standing a card depicting marbles. Six narrow slots located along the sides of the cards allowed the player to lock each into another to form open, rectilinear volumes that could stand tall but were somewhat unsteady; in short, they could be formed into a house of cards.

The instruction sheet of House of Cards demonstrated "building procedures": how to "interlock similar sections vertically to build tower" or to "interlock cards on flat surface to make platform."[67] The combination of flat and vertical sections could yield structures as simple as a "building," "house," or "dome," or larger constructions, such as an "arcade," "airplane hangar," "U.N. tower," or "stadium." These conglomerations—colorful on one side, blank (except for an asterisk) on the other—did not resemble their namesakes in any significant way. Instead, they presented a clash of configurations and images—graphic patterns, household objects, antiques—of a kind that cannot, at first, be easily grasped. There was no sequence to the graphics, no numbering system or continuity of scale that could help the player determine an explicit order (fig. 114). There was, however, an intrinsic order in every card. Ray Eames and Alexander Girard had processed the familiar landscape through a visual sieve: they had carefully selected, photographed, and transformed it into patterns with which to play (fig. 115). The eye moved between the frames—spools of thread, buttons, red-tipped kitchen matches, and snail shells—wandering within the substance of everyday life.

Different versions of the House of Cards followed the original. The Giant House of Cards (1953) was comprised of twenty-seven large cards, 7 by 11 inches each, made of thick, 8-ply cardboard. Slotted like the smaller version, these larger cards, printed with "Graphic Design Taken from the Arts * The Sciences * The World

Fig. 113. House of Cards: Pattern Deck (*top*) and Picture Deck (*bottom*), Charles and Ray Eames, 1952.

Fig. 114. House of Cards/
Wolken Kuckucks *Haus,*
Charles and Ray Eames,
published by Otto Maier
(Ravensburg), ca. 1961,
photolithographed
paper laminate.

Fig. 115. The desk of
Ray Eames during the
making of a card.

173

Around Us," could be assembled into larger and sturdier structures.[68] That House of Cards was, by 1968, a very famous architectural artifact is reflected by the copious articles that appeared in the daily press, popular magazines, and architectural journals. In 1968 the cards were reissued in Germany,[69] and in 1970 a Computer House of Cards was produced for IBM and given away as a souvenir at the World's Fair in Osaka, Japan.[70] The images on that deck of cards were based on a 1968 film by Charles and Ray Eames, *A Computer Glossary, or Coming to Terms with the Data Processing Machine*. The film illustrated the path that data traveled and defined various terms necessary to understand the computer, thus creating a glossary. Following IBM's lead, several companies including Lufthansa, Telefunken, and Fiat expressed interest in issuing their own sets. "The House of Cards," the German publisher wrote to the Eameses, "has been discovered by several large industrial firms for advertising means."[71] Replacing the pictures of marbles, spools of thread, and old toys with images of computer parts or the details of cars, the cards became an atlas of technological progress. The close-up photography of computer elements and the repetitive organization of Computer House of Cards reinforced the Eameses' notion that aesthetic constructs existed within every discipline. The cards acted as a powerful transmitter of information and visual knowledge—as well as advertising—and attested to the fruitful marriage of play and display.

The House of Cards stood between two experimental phases of the Eameses' architectural design. The cards with their multiple images intimated the mediatic spaces that Charles and Ray Eames were interested in implementing in their work. Simultaneously, the parallel and rectilinear cardboard panels of the House of Cards were evocative of experiments in prefabrication that engaged the Eameses, Buckminster Fuller, and Konrad Wachsmann, as well as many other architects in the United States after World War II. With a children's toy, novel spatial concepts were brought into the home, where they would become familiar. The colorful cardboard parts could be assembled, moved around, and taken apart to mirror the construction processes associated with prefabricated building. As early as 1944, Charles and Ray Eames, along with guest coeditors Eero Saarinen and Buckminster Fuller, had begun to wonder out loud about the role of prefabrication in creating a new domestic architecture. In the July 1944 *Arts and Architecture* special issue devoted to prefabrication, they inquired, "What is a House?" Was it to perform an act of "materials and miracles"? Was it a "Montage"? (fig.

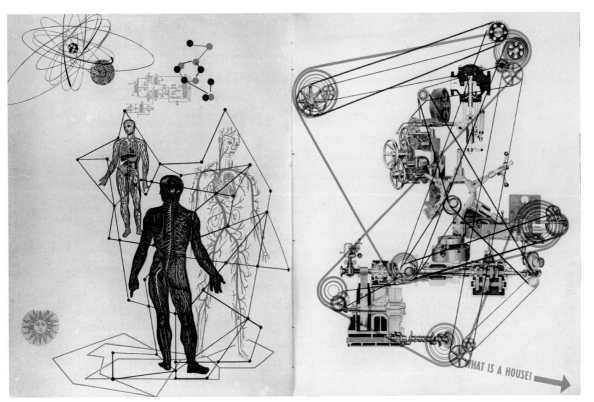

116).[72] The House of Cards, just like experiments in prefabrication, exemplified attempts to build with light panels, while it simultaneously questioned the very nature of the house.

By the early 1950s, prefabrication had gone through numerous experimental phases: most of these initial efforts—like houses of cards—collapsed. Mainly, it was becoming clear that the great domestic housing shortage, begun during World War II and exacerbated by the return of the GIs to American soil, would not be resolved immediately, as many had hoped, with the advent of the factory-made house. "We are concerned with the house as a basic instrument for living within our own time," stated the editors of the special issue. They resolved to design a house that would be contemporary both structurally and technologically. They estimated that a total of 50 million families around the world would be in need of shelter in the ten years following the war and that thanks to the acceleration of industry related to military purposes, the industrial production

Fig. 116. *"Montage, by Herbert Matter," Arts and Architecture, July 1944.*

of a house would be made possible. "NOW," they admonished, "is the time in the world when all necessary circumstances and conditions exist in such relationship to one another that we can attack, on an inclusive, over-all scale, the problem of mass housing with a better than good chance for success"[73] (fig. 117).

Efficiency was nonexistent with the conventional modes of fabrication, and as such, the editors observed, "the envelope which encases the most important of our life's functions, we think of in terms of indulgence rather than good sense."[74] But prefabrication did not mean efficiency of production only, as the editors explained:

> Prefabrication IS NOT . . . merely an ingenious *mechano-set of parts* which, when put together, form walls, roofs, shells of buildings . . . Modern industrialized prefabrication, by its very nature, cannot be disassociated from any of the functions of living related to the house. It is, then, the complete use of all the facilities of mass production aided by the best research, the best techniques, and the best materials available, to the end that every living activity will receive the benefits of our enormous industrial energies. It is through the complete integration of all these forces that we will arrive at the form of the product. Form, then, will be the by-product of the end result of our best intellectual and industrial energies rather than a point of departure.[75]

The editors thus implied that changes in the conception of the house would proceed from industrialization and technological progress, but these would only provide a point of departure. House of Cards suggested lighter means of construction and endorsed prefabrication, but it also carried messages hinting at additional spatial transformations.

The Eameses were indeed involved with the search for alternative forms of living. They answered the call for action instigated by John Entenza in January 1945 and sponsored by *Arts and Architecture* magazine. The Case Study House Program commissioned houses from young California architects. Experimenting with standardization, the Case Study House designs provided low-cost housing solutions, as well as proposals for dwelling environments for the future. The intent of the program—in which Charles and Ray Eames took part—was to generate ideas for the new postwar house. Although the program did not answer the immediate need for millions of mass-produced dwellings, it did offer a glimpse of a possible house for the future. Looking back at its impact, the design historian Reyner Banham wrote in 1971 that the future promised by these houses encompassed simple detailing, trust in the craftsman's judgment, and a lack of monumentality. In a chapter of his book *Los Angeles: The Architecture of Four Ecologies* entitled "The Style That Nearly . . .," Banham described the Case Study Houses as an architecture of omissions, of "less is more," of frankness and anti-authoritarianism. It is an architecture that "reveals again the absence of that heroic-style creative angst of the European-based modern movement, and gives an improvisatory air to the whole fabric."[76] In his eyes, this architecture of informality "nearly" became typical of a regional idiom, but did not quite succeed. Yet, it was an architecture that suggested, according to Banham, the possibility of change, constantly. Such a playful attitude, mirrored by the Eameses' House of Cards, was not the common view of industrialization and prefabrication at the time, which had been established largely by the questionable success of the geographically remote Levittown.[77] Although Levittown provided a solution to the great housing shortage, it was a developer's solution that failed to engage the interests of architects involved in rethinking the relationship between industry and housing promised by prefabrication, and in reimagining the concept of the house.

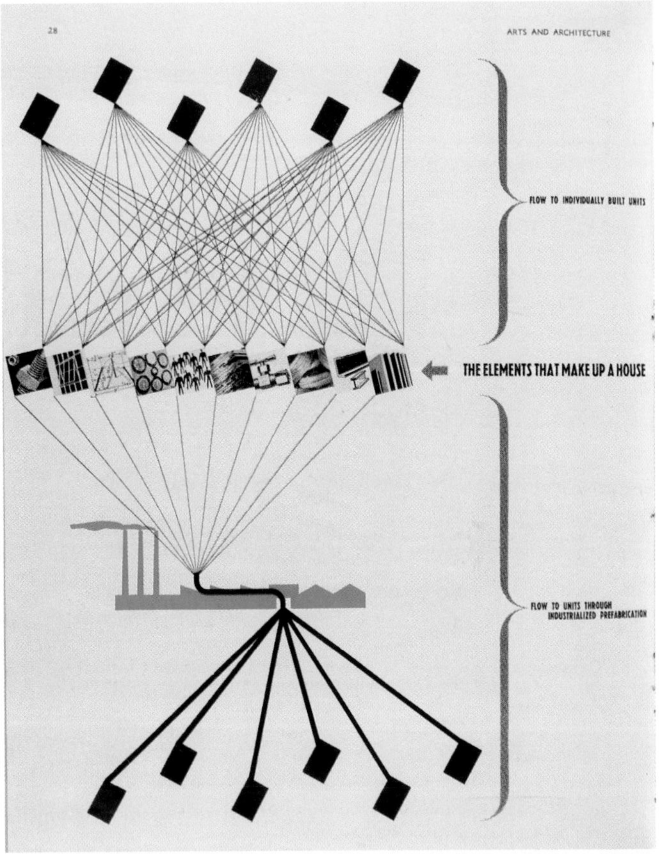

Fig. 117. The elements that make up a house in "What Prefabrication Is Not," as illustrated in *Arts and Architecture,* July 1944.

Between 1944 and 1951, other attempts at prefabrication took place that embodied more creative and innovative architectural endeavors. All of them followed, formally and technologically, the challenge posed by the writers of the July 1944 issue of *Arts and Architecture,* yet all failed to generate a mass-produced house on a large scale. The Lustron House (1948–51), a prefabricated house covered with enameled steel panels, never became affordable enough to compensate for its feeling of apparent "temporariness" (fig. 118).[78] The Acorn House—a pre-

Fig. 118. All the parts that make up one Lustron House, 1948-51.

fabricated home developed at Massachusetts Institute of Technology between 1948 and 1951—faced a similar fate. Made of fir plywood bonded over a honeycomb of kraft paper, the various components folded to fit exactly on a standard trailer truck for transport. Unfolded on-site, the two-bedroom unit measuring approximately 800 square feet could be erected by four workers over the course of a single day (fig. 119). Despite its low cost, and the initial, positive reception, the Acorn did not succeed in penetrating the housing market. Like the Lustron, and all other attempts at prefabrication, it did not comply with existing building codes, was opposed by local trade unions, and was viewed negatively by home builders whose cultural preferences ran toward familiar wood-frame or masonry construction.[79] The prefabricated solutions also failed because no one recognized the need for devising an adequate distribution system; high production costs of the components led to escalating prices, which rendered the system less favorable in the eyes of the buying public; furthermore, the existing system of house mortgages did not make it easy for buyers to purchase a prefabricated house.

The Eameses' own attempt at prefabrication took place in 1951, one year prior to their design of House of Cards. The Kwikset House was to be a low-cost pre-

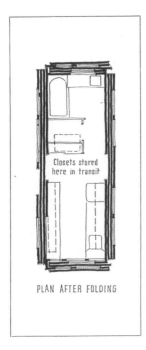

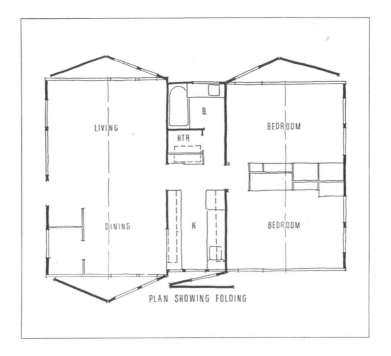

Fig. 119. Acorn House, Carl Koch, 1950. From "Do Small Houses Afford Satisfactory Practice?" *Architectural Record,* May 1950.

fabricated unit, "constructed with off-the-shelf parts and hardware, manufactured in quantity and sold as a kit."[80] The design consisted of a one-story structure with a curved roof of laminated plywood supported on laminated plywood beams (fig. 120). The form was meant to maximize, in terms of square footage, the eight-hundred-dollar budget set for the house. In fact, the space enclosed was twice as large as that of a house of similar budget built with regular masonry construction. The structure—roof and columns—was to be left exposed. A modular open plan was divided by free-standing storage walls, while the front façade was designed as a metal framework fitted with modular panels—including the door—of translucent and wired glass. Despite the great investment of the Eames Office in the project, the Kwikset Company dissolved, and the Kwikset House never materialized. Unlike the numerous mass-produced furniture projects of Charles and Ray Eames, but just like other experiments with the prefabricated house, this proposal for a house as a kit of parts collapsed.

Prior to the Eameses' attempt at prefabricating a home, Konrad Wachsmann and Buckminster Fuller tackled the problem in their own original way. Wachsmann, together with Walter Gropius, designed and attempted to

Fig. 120. Kwikset House, Charles and Ray Eames, 1951.

manufacture the Packaged House between 1942 and 1951. The search for a rational, prefabricated system comprised of a series of components that would be organized hierarchically occupied Wachsmann for the greater part of his career, and before designing the space-frames that led to the construction of the U.S. Air Force Hangar in 1955, he applied a modular prefabricated system to the design of a house. The Packaged House consisted of a kit of parts with a very limited number of components (fig. 121). The panels could only connect one to another and could not incorporate outside elements; nevertheless, the system was flexible, and the process of construction iterative and open-ended, generating a wide array of design options rather than a set of standard house plans.[81]

Wachsmann started developing the elements of his system during World War II, when there was already an urgent need for housing, but his extensive, attempts to perfect a universal four-way joint with which to connect the panel components prolonged the design process. Like the other attempts at prefabrication, the Packaged House failed, despite the great architectonic beauty and ingenuity of Wachsmann's eventual joint solution. It failed for all the same reasons that the other attempts had failed, and also because it missed the time of greatest demand: Wachsmann got lost in play and could not stop toying and tin-

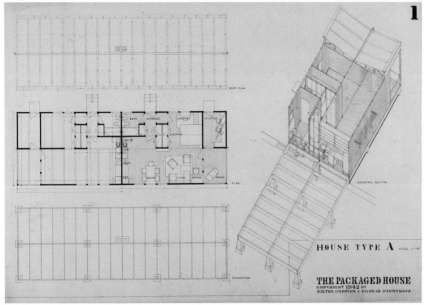

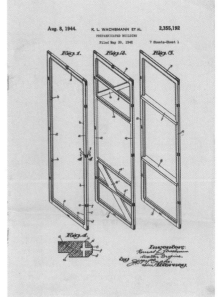

Fig. 121. The Packaged House, Konrad Wachsmann and Walter Gropius, 1942–51, House Type A (*left*) and prefabricated building panels (*right*).

kering with the system's joints. Production of the Packaged House was finally attempted in California in 1950, as Wachsmann could be seen wearing a mask and dancing with Ray Eames (see fig. 101).

The development of Fuller's Wichita House in 1946 as a prefabricated home also failed to reach manufacture beyond the initial prototype. Like Wachsmann, Fuller treated his project as an ongoing experiment and kept redesigning its parts, which caused investors and bankers to lose active interest in it. Nevertheless, the project led to Fuller's development of another prefabricated structure: the geodesic dome. Although the dome is best known in aluminum and steel, throughout the 1950s Fuller designed numerous variations using lighter and cheaper materials (fig. 122). In 1952, the Yale Collaborative of Architects and Painters, under Fuller's direction, developed a waterproof, high-strength, corrugated cardboard dome: the Cardboard House. This house was composed of 276 flat sheets of cardboard, cut and scored. The base unit was a flat, rectangular sheet of cardboard or fiberboard that, when bent, could assemble with the other rectangles. The entire package weighed 135 pounds and cost approximately seven hundred dollars.

Easily erected anywhere, Fuller maintained, the dome would offer an alternative kind of living for artists, who could pack the cardboard sheets in a car and

Fig. 122. A paperdome, Buckminster Fuller, 1950s.

go. Just as the city was being enlivened by artists turning the derelict warehouse spaces of some neighborhoods into lofts, the open, uninhabited spaces of the country could serve as new loci for experimentation. The house-dome could provide artists with the freedom to explore nature while remaining secure against the elements. A new kind of country living would be instigated, he suggested, by the very spacious yet adaptable paper house. Far cheaper than aluminum domes, the Cardboard House formed part of Fuller's continuous investigation of economical building structures that would be lightweight, easily transported, and viable around the world. Like the other proposals, this project remained a playful experiment. Nevertheless, Fuller continued to design and patent the paperboard domes, as well as heavier plydomes, throughout the 1950s (fig. 123).[82]

In its tentative nature and in the threat it posed of imminent collapse, House of Cards resembled the prefabricated house. And by 1951, it had become clear that, after numerous attempts, prefabrication and mass production had failed to change, on a large scale, the nature of the house. The toy's playful and experimental design process was also similar to that of the prefabricated house, in which the

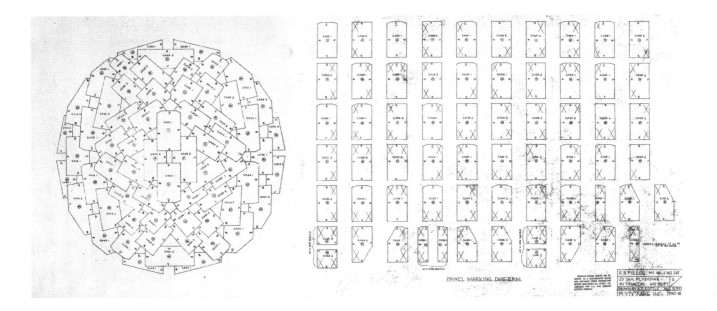

PANEL MARKING DIAGRAM.

efforts of architects and engineers did not result in the successful formation of a house but remained instead an ongoing, tentative material assemblage.

Designed in 1952, House of Cards could be used to create tentative spaces that could be seen as standing between mass-produced housing initiatives, which by 1951 had generally proved unstable, and imaginary spaces of information based on communication theory. In 1953, the Eames Office began designing a series of exhibitions and multimedia presentations on a variety of subjects encompassing the sciences, the arts, and everyday life. Just like an interactive game, these exhibitions would captivate the audience by presenting the spectator with an information wall loaded with material to see, read, and touch. Facing it, the viewer would seem to engage in a battle, catching the "bits" of information that were projected from the display. Assailed by a barrage of images, each viewer became a player, free to choose an individual path in the midst of the visual bombardment.

Many of the Eameses' projects—films, exhibitions, and lectures—began to incorporate technology that was based on the newly defined space of "information": multiscreen projections presenting a multiplicity of viewpoints and confounding the traditional linear approach to displaying a subject. House of Cards

Fig. 123. *Twenty-Nine-Foot-Diameter Plydome,* R. Buckminster Fuller, 1959, panels and assembly.

Fig. 124. *A Rough Sketch for a Sample Lesson for a Hypothetical Course,* Charles Eames and George Nelson, 1953.

presented such a display of stuff: ordinary objects and views for the player to connect, relate, and match. It presented a system of visual communication alluding to Charles Eames and George Nelson's *A Rough Sketch for a Sample Lesson for a Hypothetical Course* (1953), the first in a series of multimedia experiments, the pedagogical aim of which was to enhance the learning experience by exposing in parallel, diverse aspects of the lesson, creating multiple windows and points of view at once (fig. 124).[83]

The simultaneous use of slides and film to convey the complexity of our environment spanned the Eameses' career and was included in all of their lectures and exhibitions.[84] This approach was spurred on by Charles Eames's interest in the "mathematical theory of communication," formulated in 1948 by the American mathematicians and electronic engineers Claude Shannon and Warren Weaver.[85] In 1953, the Eames Office produced a film, *A Communications Primer,* based on that theory. Eames wished to make the "mathematical theory of communication" known to architects and planners, as an example of effectively processing the multiplicity of factors, signals, and information involved in any architectural project. The theory explained the ways by which a message, selected from many possible messages, was transmitted by the information source—a transmitter—through a communications channel, to a destination—a receiver. This type of "transistor" system was to convey information, which, in "communication theory[,] relates not so much to what you *do* say as to what you *could* say."[86] The authors explained further that "information is a measure of one's freedom of choice when one selects a message."[87] Furthermore, they maintained, "information in communication theory is associated with the amount of freedom of choice we have in constructing messages."[88] Less freedom of choice implied less information.

In communication theory, freedom of choice in the formation of messages brought about the concept of entropy. Shannon and Weaver explained: "In the physical sciences, the entropy associated with a situation is a measure of the degree of randomness, or of 'shuffledness' if you will, in the situation; and the tendency of physical systems to become less and less organized, to become more and more perfectly shuffled."[89] All messages were considered equal in terms of content, yet the higher degree of entropy, the greater the amount of information. Thus, if a situation were highly organized, presenting no randomness of choice, the entropy—and hence the amount of information—would be very low.

As opposed to linear communication—such as speech conveyed through the telephone—this visual system of communication would allow for a multiplicity of messages to be delivered all at once. By applying this system to planning and architecture, the Eameses proposed nothing short of the creation of a new kind of space. Labeled "the Eameses' multimedia architecture" by Beatriz Colomina, it consisted of "a framework in which objects can be placed and replaced."[90] There, she notes, "spaces are defined as arrays of information collected and constantly changed by the users."[91] The overlaps of information—the multiplicity of viewpoints—had the potential to change the nature of human habitation. Departing from a formal definition, space could result from constantly changing factors, including visual memories and associations drawn equally from personal experiences, the sciences, and the arts. Assailed by a barrage of options, exemplified by the images in House of Cards, the occupant of a house could become a player, free to choose an individual path from the bombardment of visual possibilities. Playing with House of Cards elucidated such a practice, where freedom of choice was left to the player, while the framework—here, the regular system of connections and parallel frames—remained stable and intact.

Fig. 125. *Parallel of Life and Art* exhibition at the Institute of Contemporary Art, London, 1953.

Parallel of Life and Art, an exhibition that opened in London during the fall of 1953, developed in parallel with the design of House of Cards, yet without knowledge of its existence. The exhibition shed light on the meaning of the multiplicity of images and the scaffolding of messages (fig. 125). Eduardo Paolozzi, Nigel Henderson, and Alison and Peter Smithson—the curators, all members of the Independent Group—were first brought together in London in the fall of 1952 by Reyner Banham, who set them to question the basic premises underlying the modern movement, which—they all agreed—had failed to deal adequately with the history of science, changing technologies, popular taste, and consumerism.[92] The curators approached their work on the *Parallel of Life and Art* exhibition through a shared enthusiasm for the extraordinary aspects of the ordinary; they "gloried in the disorder of human existence as opposed to the preciousness of metaphysical art."[93] They rejected the modernist premise that design exhibited timeless qualities. To them, after a few years, everything became dated and technologically obsolete. Their concept of the "expendable aesthetic" posed "a radical challenge to modernism in its recognition of the constantly changing nature of style." "The longevity of a design," as Anne Massey has explained, "was no guarantee of quality" for this formidable foursome.[94]

Parallel of Life and Art consisted of a series of black-and-white photographic reproductions—grainy enlargements of images from nature, industry, building, and the arts—exemplifying the group's interest in images that were not usually considered as having artistic meaning.[95] Resonant in their spatial interrelation with House of Cards, the photographs were hung on the wall at different angles and suspended from the ceiling by an intricate network of wires, juxtaposed in such a way that no narrative was stated, but instead series of cross-relationships were established, offering analogies and associations. At the time, the "as-found quality," as the Independent Group approached it, was a new way of viewing the ordinary, in which an awareness of mundane and banal things could become part of one's creative activity. It was an extreme way of paying attention to things, enforcing no singular perspective and understanding everything only in terms of relations. The press release of the exhibition explained: "There is no single simple aim in this procedure. No watertight scientific or philosophical system is demonstrated. In short, it forms a poetic-lyrical order where images create a series of cross-relationships."[96] The curatorial practice of the organizers, Henderson, Paolozzi, and Alison and Peter Smithson, became a game of matching and associating parallels spontaneously.[97]

As with House of Cards, the exhibition-goer became an active player who placed and replaced frames and moved objects around the field in a designated playground. Neither designers nor curators were engaged in an antagonistic relationship to the viewer. They neither imposed a vision nor framed a particular view but rather offered a multiplicity of messages. The spectator was a participant engaged in creative viewing, in a spatial game of making choices among the multiplicities of options, to forge his or her own meanings. In this sense, House of Cards and *Parallel of Life and Art* were parallel inventions.[98] They both countered the supremacy of the designer and assigned to the viewer the role of key player. Endowing the field with a freedom of choice, the fixed modernist framework could be redefined, suggesting new, flexible scaffolding for inhabitation: an innovative way of engaging the house. This original template proposed spaces that would not be generated by set geometries and proportions but instead would be based on relationships that would question the rules of assembly and composition at all times. The only rules were those of flexibility and transformation.

House of Cards—and *Parallel of Life and Art*—did not offer formal suggestions for form or structure but instead educated players and participants in change and alternatives in design.

House of Cards proposed an aesthetic for years to come: times that, as Peter Smithson wrote, would require a "practical response to the glut of objects, the proliferation of systems of information."[99] House of Cards claimed space as a ground of free choice, of personal freedom. By drawing parallels between life and art, and between communications and design, a new landscape of building could emerge in answer to the question, "What is a house?" Like a house of cards, this new domestic architecture may not always be fixed and stable, but, as on a playground, the spaces would balance continuously to accommodate aspects of change and new modes of life.

In his poem "Memorial Day 1950," the American poet Frank O'Hara (1926–1966) juxtaposes the war and destruction that marked the first half of the century with the tremendously inspiring acts of creativity and play of the artistic avant-garde that developed during that exact same time. Blood and toys overlapped:

> At that time all of us began to think
> with our bare hands and even with blood all over
> them, we knew vertical from horizontal, we never
> smeared anything except to find out how it lived.
> Fathers of Dada! You carried shining erector sets
> in your rough bony pockets, you were generous
> and they were lovely as chewing gum or flowers![100]

In a parallel fashion, on the pages that preceded "Building Toy" in the July 16, 1951, issue of *Life* magazine, a large color photograph showed a huge orange ball of fire exploding in pink flames (fig. 126). The short descriptive article "Atomic Bomb over Nevada" described in matter-of-fact terms the workings of the A-bomb, as demonstrated in a recent test explosion. It explained how, following a detonation, a ball of fire begins to rise:

> [In] a few seconds [it] will be climbing at a speed of almost 200 mph. The
> reddish column beneath the fireball is formed by dust sucked up from the

ground below. This dust churning upward with the fireball will later help form the familiar mushroom cloud of atomic explosions. . . . The bomb's fission products (fragments of plutonium or uranium atoms) are already so intensely radioactive they can cause air to glow. And since they were vaporized in the first instant of the explosion, they may have been carried even higher than the fireball itself to produce the mysterious purple haze at the top.[101]

On the pages that followed, the orange and pink panels of The Toy's light, prismatic forms cast their glow. The shift from seriousness to play, from destruction to construction, is abrupt but revealing.

The philosopher John Dewey, whom Charles and Ray Eames read, wrote in *Art as Experience* (1934) about the relation between past experience and play with building blocks. Play involves "an ordering of materials," he wrote.

> In playing with blocks the child builds a house or a tower. He becomes conscious of the meanings of his impulsions and acts by means of the difference made by them in objective materials. Past experiences more and more give meaning to what is done. The tower or fort that is to be constructed not only regulates the selection and arrangements of acts performed but is expressive of values of experience. Play as an event is still immediate. But its content consists of a mediation of present materials by ideas drawn from past experience.[102]

In an era of nuclear experiments, construction toys presented a way actively to counteract the destruction so visually prevalent after the war.

In 1950, the Dutch historian Johan Huizinga's seminal book on play, *Homo Ludens,* was translated into English and published in the United States.[103] According to Huizinga, *homo ludens* ("man the player") was essentially a fun-seeker, and play was a primary category of life and an integral part of culture. Voluntary—never imposed by necessity, duty, or obligation—play embodied a sense of freedom. Nevertheless, it absorbed the player so fully and intensely that, inevitably, seriousness came into play. The notions of playfulness and seriousness were thus bound together in a continuously oscillating relationship: "Play turns into seriousness and seriousness into play."[104] And

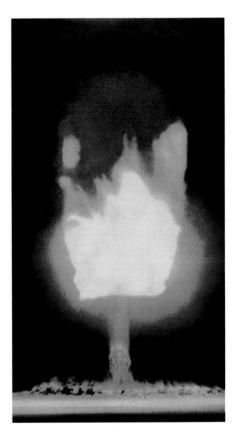

Fig. 126. "Atomic Bomb Testing over Nevada," *Life,* July 16, 1951.

although seriousness was usually considered superior when contrasted with play, "play may rise to heights of beauty and sublimity that leave seriousness far beneath."[105]

Huizinga defined the "play-ground," or space where play took place, in the following terms: "The arena, the card-table, the magic circle, the temple, the stage, the screen, the tennis court, the court of justice, etc., are all in form and function play-grounds, i.e. forbidden spots, isolated, hedged round, hallowed, within which special rules obtain. All are temporary worlds within the ordinary world, dedicated to the performance of an act apart."[106] Thus, in play one actually "stepp[ed] out of 'real' life."[107] Battle and play were related, Huizinga added, in a chapter called "Play and War." "Indeed, all fighting that is bound by rules bears the formal characteristics of play by that very limitation," he wrote.[108] For example, "the spot where the duel is fought bears all the marks of a play-ground; the weapons have to be exactly alike as in certain games; there is a signal for the start and the finish, and the number of shots is prescribed."[109] And just as order was imperative in battle, a formal discipline existed within the play-ground. Huizinga described: "Inside the play-ground an absolute and peculiar order reigns. Here we come across another, very positive feature of play: it creates order, *is* order. Into an imperfect world and into the confusion of life it brings a temporary, a limited perfection. Play demands order absolute and supreme. . . . The profound affinity between play and order is perhaps the reason why play . . . seems to lie to such extent in the field of aesthetics."[110] Thus, it is in the formal necessity of order and organization—and in their inherent aesthetic qualities—that "play is battle and battle is play."[111]

Playground and battleground were words used at the time to describe works of architecture. In October 1950, *Arts and Architecture* displayed a layout of "Chairs by Charles Eames" (fig. 127).[112] The images—a field of fiberglass and resin shells with webs of different bases—were displayed across from a text in the form of a poem, entitled "Architecture and Technology," by the director of the Department of Architecture at Illinois Institute of Technology, Mies van der Rohe. He wrote:

I hope you will understand that architecture
has nothing to do with the inventions of forms.
It is not a playground for children, young or old.
Architecture is the real battleground of the spirit.[113]

Fig. 127. "Chairs by Charles Eames," *Arts and Architecture,* October 1950.

If the first Eames chair seemed to be born out of a battleground—when it was first molded and stamped, "people in the neighborhood reported dishes rattling in their cupboards and thought the shaking was caused by earthquakes; local electrical power levels dropped substantially due to the overload"[114]—the Eameses' practice echoed a playground. Battleground and playground coexisted. While the designers implemented military technology in the development of the chair and of their house, they filled their office with toys and kites that they collected and designed. Furthermore, relaxedness, experimentation, improvisation, and lack of monumentality—attributes associated with play rather than with battle and characteristic of numerous Eames designs—transformed the office into a playground.

A lecture Charles Eames gave in June 1951 at the Aspen Design Conference is helpful in understanding the meaning of the "playground" and the "battleground" in architectural practice, and the relation of both to the "invention of form" and to the Eameses' toys. In the lecture, entitled "Design, Designer and Industry," Eames talked about true invention and originality in design. As an example, he showed one of Herbert Bayer's advertisements, which he commended because it was not the result of trying to be original but, instead, of having "a real conception, a big idea."[115] The 1944 ad for the Container Corporation of America showed a fragile house of cards balancing precariously, from which lines extended and converged toward a sturdy cardboard box (fig. 128). The caption proclaimed, "From Weakness to Strength," suggesting that, during a time of war, it was important to leave behind the weakness of a house of cards—a toy construction—and move forward, joining forces with powerful American industry, toward the enclosed container—the more solid box.

During his talk, Eames discussed other friends—great thinkers of the time—whose work, like Bayer's, embodied great invention in design. He recalled: "I believe it was George Nelson who once said, 'You know, Bucky somehow has the

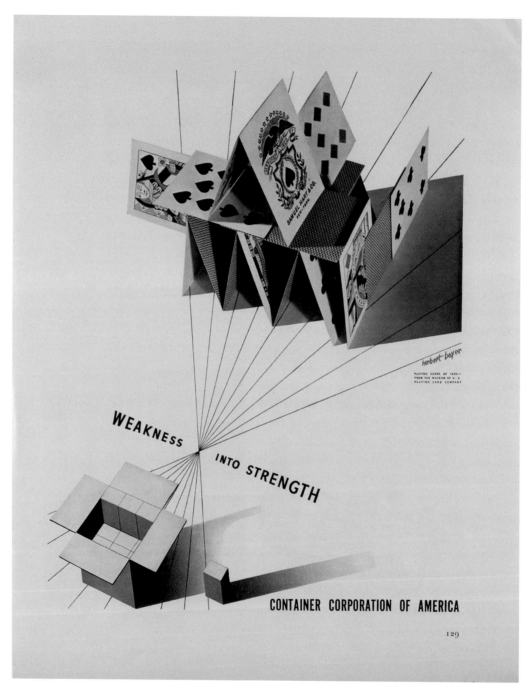

Fig. 128. "Weakness into Strength," Herbert Bayer, advertisement for Container Corporation of America, 1941.

quality of looking at everything he sees as a child looking at it for the first time.' What a great faculty that is!"[116] Charles and Ray Eames did the same. They questioned the nature not only of construction toys but of the house and, by extension, of all architectural design. The houses they proposed—toy-sized or full-scale, to be built with kits of parts—did not make up a solid box. Six years following Bayer's advertisement, Charles and Ray Eames reversed the equation and endorsed a "house of cards" to speak to the possibilities inherent in lightness and flexibility in design. In his Aspen lecture, Charles Eames recounted, "[Fuller] says that the great advantage that education can provide to a student is 'security in change.' What a great gain that is over safety in the *status quo!*"[117] The Toy and House of Cards educated to possibilities of change in design through the use of lightweight materials, modular frames, flexible connections, and standardized parts. They also educated to changes in the process of design: the inhabitant or designer would become a player taking active part in shaping the environment, playfully assembling its constituent parts.

Although play usually embodied freedom from subordination to a required aim or purpose, Dewey claimed in *Art as Experience* that creativity could only be experienced within a climate of imposed limitations. He wrote about the creative individual: "Individuality itself is originally a potentiality and is realized only in interaction with surrounding conditions. . . . The individuality of the artist is no exception. If his activities remained mere play and merely spontaneous, if free activities were not brought against the resistance offered by actual conditions, no *work* of art would ever be produced."[118] Play with The Toy and House of Cards was free and open-ended, yet directed. The set building materials and joints offered resistance to explore new possibilities along architectural lines and opened the way to establish parallels between the work of architecture and the work of art.

In 1952, six years after the war, Charles and Ray Eames recruited children with a toy that enlisted them to the task of acknowledging once again works of architecture as a territory for exploration: of testing and redefining the "living-grounds" through play. Handling The Toy and House of Cards implied that one could reclaim architecture as a playground.

OPENING SCENE BEGINS BY
SHOWING A SINGLE KID PLAY-
ING WITH BLOCKS IN A HOME
SITUATION.

CHILDS MOTHER BECOMES PART
OF THE SCENE SHORTLY AFTER
OPENING SCENE AS SHE IS
READING IN A NEARBY CHAIR.

AS PRECEDING SCENE BEGINS TO DRAG
MOM GETS UP & ESCORTS THE CHILD TO
BED, WHERE SHE TUCKS THE YOUNG-
STER IN & HE QUICKLY FALLS ASLEEP.

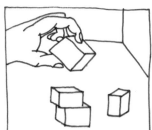

DREAM SEQUENCES BEGIN TO
APPEAR WITH CHILD IN THE
FOREGROUND, DREAMING OF A
SITUATION SIMILAR TO OPENING SCENE

AS THE SLEEP DEEPENS, DREAM BE-
COMES LESS REAL-LIKE & MORE & MORE
FANTASY. FANTASY OR DREAM
SEQUENCE FILLS UP ENTIRE FRAME.

SUBSEQUENCES SEQUENCES CHILD
BEGINS TO REEMERGE IN HIS DREAMS
AS AN ACTIVE PARTICIPANT AS IN
FORM OF AN ARCHITECT, GLADISTOR,
MATHEMATICIAN/SCIENTIST.

tempo/rythom starts out slowly
showing blocks as simple stable
forms _ child is shown
stacking several cubes

tempo quickens — multiplicity of
blocks being shown & complexity
of form being sequentially
heighten.

Brief — almost momentary
patches of blocks on a more
grandiose scale are shown
intermitsntly - (stills from slides)
between smaller scale toy blocks

towers, puzzles, grow, expand,
etc. on their own _____

NO HANDS BEING SHOWN

TO VARYING HEIGHTENS
& COMPLEXITIES

(slowly)

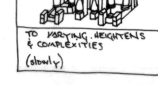

SOME OF THE TOWERS &
PUZZLES COLLASPE TO THEIR
(slowly) most stable, static
form.

Conclusion

"Blocks" was the name of a proposed film featuring different architectural toys, blocks, and construction sets, to be produced in 1976 by Charles and Ray Eames. The designers had prepared various alternatives for the development of the plot, as numerous storyboards attest, yet a few scenes were identical to all (fig. 129). These portrayed a child who plays with blocks just before being accompanied to bed by his mother. Once the child is asleep, a dream sequence begins: a single cube comes into focus and falls through the air; other blocks appear, and together they form large rectilinear conglomerations. "As the sleep deepens," one storyboard relates, "dream becomes less real-like and more and more fantasy," and the "fantasy or dream sequence fills up entire frame."[1] Next, historic-looking castles reminiscent of Anchor Blocks structures take shape, which in turn are succeeded by polyhedrons that grow and grow endlessly. "Buildings begin to appear from seemingly nowhere as they soar into existence," the storyboard goes on, and "soon, an entire city is fashioned." Rapid changes set the pace of the dream, as structures collapse, tumbling in slow motion to the ground, and new ones are constructed in their place. Before long another transition occurs, and a new city is built up with a different set of building blocks. Then, one by one, these constructions topple to the ground as well.

The film's repertory of blocks would include a variety of wooden bricks, alphabet cubes, Anchor Blocks, Lincoln Logs, and other architectural toys, most likely taken from the extensive toy collection of Charles and Ray Eames.[2] Played with

Fig. 129. Storyboard for the proposed film "Blocks," Charles and Ray Eames, 1976.

and filmed in succession, these toy constructions would demonstrate the endless possibilities of building, or, as Charles Eames wrote in the notes accompanying the storyboards, the "infinitum of blocks." The sense of order existing in play was more apparent with building blocks than with other toys since, according to him, blocks indicated that "throughout history man has been a builder, an orderer of things." Blocks and construction toys emphasized the "development of a dialogue between fantasy and real"—a dialogue constantly present in the architectural projects of Charles and Ray Eames. Unfortunately, "Blocks" would never develop beyond the storyboards to reveal succinctly the mystery of the ordinary object as do the couple's other films. Charles Eames passed away in 1978, and this project clearly required the kind of inventive synthesis that only collaboration between the two designers could produce. The plans for the film nevertheless attest to the couple's thinking that in play an imaginary world could be accessed, and through the repetitive process of building up and tearing down, inventive new structures could be realized.

More than one hundred years earlier, in 1836, Friedrich Froebel put forth the message, "Come, let us live with our children,"[3] suggesting that adults learn from children's experience and see everything with fresh eyes. Similarly, the proposition of the Eameses' film, representing an as-if session of play in a dream where worlds are erected, torn down, and built up again, also suggests that adults learn from children, whose nonhabituated minds allow them freely to imagine and destroy. The film creates a seamless succession of all the different historic moments of block building as one construction set fades into another. Similarly, each of the previous chapters in this book focuses on a different building set, in chronological order; nevertheless, each pursues a distinct historical trajectory particular to the circumstances in which each architectural toy was invented and produced. No encompassing theme binds all construction sets into a single continuity; instead, specific historical interrelationships between the toy and a broader set of concerns are traced, reflecting the different cultural contexts that pertain to each different toy. The chapters draw on a wide array of historical literature, to unravel the different backgrounds at the basis of the toys' invention— from nature to emerging technologies.

The Gifts (1836) attest to Froebel's belief that playing with crystalline forms would engrain in children a better understanding of the solid world. Manipulating prismatic volumes in a prescribed and controlled manner within the setting of the new kindergarten would elicit an innate understanding of nature and its material organization. Inner structure and outer phenomena would thus echo each other and reinforce a child's grasp of the physical world.

Anchor Stone Building Blocks (1887) allowed children to manipulate a real building material—stone. By reproducing civic structures with miniature bricks, players approximated the task of "real" architect-builders. At the end of the nineteenth century, tremendous technological changes were taking place—changes that allowed for faster displacement of people and things outside of the city and around the world. This affected one's perception of space and the environment. The time-consuming construction—and rapid destruction—of a heavy miniature structure that hinted at the possibilities of modularity, prefabrication, and hence mass production in architecture would alert the player to the dichotomies of the age: a slow, sedentary existence contrasted with the promise of lightness, speed, and displacement.

Structures built with Meccano and Erector Sets (1901, 1911), on the other hand, could not be easily broken. Painstakingly assembled with nuts and bolts, the metal pieces telegraphed the sturdiness of contemporary iron and steel structures. Rather than demonstrating different forms—such as "Forms of Beauty" or "Forms of Knowledge" with Froebel's Gifts, or the design of civic structures with Anchor Blocks—the structural-mechanical toys would enable hands-on experimentation with the new technology. Cranes, elevators, bridges, and skyscrapers conveyed the image of the future, and handling them promised a hold on stability in the face of perilous modernity.

At midcentury, The Toy and House of Cards (1951, 1952), the architectural toys designed by Charles and Ray Eames, presented endless and flexible play and encouraged the making of abstract forms. Made of pliable materials—paper and cardboard—these colorful, whimsical compositions attested to new interests in the postwar period: mobility, fast construction, and prefabrication. The absolute purity of modernist grounds was let go in favor of a colorful playground amalgamating experimentation with instability and impermanence.

In each chapter, I traced the distinct historical paths of the toys during their first years of production. I then used the theories of play contemporary to their inception as tools for reading the toys' pedagogical aims, which lead in each case to a different understanding of the interrelationship between toy construction and environment. The interpretations of play have perpetually shifted, coinciding and then changing in a constant contest of definitions. Yet, despite the differences, there are modes of doing that are common to most building toys, and this concluding chapter focuses on what unites architectural toys. Disparate writings by philosophers, cultural historians, and anthropologists have alluded to themes that the trajectory taken in this book has helped consolidate as most crucial to construction toys. The following concepts are always at play when handling architectural toys.

CONSTRUCT. DESTRUCT. REPEAT.

A note in the margin of one of the storyboards for the Eameses' proposed film "Blocks" reads, in Charles Eames's handwriting: "Building 'em up—building 'em up—& up & up & knocking them down," followed by, "Death in the end." Construction and collapse, erection and failure: the repetition of these acts, over and over again, was the predominant theme that Charles and Ray Eames hoped to convey in the film. But "Death in the end"? What could Eames possibly have meant? The end of the fantasy? The end of play?

Writing about toys in *Mythologies* in 1957, Roland Barthes pointed to the importance of building blocks. With their verisimilitude and literalness, he explained, most toys present normalized experiences with an even tone: the soldier holds a gun, and the doll urinates. Children, as a result, are prepared for experiencing their lives as "future roles"—"actions without adventure, without wonder, without joy."[4] With that kind of play, children are neither creators nor discoverers but only the users of those seemingly "meaningful" toys. In opposition to those toys, Barthes positioned simple building blocks. Only with the blocks, he wrote—especially if they were not refined, if they were made of wood and not of "a graceless material [that was] the product of chemistry"[5]—could the child become an inventor. Only with blocks that did not mean anything—that were not invested with preestablished meaning—could the child truly create new, unknown forms. Only if the blocks were not based in imitation would they, indeed, provide learning and benefit the child, since with them "the actions he performs are not those of a user but those of a demiurge. He creates objects which walk, which roll, he creates life not property; objects now act by themselves."[6] Hence, by extension of Barthes's argument, simple building blocks would also *mean something,* and that meaning would mainly be "construction"—the "positive," constructive act of building up. Thus, the "positive" aspect of the building set is that it presents a site where the expectation would be to build up, add, and assemble rather than to destroy. The different architectural toys presented in this book are hardly as simple as plain wooden blocks. They are refined, and some are based in imitation. Nevertheless, with such versatile abstract parts the child could create spaces and construct new forms.

Yet there was "death in the end": it seems that Eames also found "meaning" in the demolition of the toy structure. Just like the positive act of construction, the opposite act of destruction, of breaking down, has been presented as equally "meaningful" with regard to the architectural toy. It is destruction rather than construction—as it is immediate and impulsive and never presented in an instruction booklet—that would better construe for children an act of free play. Froebel had observed over a century earlier that the child's "greatest delight consists in the quick alternation of building up and tearing down," as the child repeatedly enjoys seeing "forms built up and arranged together . . . soon torn down and separated again."[7] And Baudelaire, too, when he recalled his childhood experience with toys, wrote of the behavior common to all children that entailed taking apart and breaking almost instantaneously any kind of toy:

> The overriding desire of most little brats . . . is to get at and *see the soul* of their toys, either at the end of a certain period of use, or on occasion *straightaway*. I cannot find it in me to blame this infantile mania: it is the first metaphysical stirring. When this desire has planted itself in the child's cerebral marrow, it fills his fingers and nails with an extra-ordinary agility and strength. He twists and turns the toy, scratches it, shakes it, bangs it against the wall, hurls it on the ground. . . . Its marvelous life comes to a stop. Finally he prises it open for he is the stronger party. But *where is its soul?*[8]

Taking apart is embodied in the nature of the building toy. The different case studies in this book attest to the fact that, in play, the act of constructing a whole takes different forms and that the meaning of breakdown varies too from toy to toy. Any connection made could be taken apart in a manner that could be interpreted differently, by a different theory of play and by each different toy. A gradual, calculated division based on nature's geometry presented a fascination with natural processes and imitated in reverse natural patterns of growth. Froebel's Gifts followed such natural patterns as models for a form's breakdown. With Meccano and Erector Set, however, the act of breaking down acquired additional significance. These breakdowns were fundamentally rooted in technology. Technological constructions, seeming at times in history just as miraculous as nature, called for dismantling in order to comprehend their processes of growth.

Still, what might the "soul" of a construction toy be? What could be at the core of a small construction? Was it the uncanny spirit of familiar surroundings, appropriated through their reconstruction in miniature? Or was it the essence of an idealized space for which one truly wishes?

In *Beyond the Pleasure Principle* (1920), Sigmund Freud declared play to be an act of adaptation and a compensatory activity.[9] While the repetition of play was usually associated with the seeking of gratification, with the pleasure principle, Freud also found that through play, the child would reenact an unpleasant experience in order to master the situation. He would repeat it until he could derive some pleasure from the experience. Freud then asked, how could the repetition of a distressing event relate to the repetition arousing pleasure, in play? The "death drive," he found, was an instinct as strong as the pleasure principle, and was manifest in an organism's wish to return to a previous, inanimate, inorganic state. Also, he confirmed in later writings, these repetitions would seem to be "diverted towards the external world and come to light as an instinct of aggressiveness and destructiveness."[10] Aggressiveness and destruction were instincts that architectural toys allow a child to master.[11] By identifying the manifestation of the death instinct in play, Freud established a link between play and violence, play and destruction.

This subversion of the evolutionary theory of play away from the demiurge, or act of creation, and toward its inverse—destruction and eventually death— was most evident with the structural-mechanical toys. Their handling wavered between play as a constructive practice and play as a preemptive measure against the fear of collapse and destruction. For the toy to be constructive, one needed to be able to destroy.

Construction and collapse, erection and failure, which were intended to be included in Eames's proposed film, exemplified what has united play across generations: the "law of repetition." Walter Benjamin identified the specific rhythms that were manifested in play—in rocking, in balancing, in spinning again and again—rhythms that involve repetition and that we experience early in life. "These are the rhythms in which we first gain possession of ourselves," he wrote; "we know that for a child repetition is *the soul of play,* that nothing gives him greater pleasure than to 'Do it again!'"[12] As Benjamin notes, the child always asks for "one more time":

> The child is not satisfied with twice, but wants the same thing again and again, a hundred or even a thousand times. This is not only the way to master frightening fundamental experiences—by deadening one's own response, by arbitrarily conjuring up experiences, or through parody; it also means enjoying one's victories and triumphs over and over again, with total intensity.... A child creates the entire event anew and starts again right from the beginning.[13]

This insatiable longing to return again and again to a task could satisfy the need to master an ominous incident, to experience victory repeatedly. In Freud's terms, repetition could imply a wish to return to a prior condition or state of being. It is also possible, however, to see in the repetition happening in play, the "transformation of a shattering experience into habit," which Benjamin identified as the "essence of play."[14] "For play and nothing else is the mother of every habit,"[15] Benjamin maintained: "Habit enters life as a game, and in habit, even in its most sclerotic forms, an element of play survives to the end. Habits are the forms of our first happiness and our first horror that have congealed and become deformed to the point of being unrecognizable."[16]

Returned to repeatedly and played with over and over again, toys are vessels for habits, not only through the repetition in play that they engender, but since they immobilize—for their designer, the habituated adult—moments, acts, and moves that have been considered worth reliving and toying with. While a habit is "a settled disposition or tendency to act in a certain way, especially one acquired by frequent repetition of the same act, until it becomes almost or quite involuntary"; to inhabit is "to live habitually" or "to dwell."[17] Thus, our first habits inhabit us—"Our greatest vices make their first habit in us, from our infancie,"[18] Montaigne had said, and consequently our habits dwell in our inhabitations; as Georges Teyssot has recognized, "habitations are actually places for long habits, places where habits may be inscribed in a space that awaits them."[19]

Architectural toys play with the residue of formal habits, and, moreover, as toys that toy with inhabitation, they doubly house those repetitions. The portrayal in the building toy of inhabitations—which in fact are spaces for long habits and consequently the rebuilding ad infinitum of those "places where habits may be inscribed"—embodies a mise en abîme. With the power relegated to miniaturization, repeatedly handling from the outside those spaces, miniaturized, where our habits reside could engrain our habits, or else could erode them and erase our experiences. For although one may gain possession of oneself through repetition, the wish still exists to start anew, go back in time, become a child, and obliterate one's history and habits.

Would the Eameses' film present the refusal to accept and adapt to present environments? Would that then be the wish, protected by its presentation as a dream, to demolish habits and start anew? Only through the acts of a child in a land of play or dream could destruction be deemed so acceptable and attractive.

BRICOLAGE

The reproduction, and hence repetition, that Walter Benjamin first described and that has become omnipresent in our postindustrial world presents a multiplicity that comes to replace the loss of tradition and of habits.[20] It has been suggested that the puerile character of repetition is an aspect of contemporary life that borrows from the repetition of play in childhood.[21] Since the advent of industrialization, repetitive means of production, mechanically reproduced artifacts, and the repetitive motions engendered by their use have in themselves become habits. Roger Caillois has described an aspect of play that relates most specifically to this kind of repetition and that is manifest in some architectural toys:

> Industrial civilization has given birth to a special form of *ludus,* the hobby, a secondary and gratuitous activity, undertaken and pursued for pleasure … an occupation that is primarily a compensation for the injury to personality caused by bondage to work of an automatic and picayune character. It has been observed that the hobby of the worker-turned-artisan readily takes the form of constructing complete scale models of the machines in the fabrication of which he is fated to cooperate by always repeating the same movement, an operation demanding no skill or intelligence on his part.[22]

Caillois considers the hobby one of the highest manifestations of the play instinct, since it provides an opportunity for the player to interact with new technological worlds; the player thus "avenges himself upon reality, but in a positive and creative way."[23] Anchor Blocks, Meccano, and Erector Set—those sets that have closely implemented the industrial and innovative means of production of their times—have become collectors' items, subjects of meetings and exchanges between nostalgic players. As hobbies, they have been preserved in their boxes, and if built, these complete scale models were usually exhibited rather than played with. And although, like construction toys, "hobbies reflect the rare qualities that make their development possible,"[24] this book has considered the reception of the toys during the first few years following their invention. The toys were then intended as valuable pastimes for children to play with in the spirit of discovery and then dismantled, broken, or forgotten.[25] The existence of these toys today as collectors' items highlights the resemblance between the childish character of playful repetition and some trifling aspects of collecting a construction toy as hobby.

As opposed to hobbies that are modeled on replicas of the adult's realm, almost anything in the world can attract a child's attention and become a toy. Children, in fact, can find a potential playground anywhere, and even as toys have become more sophisticated, children's attitudes have not changed. The child, according to Walter Benjamin, sees the world of playthings as a utopian realm, where every toy—the shiniest trinket or the dullest-looking piece of cardboard—presents an equal promise for play. For children, Benjamin wrote, any site has the potential of becoming a "construction site": "For children are particularly fond of haunting any site where things are being visibly worked upon. They are irresistibly drawn by the detritus generated by building, gardening, housework, tailoring, or carpentry. In waste products they recognize the face that the world of things turns directly and solely to them."[26]

The philosopher and political theorist Giorgio Agamben noted years later that children were attracted to play with anything that came their way, since for them anything had the potential of becoming a toy: "A look at the world of toys shows that children, humanity's little scrap dealers, will play with whatever junk comes their way. . . . Everything which is old . . . is liable to become a toy."[27] Thus, the "construction site" of the building toy is a site in constant formation, transformation, and doing; it is a site where forms are assembled, where parts are connected and taken apart over and over again. It is where "plans" are made and then changed as construction grows. This kind of play also entails an organization of sorts, for the builder needs to take stock of his building elements. One structure built may include the same pieces as the next, or it may not; the result may be slightly different, or it may not. Nevertheless, using similar elements will certainly give the next structure built an air of general resemblance to the one that came before it.

This mode of doing is reminiscent of "bricolage," as Claude Lévi-Strauss described it in *The Savage Mind* (1962). Bricolage is a mode of activity analogous to a "primitive" kind of scientific thought, Lévi-Strauss explained, in which different models of observation and reflection lead to a "speculative organization of the sensible world."[28] Although largely intuitive, these classifications—just like the exact sciences—entail discoveries and results that with time have acquired cultural validity, and in addition have led to highly aesthetic taxonomies and orderings. It is a mode of thought that was employed in various popular attempts at grasping and "structuring" the physical world, in both the sciences and the arts. To engage in "bricolage" is thus to take part in a mode of activity analogous to this "prior" form of thought; the "bricoleur" who assembles such "speculative organizations" in our time remains "someone who works with his hands and uses devious means compared to those of a craftsman."[29] Lévi-Strauss explained that, unlike the engineer's realm, in which he himself designs his tools and materials according to each project and its specific requirements, the bricoleur's universe of materials is "closed":

> The rules of his game are always to make do with "whatever is at hand," that is to say with a set of tools and materials which is always finite and is also heterogeneous because what it contains bears no relation to the current project, or indeed to any particular project, but is the contingent result of all the occasions there have been to renew or enrich the stock or to maintain it with the remains of previous constructions or destructions.[30]

Just like the bricoleur's world, the universe of materials and tools at the disposal of the builder armed with a building block set is finite. New structures are limited by the materials and parts chosen from prior architectural models, and the player, like the bricoleur, surveys his entire inventory of forms for potential assemblies and combinations. Since the elements in the bricoleur's collection are limited to parts chosen from other assemblies—a "collection of oddments left over from human endeavors" that used to hold different meanings—each of his combinations differs from the other only in the disposition of its parts.[31] Such is the work of the player with building blocks: each toy structure is made with whatever material is at hand and differs from another only in the form and dis-position of the different elements.

The defining feature of bricolage, Lévi-Strauss added, "is that it builds up structured sets, not directly with other structured sets but by using the remains and debris of events: in French 'des bribes et des morceaux,' or odds and ends in English, fossilized evidence of the history of an individual or a society."[32] Thus, if the term "bricolage" were applied to the activity of building with construc-tion toys, it would imply toying with the "odds and ends" of architecture, play-ing with the "remains and debris" of architectural history. Overall, then, the bricoleur is an apt description of the player—the child—on whom the detritus of architecture has been bestowed. "Odds and ends" of the built world—bricks, columns, girders, trusses, joints—are miniaturized and then manipulated in an act of bricolage.

Yet with toys in general and architectural toys in particular, bricolage assem-bles and combines additional dimensions beyond the material ones. Toys embody different historical times by reflecting contemporary materials and manufactur-ing technologies, as well as different forms, parts, and joints. Furthermore, toys evoke past use and have thus the ability to convey temporality in a direct man-ner. Writing in "In Playland: Reflections on History and Play" (1978), Agam-ben described the particular kind of temporal bricolage that the toy enabled and established the toy's distinct relation to human time. The toy is capable of embodying human temporality like no other object can since manipulating min-iature versions of objects that had once belonged to the sphere of use allows for the handling of historical time and, as such, exemplifies bricolage with human temporality. Playing with the toy thus embodies a specific act of temporal bri-colage: through miniaturization, the "crumbs" of history are manipulated and played with. As Agamben writes, the (architectural) toy materializes qualities of human and historical time.[33]

Like all toys, then, architectural toys play with the history of technology and the history of architecture, but more specifically, architectural toys also allow for manipulating "human time."[34] One temporal dimension derives from the "odds and ends" of the history of architecture, of bits of masonry, miniature stereometrical pieces, and steel structures that allow for the tangible manipulation of architectural periods; other "bits and pieces" relate to the moments of play of the person whose imagination once yielded a structure that was toyed with—inhabited in the mind and then ignored or discarded. Thus, architectural toys are like spatial crumbs, embodying bits and pieces of architectural history as well as condensed human time.

THE CHILD'S WORLDVIEW

The player with a finite set of building blocks can be likened to the bricoleur, who attempts to grasp the world and create a sensible organization with "odds and ends," "remains and debris" of events or things. But the "organization of the world" that the player creates, as seen through the physical constructs he makes, can be understood as part of another tradition of form making.

In the early 1950s, the art historian Ernst Gombrich questioned the absolutes that were used in the analysis of art form, and in his essay "Meditations on a Hobby Horse" proposed to look at the origins of form making by probing an age-old toy—the hobbyhorse.[35] Gombrich's focus on the toy horse, rather than another toy animal or toy car, points to the prevalence of the horse figure in art dating back to cave paintings. And while the image of the horse was present in art and in the nursery, the horse had been part of the city's landscape for years, providing power for work and means of transportation. In time, the horse figure was subjected to varying degrees of representation and abstraction. Portrayed in monumental equestrian sculptures, paintings of battle, and time-lapse photography, the horse became a favorite object of study—it was drawn, cast, investigated, and analyzed. The toy horse, however, was the opposite of the monument: it was not venerated or admired from the bottom of a pedestal but was used, toyed with, broken, and knocked down.

The hobbyhorse was also a "Dada" object—meaning also *horse,* in French, in the language of children—and as such it implied another tradition of form making—one that died in 1923 but of which Tristan Tzara wrote retrospectively in 1953: "Dada tried to destroy, not so much art, as the idea one had of art, breaking down its rigid borders, lowering its imaginary heights—subjecting them to a dependence of man."[36] Thus, Gombrich chose to take apart the hobbyhorse, a particularly meaningful figure in the history of representation, which has endured analysis and deconstruction before, to exemplify a different understanding of the origins of form making.[37]

The hobbyhorse is not an image of a horse, Gombrich claimed. Rather, it is a representation of a horse only to the extent that a representation could provide a "substitute" for the original.[38] Function, rather than form, is the aspect that relates the "substitute" to its model, and thus a hobbyhorse would relate to its model if the maker—and later, player—were able to "ride its back" as if it were a horse. Gombrich associated that assembly of forms with the cave dweller's drawings of animals, conjured out of hunger or fear and produced as responses to the basic needs and demands of their creator's organism. The creation of a "substitute" hence entailed making what Gombrich called a "conceptual image" that was psychologically meaningful to the maker and more potent than any formal abstraction. Gombrich also labeled "substitute" and "conceptual image" as "significant form." The act of creating this form preceded communication, since it was not yet possible for the "substitute" to convey an idea to an audience. It was with the use of a "significant form" that the "substitute" came closer to primitive art, constructing numerous representations with a limited vocabulary of simple shapes. Thus, according to Gombrich, the "substitute," or "conceptual image," was the starting point of image making, before any other universally accepted abstract or figurative form. It entailed a basic material organization and embodied the minimal set of elements made with certain materials that would allow the hobbyhorse to fit in a "psychologically meaningful lock" for its maker.[39] Made with a vocabulary of basic forms, this "conceptual image" also exemplified the perception of the child. Without this basic organization, Gombrich explained, "the 'innocent eye' which should see the world afresh would not see it at all. It would smart under the painful impact of a chaotic medley of forms and colours. In this sense the conventional vocabulary of basic forms is still indispensable to the artist as a starting point and focus of organization."[40] Furthermore, any work depended entirely on the individual and the situation in which it had been created; it did not simply entail manipulating forms. "One thing would be denied even to the greatest of contemporary artists," Gombrich claimed: "he could not make the hobby horse mean to us what it meant to its first creator."[41]

A construction with building blocks could also be seen as a "substitute," or a "conceptual image." It would embody a focus of organization and a way to sort out the chaotic medley of everyday forms. The small "construction site" would involve the combination of a minimal set of elements and a basic vocabulary of forms. And thus the construction toy, also in the family of the hobbyhorse, would mean the most to its creator—it would be assembled according to the toy's meaning to its maker-artist-conjurer of form.

Gombrich's understanding of the origins of form allowed countering the absolutes posited by modernism, since any combination made was meaningful and could be deemed the beginning of a new creation. His position brought forth an experimental vision akin to the child's discovery of new patterns, new means of communication, new field conditions.

A few years after Gombrich wrote his essay on the hobbyhorse, György Kepes also encouraged an experimental mode of vision in his *The New Landscape in Art and Science* (1956). He wrote of the special abilities of the child:

> To children and primitives the significance of objects is their potential for practical use, fantasy or play. The older our children grow, the more they see characteristics like size, shape, color and substance, rather than the dynamic relation between subject and object. . . . It would seem that to perceive the expanded world we need to return to our prior mode of perception, and, as children do, see interactions rather than things.[42]

Hence, the call in the 1950s to see like a child meant adopting a playful vision and questioning accepted ways of form making. Whereas in the 1830s, the pedagogical method instituted by Heinrich Pestalozzi and then Froebel entailed bringing out the pattern imprinted in one's mind, more than one hundred years later, the desire was to capture the structure of the world anew. The child, whose perception had not been shaped by a prior knowledge of absolutes, became an agent of change. The adult could learn from the child, who, with fresh eyes, would play, build, and establish new connections, material organizations, and assemblies of forms.

Well before the 1950s, Immanuel Kant had acknowledged the significant role of play and defined the vital role of the imagination. In his 1798 essay *Anthropology from a Pragmatic Point of View,* Kant described different states of mind in which one lost all touch with reality; he referred to these as "faults of the cognitive power," or "mental deficiencies."[43] He also described another milder condition—an escape from the world—which he defined as "the slightest of all excursions beyond the border of sound understanding."[44] This was embodied, he wrote, by the hobbyhorse, which could be seen as

> a fancy for occupying oneself diligently, as with a serious business, with objects of imagination that understanding merely plays with to amuse itself, a busy idleness, so to speak. For old people retired in comfortable circumstances, this frame of mind, which is like withdrawing again into carefree childhood, not only promotes health, as an agitation that keeps the vital force constantly moving; it is also lovable. It is laughable, too, but in such a way that the person we laugh at can laugh good-naturedly along with us.—But riding a hobbyhorse serves as relaxation even for younger people and people who work, and anyone who cavils at such innocent little follies and censures them with pedantic gravity deserves *Sterne's* reprimand: "Let everyone ride his hobbyhorse up and down the streets of the city, *as long as he doesn't force you to sit behind him.*"[45]

Years later, when the psychologist Erik Erikson (1902–1994) followed the constructions of children playing with blocks, he saw in them "condensed bits of life" and "the creation of new things . . . that are constructed within the individual himself."[46] In play, he believed, the child and the adult could reinvent an experience and change its course. Like the child, the adult, Erikson wrote, "must on each level renew some of the playfulness of childhood," and remaining playful must be at the center of his concerns. For the adult, play relates to the "opportunities to renew and increase the leeway and scope of his and his fellow man's activities." That potential increase in man's range of action Erikson called "Spielraum," not to be translated literally as "play-room" but, according to him, as "a *leeway of mastery* in a set of developments or circumstances."[47] It was a place where man could test himself against given conditions. Thus, within the space of play, both adult and child could test the latitude and freedom of the world, and expand it. That "leeway of mastery," which at times could be seen as a ride on a hobbyhorse or perhaps as a flight of fancy, was a private endeavor, most meaningful to its owner and creator. Anyone could build a castle in the sky; that castle was a Spielraum, a private space, a place to grow and expand, but guests may not be able to enter.

Up to the last year of their architectural practice, Charles and Ray Eames addressed toys with utter seriousness. After World War II, they paved the way for other designers who would come to see play as instrumental to daily experience. But even prior to that time, Adolf Behne recognized the interrelation of play and architecture, as evidenced by the preface of his *The Modern Functional Building,* written in 1923. Behne, an architectural historian and theoretician, strove to define the characteristics of the modern movement and differentiate them from contemporary trends of functionalism. He presented a dichotomy of two objects—the toy and the tool—and positioned the house right in between, as it should ideally have characteristics of both. Behne wrote that man's "early buildings are purely functional in character; they are in their nature essentially tools."[48] He maintained, however, that "the instinctive joys of play cannot be separated from practical matters": "Primitive man is not strictly utilitarian. He demonstrates his instinct for play even in his tools, which he makes smooth and beautiful beyond the demands of strict necessity, painting them or decorating them with ornaments. The tool called 'house' is no exception to this. From the very beginning the house has been as much a toy as a tool."[49] Conceptualizing the house as a tool assumes a strict focus, in its design, on functional requirements; imagining it as a toy embodies, for Behne, a demonstration of fantasy, or extreme play with forms. A balance should be reached between the two, he proposed, although rarely in history had such equilibrium been reached. A period of fantasy and expressionism, as embodied by some works in the early 1920s that preceded Behne's writings—the imaginary Crystal Chain structures or Kurt Schwitters's *Merzbau*—was characterized by forms that were so fixed that they overpowered the role of function, he explained. After this period, works began to embody the belief that following function would innovate and revolutionize form. Aspects of play were to oppose notions of function, and finding the right balance between the two was thus paramount in order for the house to be a successful work of architecture, Behne concluded in his preface.

With a tool one sets out to accomplish a specific task, whereas with a toy and in play one is most likely to deviate from a projected path. Nevertheless, both tool and toy are handled and manipulated with one's hands, and likening the house to either object suggests that architecture could be actively grasped. The architectural toy, this book proposes, is in itself a tool. With that tool one can handle reality—take hold of the environment—and conduct miniature experiments with the built world. As a tool, the architectural toy specifically allows one to manipulate and tinker with space, literally grab and toy with morsels of architecture without a specific goal or task. But unlike a tool, the architectural toy can subvert function, since in play one often deviates from the prescribed path. Le Corbusier wrote in 1935: "The great discoveries are disinterested, their consequences not being predictable. The inventor, the creator, pursue a chimera of the spirit: it so happens that they come on it unawares at a cross road, and then their eyes must see it and their hands grasp it."[50] Certainly one may, through the toy, grasp aspects of the histories of architecture and technology. But perhaps through the seemingly disinterested manipulation of an architectural toy, without setting out on a specific task, one may also glimpse intimations of modernism.

Behne mentioned "toy" and "play" in relation to the architecture of the modern movement. But building toys in themselves were hardly modern. They have rarely represented the most recent, significant stages of architectural development and have seldom exhibited innovations before they were seen full-size, maintaining as such the toy's secondary and marginal status in culture. But just as modernity was not a unified phenomenon, toys have not uniformly presented the "modern" viewpoints of the world they reflected. While Froebel's Gifts embodied visions of the modern, other toys' representations lacked unity and did not reflect current architectural and cultural trends, instead presenting historicisms and regressions. Some toys embodied a vision that at times rejected history but at other times venerated the past. Architectural toys shared neither specific formal attributes nor precise geometrical or structural features: their defining characteristic was that they renewed themselves endlessly, continuously building on what had been destroyed.

The pedagogical contribution of Froebel's blocks, how they transformed the imagination of the pioneers of modern art and architecture, established the Gifts as the forebears of modernism and set the expectation for similar pedagogical underpinnings for all subsequent construction toys. And while there are accounts of prominent scientists and engineers playing in childhood with Anchor Blocks and Erector Sets, it would be a stretch to suggest that these toys—as educational as they were—substantively contributed to the creation of a new architecture, or to novel developments in engineering and the arts. Still, architectural toys have provided a testimony to the ways we viewed the world and how we have handled it—manipulating small parts, grasping them over and over again, constructing worlds and tearing them apart. These acts would not always embody invention or starting anew but, rather, a continuous and constant handling of stuff, in an attempt to relate to the present time. Perhaps this is a reflection of our culture: while some true—or even remarkable—innovation may occur, more generally we create minor interventions, tooling and toying in a constant act of "bricolage."

It is the experience of history that the toy allows, and it is the focus on this experience that has inspired the treatment of toys and of building culture in the present study. This work is not a recounting and exposition of archival material but an attempt to reconstruct play sessions with building blocks and, through them, to grasp aspects of history. When Giorgio Agamben defined the essence of the toy, he claimed that the temporality of history actually was better grasped through a toy than through an archival document since, with the toy, "what children play with is history." "Play," he maintained, "is a relationship with objects and human behavior that draws from them a purely historical-temporal aspect."[51] This is the main difference between this and prior studies of toys: this emphasis on the haptic dimension of architecture, making architectural history tangible and easily grasped. And while the toy is primarily a historical object that belongs to the past, the nature of the toy "construction site" shifts from being a miniature storeroom of historical forms to a modern, avant-garde, and tangible terrain of experimentation and thought.

Notes

INTRODUCTION

1. Maria Edgeworth and Richard Lovell Edgeworth, *Practical Education,* 2nd ed., vol. 1 (London: Printer for J. Johnson, St. Paul's Church-Yard, 1801), 1. The first edition of *Practical Education,* published in 1798, does not contain the paragraph relating to building bricks.

2. Ibid., 38.

3. Ludwig Wittgenstein, *Philosophical Investigations* (New York: Macmillan, 1953), 31–32.

4. Frank Lloyd Wright, *An Autobiography* (New York: Duell, Sloan and Pearce, 1943), 13–14. See also Edgar Kaufman, "'Form Became Feeling': A New View of Froebel and Wright," *Journal of the Society of Architectural Historians* 40, no. 2 (May 1981): 130–37; Jeanne S. Rubin, "The Froebel-Wright Connection: A New Perspective," *Journal of the Society of Architectural Historians* 48, no. 1 (March 1989): 24–37; and Jeanne Spielman Rubin, *Intimate Triangle: Architecture of Crystals, Frank Lloyd Wright and the Froebel Kindergarten* (Huntsville, Ala.: Polycrystal Book Service, 2002).

5. Marc Solitaire, "Le Corbusier et l'urbain: La rectification du damier Froebelien," in *La ville et l'urbanisme après Le Corbusier* (conference proceedings), ed. H. Allen Brooks (La Chaux-de-Fonds, Switzerland: Editions d'En Haut, 1993).

6. The advertisement for the school also appears in Adolf Max Vogt, *Le Corbusier, the Noble Savage: Toward an Archaeology of Modernism* (Cambridge: MIT Press, 1998), 291. In original: "Mlle Louise Colin, ayant participé au Cours normal froebelien de Neuchâtel, prévient les parents qu'à l'avenir son école répondra aux exigences de la nouvelle loi scolaire. Dirigée d'après cette méthode etudiée en vue de nos mœurs et appliquée à nos besoins industriels, rien ne sera negligé quant au développement intellectual des élèves. Education intuitive et morale. Matériel Froebel."

7. Pat Kirkham, *Charles and Ray Eames* (Cambridge: MIT Press, 1998), 10–11.

8. From the video *Buckminster Fuller: Thinking Out Loud,* prod. and dir. Karen Goodman and Kirk Simon (New York: Zeitgeist Films, 1996).

9. Norman Brosterman's book *Inventing Kindergarten* (New York: Abrams, 1997) has been instrumental in bringing forth the familiarity of numerous artists and architects with the Froebel

material at the beginning of the twentieth century.

10. The members of the Crystal Chain, or Glaeserne Kette—including, among others, Walter Gropius, Hans Scharoun, Wenzel Hablik, and Herman Finsterlin—took on pseudonyms such as Glas or Stellarius and swore to secrecy, as if partaking in a Masonic order. To play with the glass metaphor, one had to abide by the Crystal Chain rules. For more on the Crystal Chain, see Iain Boyd Whyte, *The Crystal Chain Letters: Architectural Fantasies by Bruno Taut and his Circle* (Cambridge: MIT Press, 1985).

11. In recent years, the Vitra Museum reissued Bruno Taut's Dandanah. Hoffmann's Fabrik is held in the collection of the Canadian Centre for Architecture, Montreal.

12. Benjamin's review of Karl Gröber's book originally appeared in *Die literarische Welt,* June 1928, and was translated in Walter Benjamin, "Toys and Play" (1928), in *Selected Writings,* ed. Marcus Bullock and Michael Jennings, vol. 2, *1927–34* (Cambridge: Belknap Press of Harvard University Press, 1996–2003), 118. Karl Gröber, *Kinderspielzeug aus alter Zeit: Eine Geschichte des Spielzeugs* (Berlin: Deutscher Kunstverlag, 1928); English version: *Children's Toys of Bygone Days: A History of Playthings of All Peoples from Prehistoric Times to the XIXth Century,* trans. Philip Hereford (London: B. T. Batsford, 1928).

13. For the history of toy production, see Gröber, *Kinderspielzeug aus alter Zeit;* as well as Antonia Fraser, *A History of Toys* (London: Weidenfeld and Nicolson, 1966). For a philosophical take on toy production, see Walter Benjamin, "The Cultural History of Toys," in *Selected Writings,* vol. 2, *1927–1934,* ed. Marcus Bullock and Michael Jennings (Cambridge: Belknap Press of Harvard University Press, 1996), 113–16.

14. See, for example, *Games of Architecture,* ed. Jane Harrison and David Turnbull (London: Academy Editions, 1996); the exhibition catalogues *Kid Size: The Material World of Childhood* (Milan: Skira and Weil am Rhein: Vitra, 1997) and *Century of the Child: Growing by Design, 1900–2000,* ed. Juliet Kinchin and Aidan O'Connor (New York: The Museum of Modern Art, 2012); as well as Amy Ogata, *Designing the Creative Child: Playthings and Places in Midcentury America* (Minneapolis: University of Minnesota Press, 2013).

15. For the development of the play concept and its relation to prerational and rational thought, see Mihai I. Spariosou, *Dionysus Reborn: Play and the Aesthetic Dimension in Modern Philosophical and Scientific Discourse* (Ithaca: Cornell University Press, 1989). Spariosou contends that the split nature of Western mentality—being composed of prerational and rational values—is reflected in the split nature of play concepts. Since Schiller's reintroduction of the concept of play in the late eighteenth century, the understanding of play has shifted between those two poles.

16. Johan Huizinga, *Homo Ludens: A Study of the Play Element in Culture* (Boston: Beacon, 1955), 8.

17. Ibid., 9.

18. Ibid., 10.

19. Ibid., 13.

20. Roger Caillois, *Man, Play and Games* (Urbana and Chicago: University of Illinois Press, 2001), 21 (English translation by Meyer Barash, 1961). Originally published in French: Roger Caillois, *Les jeux et les hommes* (Paris: Librairie Gallimard, 1958).

21. Caillois, *Man, Play and Games,* 15.

22. Ibid., 29. Agôn is also present within the social aspect of this seemingly solitary act of playing with building blocks, as it would be strange for a solitary game to engage a person for a long time. "In reality," Caillois writes, "it is permeated with an atmosphere of competition. It only persists to the degree that the fervor of addicts transforms it into virtual *agôn.* When the latter is missing, *ludus* cannot persist independently . . . or else it risks turning into an obsession for the isolated fanatic who would dedicate himself to it absolutely and in his addiction would increasingly withdraw from society" (ibid., 32). So do avid collectors of Meccano, Erector Sets, and Anchor Blocks still share their findings on the Internet and at annual meetings, thus creating a spectacle and revivifying a certain show of agôn.

23. Ibid., 22.

24. Ibid., 29.

25. Ibid., 27.

26. Ibid., 30.

27. Ibid., 28.

28. See, for example, Karen Hewitt and Louise Roomet, *Educational Toys in America, 1800 to the Present* (Burl-

ington, Vt.: Robert Hull Fleming Museum, University of Vermont, 1979); and for a sociological perspective, see Dan Fleming, *Powerplay: Toys as Popular Culture* (Manchester: Manchester University Press, 1996).

29. Aspects of play and digital space are discussed in Friedrich von Borries, Steffen P. Walz, and Matthias Böttger, eds., *Space Time Play: Computer Games, Architecture and Urbanism: The Next Level* (Basel and Boston: Birkhaüser, 2007); as well as in Maaike Lauwaert, *The Place of Play: Toys and Digital Cultures* (Amsterdam: Amsterdam University Press, 2009).

30. Besides Karl Gröber's and Antonia Fraser's books mentioned above, see also Deborah Jaffe, *A History of Toys: From Spinning Tops to Robots* (Stroud, England: Sutton, 2006). For construction toys specifically, see the very informative work by Annette Noschka and Günter Knerr, *Bauklötze Staunen: 200 Jahre Geschichte der Baukästen* (Munich: Deutsches Museum and Hirmer Verlag, 1986); as well as Ulf Leinweber, *Baukästen: Technisches Spielzeug vom Biedermeier bis zur Jahrtausendwende* (Wiesbaden: Drei Lilien Edition, 1999). Some construction toys are presented in the exhibition catalogue *Toys of the Avant-Garde,* curated by Carlos Pérez and José Lebrero Stals (Malaga: Fundación Museo Picasso, 2010) and the copiously illustrated book featuring toys from his own private collection by Juan Bordes, *Historia de los juguetes de construcción: Escuela de la arquitectura moderna,* (Madrid: Cátedra, 2012).

31. The catalogues of the Canadian Centre for Architecture, in Montreal, include Rosemary Haddad, Brooke Hodge, and Witold Rybczynski, *Buildings in Boxes: Architectural Toys from the CCA* (1990); Norman Brosterman and Michael Lewis, *Potential Architecture: Construction Toys from the CCA Collection* (1991); Michael Lewis, *Toys That Teach* (1992); Detlef Mertins and Howard Shubert, *Toys and the Modernist Tradition* (1993); Alice Friedman and Rosemary Haddad, *Dream Houses, Toy Homes* (1995); Peter Smithson and Cammie McAtee, *Toy Town* (1997); Richard Ingersoll and Rosemary Haddad, *Cities in Motion: Toys and Transport* (2000).

32. The Deutsches Museum in Munich holds a large collection of toys as well—construction sets included—a testament that Germany was indeed the world capital of toy making before World War I.

33. Benjamin's review of the exhibit was published in the *Frankfurter Zeitung,* March 1928. In English, see Benjamin, "Old Toys," in *Selected Writings,* vol. 2, *1927–1934,* ed. Marcus Bullock and Michael Jennings (Cambridge: Belknap Press of Harvard University Press, 1996), 98.

34. This has been echoed in the famous remark by Henry Ford in 1919: "We want to live in the present and the only history that is worth a tinker's damn is the history we make today" (Terry Smith, *Making the Modern: Industry, Art and Design in America* [Chicago: University of Chicago Press, 1993], 4).

35. The reduction of scale of the miniature, Susan Stewart wrote, "skews the time and space relations of the everyday life world" (Susan Stewart, *On Longing: Narratives of the Miniature, the Gigantic, the Souvenir, the Collection* [Durham: Duke University Press, 1984], 66).

36. Gaston Bachelard, *The Poetics of Space* (Boston: Beacon, 1994), 162.

1. KINDERGARTEN GIFTS, CIRCA 1836

1. Edward Wiebé, *The Paradise of Childhood: A Practical Guide to Kindergartners,* Golden Jubilee Edition (Springfield, Mass: Milton Bradley Co., 1923). The encounter between Edward Wiebé and Milton Bradley is mentioned in the "Preface to Second Edition," 9.

2. Joachim Liebschner, *A Child's Work: Freedom and Guidance in Froebel's Educational Practice* (Cambridge, England: Lutterworth, 2001), 28. Froebel appealed continuously to women to become kindergarten teachers, as well as to serve in official roles in education.

3. Friedrich Froebel, circa 1803, qtd. in Wichard Lange, *Aus Froebel's Leben und ersten Streben* (Berlin: Enslin, 1862), 72. Translated in Liebschner, *A Child's Work,* 4.

4. For two years, from 1838 to 1840, Froebel wrote and published a weekly Sunday paper, *Sonntagsblatt,* to provide psychological and philosophical justification for play and to instruct parents and teachers on the use of his Gifts and Occupations. His *Die Pädagogik des Kindergartens,* a collection of essays published in Berlin in 1861, further illuminates his educational principles and their material form. For an English translation, see *Friedrich Froebel's Pedagogics of the Kindergarten: Or, His Ideas Concerning the Play and Playthings of the Child,* trans. Josephine Jarvis (New York: D. Appleton, 1896).

5. Wiebé, The *Paradise of Childhood,* 12.

6. Ibid., 117.

7. Ibid., 29.

8. Ibid., 12.

9. Ibid., 146.

10. Edward Wiebé, *Quarter Century Edition of the Paradise of Childhood: A Practical Guide to Kindergartners,* ed. Milton Bradley (Springfield, Mass: Milton Bradley Co., 1896), 200.

11. The first six Gifts were described by Froebel himself in his Sunday paper, *Sonntagsblatt,* between 1838 and 1840. Until his death in 1852, he published additional explanations of the Gifts in a variety of publications. For a detailed account of these publications, see Liebschner, *A Child's Work,* chap. 5, "The Gifts," 71–94. Froebel also published two short articles on stick laying in 1850, and another on paper folding, an article that appeared after his death (see Liebschner, *A Child's Work,* 99).

12. Froebel, *Froebel's Pedagogics of the Kindergarten,* 22.

13. Ibid., 123.

14. Friedrich Froebel, *Education by Development: The Second Part of the Pedagogics of the Kindergarten*, trans. Josephine Jarvis (New York: D. Appleton, 1899), 182.

15. Ibid., 188–89.

16. Ibid., 187.

17. Alexander Bruno Hanschmann, *The Kindergarten System: Its Origin and Development as Seen in the Life of Friedrich Froebel* (London: S. Sonnenschein, 1897), 59.

18. Froebel, *Education by Development,* 314.

19. Ibid.

20. Friedrich Froebel, *Autobiography of Friedrich Froebel,* trans. Emilie Michaelis (Syracuse, N.Y.: C. W. Bardeen, 1889), 113.

21. Wiebé, *Paradise of Childhood,* 24.

22. Froebel, *Education by Development,* 315.

23. Wiebé, *Paradise of Childhood,* 25.

24. Ibid.

25. Ibid.

26. Ibid.

27. Froebel, *Education by Development,* 316.

28. Ibid.

29. Wiebé, *Paradise of Childhood,* 28–29.

30. Ibid., 38.

31. Froebel, *Education by Development,* 319.

32. Wiebé, *Paradise of Childhood,* 28.

33. Froebel, *Pedagogics of the Kindergarten,* 137.

34. Ibid., 132.

35. Wiebé, *Paradise of Childhood,* 28.

36. Ibid., 35.

37. Froebel, *Education by Development,* 322.

38. Wiebé, *Paradise of Childhood,* 41.

39. Ibid., 38.

40. Ibid.

41. Froebel, *Education by Development,* 320.

42. Wiebé, *Paradise of Childhood,* 54.

43. Ibid.

44. Ibid., 61.

45. Ibid., 78.

46. Froebel, *Education by Development,* 324.

47. Wiebé, *Paradise of Childhood,* 77.

48. Froebel, *Pedagogics of the Kindergarten,* 31.

49. Froebel wrote: "Two principles . . . seized upon me with special force, and seemed to me valid. The first was the conception of the mutual relationship of all animals, extending like a network in all directions; and the second was that the skeleton or bony framework of fishes, birds, and men was one and the same plan. . . . Invariably, whenever I grasped the interconnection and unity of phenomena, I felt the longings of my spirit and soul were fulfilled" (Lange, *Friedrich Froebel's Leben und ersten Streben,* 56, translated in Liebschner, *A Child's Work,* 3).

50. Friedrich von Schelling, *Sämtliche Werke,* 2:520, 3:220, cited in Joseph L. Esposito, *Schelling's Idealism and Philosophy of Nature* (Lewisburg, Pa.: Bucknell University Press, 1977), 100.

51. John G. Burke, *Origins of the Science of Crystals* (Berkeley and Los Angeles: University of California Press, 1966), 150.

52. Ibid., referring to Friedrich von Schelling, *Von der Weltseele* (Hamburg, 1798), 189, 219.

53. Froebel, *Autobiography of Friedrich Froebel,* 87.

54. Irene Lilley, *Friedrich Froebel: A Selection from His Writings* (Cambridge: Cambridge University Press, 1967), 13–14.

55. Because the molecules were units, any plane, angle, or side could be calculated by plane trigonometry.

56. At the time, various crystallographers disagreed. Their contention was expressed by the reported angular values of the Iceland crystal. Christiaan Huygens, Jean-Baptiste L. Romé de L'Isle, Philippe de la Hire, and

William Hyde Wollaston, mineralogists and physicists, all arrived at different values (Wollaston's were actually the closest to the modern value of the crystal). Romé de L'Isle contended that cleavage and calculation, as performed by Haüy, could not take the place of direct observation and the angular measurements of the crystal as performed with the goniometer. Haüy, on the other hand, claimed that the measuring instrument—the reflecting goniometer—was in itself a device subject to error.

57. Burke, *Origins of the Science of Crystals,* 105.

58. Ibid., 149.

59. Immanuel Kant, *Metaphysical Foundations of Natural Science,* trans. James Ellington (Indianapolis: Bobbs-Merrill, 1970), 40.

60. Ibid., 49.

61. Ibid.

62. Ibid., 56.

63. Ibid., 57.

64. F. W. J. Schelling, *Sämtliche Werke,* edited by K. F. A. Schelling, 14 vols. (Stuttgart, 1856–61), 2:459, trans. Robert Stern, in the introduction to F. W. J. Schelling, *Ideas for a Philosophy of Nature* (Cambridge: Cambridge University Press, 1988), ix–x.

65. Schelling, *Ideas for a Philosophy of Nature,* 156.

66. Ibid., 165.

67. Schelling, *Von der Weltseele,* 227, translated in Burke, *Origins of the Science of Crystals,* 151.

68. According to Weiss, attractive and repulsive forces were in equilibrium in fluids. If repulsive forces were stronger, crystallization would occur.

69. Although both Huygens and Haüy referred to symmetry in their analysis of crystals, they never conceived of more than one crystallographic axis.

70. Weiss's dissertation was published in Latin (Lipsiae: Impressit Carolus Tauchnitz, ca. 1809), translated into French in 1811 by Brochant de Villiers, Haüy's assistant, as *Mémoire sur la détermination du caractère geometrique principal des formes cristallines,* and published in *Journal des Mines,* 19 (1811): 349–91, 401–44.

71. Those translations are given by Clive Ashwin in his *Drawing and Education in German-Speaking Europe, 1800–1900* (Ann Arbor, Mich.: UMI Research Press, 1981), 2.

72. Rousseau had already advocated drawing from nature. In *Emile, or On Education,* Rousseau endorsed the protagonist's mode of education: "Nature should be his only teacher, and things his only models. Let him draw a house from a house, a tree from a tree, a man from a man, etc." Original publication: Jean-Jacques Rousseau, *Émile, ou de l'education* (Amsterdam: Jean Néaulme, 1762), 108, translated and qtd. in Ashwin, *Drawing and Education,* 16.

73. Pestalozzi, *Werke,* 1803, 13:283, translated and qtd. in Ashwin, *Drawing and Education,* 10.

74. Ashwin, *Drawing and Education,* 16.

75. Pestalozzi, *Werke,* 1803, x, translated and qtd. in Ashwin, *Drawing and Education,* 15.

76. Pestalozzi, *Werke,* 1803, 13:253, translated and qtd. in Ashwin, *Drawing and Education,* 13.

77. Pestalozzi, *Werke,* 1803, 13:236, translated and qtd. in Ashwin, *Drawing and Education,* 13–14.

78. Pestalozzi, translated and qtd. in Ashwin, *Drawing and Education,* 19.

79. Ibid.

80. Samuel Georg Mellin, *Encyclopädisches Wörterbuch der kritischen Philosophie* (Zullichau und Leipzig: F. Frommann 1797–98), mentioned in Ashwin, *Drawing and Education,* 18.

81. Immanuel Kant, *Critique of Pure Reason,* trans. Norman Kemp Smith (New York: St. Martin's, 1965), 65–66. Original publication: *Kritik der reinen Vernunft.*

82. Ibid., 68. Similarly, Kant proves that time is another "pure form of sensible intuition" and that both space and time "serv[e] as principles of *a priori* knowledge" (ibid., 67).

83. Ibid., 71.

84. Ibid.

85. Ashwin, *Drawing and Education,* 22.

86. Karl Heinrich Giesker, *Der Zeichenunterricht an der schweizerischen Volksschule im 19. Jahrhundert* (Zurich: University of Zurich, 1938), 49, translated and qtd. in Ashwin, *Drawing and Education,* 21.

87. See Froebel, *The Education of Man,* in a section entitled "Drawing on a Grid According to Apparently Necessary Laws." For a discussion of net drawings, see Ashwin, *Drawing and Education,* 128. The architect and professor of architecture Jean-Nicolas-Louis Durand attempted to systematize architectural knowledge by classifying edifices and drawing them on a grid. It is not known whether Froebel was aware of Durand's books, published as early as 1800. For more on Durand, see chapter 2.

2. ANCHOR STONE BUILDING BLOCKS, 1877

1. *Bestelmeiers Magazin,* a catalogue presenting the goods of the large toy house of Georg Hieronymus Bestelmeier in Nuremberg, is the earliest-known catalogue of German toys. It contained more than 1,200 artifacts and was mentioned in Karl Gröber, *Kinderspielzeug aus alter Zeit: Eine Geschichte des Spielzeugs* (Berlin: Deutscher Kunstverlag, 1928) In English: *Children's Toys of Bygone Days: A History of Playthings of All Peoples, from Prehistoric Times to the XIXth Century,* trans. Philip Hereford (London: B. T. Batsford, 1928), as well as in Ulf Leinweber, *Baukästen: Technisches Spielzeug vom Biedermeier bis zur Jahrtausendwende* (Wiesbaden: Drei Lilien Edition, 1999). In the United States, construction sets of the same period also were made of wood, but unlike the German blocks, they did not allude to Greek or Gothic orders. The Log Cabin Play House, 1865, a painted wood and metal set, consisted of logs that assembled with a notched-dowel system; Crandall Blocks, 1870, presented mainly flat wooden rectangles that assembled with a tongue-and-groove system at their edges; while Kinsey's Ornamental Lock Block and Toy, 1875, assembled with a pinwheel tongue-and-groove system. These last two sets could yield abstract compositions, but not necessarily buildings. Apparently, no manual of instructions existed to suggest how to combine the geometrical pieces into recognizable structures.

2. *Anchor Designs for Architectural Models,* no. 4 (Rudolstadt, Thüringen), instruction booklet reprinted circa 1996. A fantastic book with a great wealth of information useful for collectors was published online. See George Hardy, *Richter's Anchor Stone Building Blocks* (Charlottesville, Va., 2007). It can be found online at www.ankerstein.ch/downloads/CVA/Book-PC.pdf. In the book, Hardy details the change of the blocks from the 20mm module to the 25mm module in the hands of Richter.

3. The Basic Box, set no. 4, contained 55 stones, while the first, medium-size castle could be built with set no. 14, which contained 214 stones. The last page of each instruction booklet revealed more advanced structures that could be built with the following set. In the first years of the twentieth century, additions were made to the sets, incorporating steel and iron pieces.

4. Anna and Gustav Lilienthal described the division of labor, as well as the process leading to the manufacture of the first stones, in the family biography of 1930 (see Anna Lilienthal and Gustav Lilienthal, *Die Lilienthals* [Stuttgart and Berlin: J. G. Cotta'sche Buchhandlung, 1930], 24–30).

Otto Lilienthal's flight experiments have been documented extensively. Nevertheless, the toy endeavors of both brothers and the architectural oeuvre of Gustav Lilienthal have been mentioned in only few sources. Besides the family's own biography, these include *Gustav Lilienthal, 1849–1933: Baumeister, Lebensreformer, Flugtechniker,* ed. Hans J. Reichhardt (Berlin: Stapp Verlag, 1989); and, specifically about Gustav Lilienthal's architectural work, a short article by Lilienthal himself, published in 1889 in *Prometheus,* an illustrated weekly covering developments in science and technology; an essay by Julius Posener, written for the daily newspaper *Der Tagesspiegel* on June 13, 1971, and prompted by the one-hundredth anniversary of Lichterfelde; and the essay by Wolfgang Schäche, "Gustav Lilienthal und das Bauen," in *Gustav Lilienthal,* ed. Reichhardt, 91–118.

5. See Samuel Smiles's *Self-Help* and the play movement in the United States, also discussed in chapter 4 in relation to Meccano and Erector Sets.

6. The blocks were first called Patent-Baukasten, before the name was changed to Anker-Steinbaukasten. In 1880, the Prussian government assigned patent number 13770 to Richter, "for the production of artificial stones from a mixture of sand and chalk with the appropriate addition of varnish and coloring ingredients, which by the addition of glue and strong stirring gets worked into a damp powder and pressed into moulds and dried for 8 days at a temperature of 100–150 degrees Celsius" (Annette Noschka and Günter Knerr, *Bauklötze Staunen, 200 Jahre Geschichte der Baukästen* [Munich: Deutsches Museum and Hirmer Verlag, 1986], 54). The translation of this and all subsequent passages from the German are by Kathryn Schoefert and Tamar Zinguer.

7. An early advertisement read, "It is the only solid toy that even the poorest father can put on the Christmas table for his darlings" (catalogue of the firm, reprinted in Noschka and Knerr, *Bauklötze Staunen,* 53).

8. Max Born, *My Life: Recollections of a Nobel Laureate*

(New York: Scribner, 1978), 55. Born won the Nobel Prize in physics (1954) for his work on quantum mechanics. Born's personal account was originally written for his family and was published after his death.

9. Ibid. Born added: "For the older generation the look of these buildings was according to the styles they were used to, and the sets had great educational value because if one made a single error in a single cross section and used the wrong stone, then one later ran into difficulties and could not complete the structure.... The results were admittedly, considered from an aesthetic point of view[,] quite a bit more dreadful than the printed plans and thus reaped ironic comments from the older generation, such as aunts and uncles. Therefore I decided to discover something new and wonderful which also satisfied me. It resulted in a new method, using building stones whose longest dimension was not more than seven or eight centimeters, of building bridges with a wide span (about one meter). I used no cement of any kind, rather applied the arch principle whereby I used small, wedge-shaped, blue building stones (which are normally used for roofs) as supports."

10. Gustav Lilienthal's then fiancée (and later wife) interpreted the failure of his toy inventions in Paris, in Lilienthal and Lilienthal, *Die Lilienthals,* 24–30.

11. Lilienthal had set up trade agreements with Belgium, England, Portugal, China, the United States, and other countries before his loss at trial in 1887; Richter would later profit from these agreements. The original factory shut down in 1963, but manufacture started there again in 1995 in response to demand for the blocks. The Friends of Anchor Club, most of whose members are adult men, is still very active today (see www.Ankerstein.org). The association issues a newsletter, maintains a website, and exchanges information about the construction of new models.

12. For a discussion of the tectonic, see Kenneth Frampton, "Rappel a l'ordre: The Case for the Tectonic," *Architectural Design* 60 (1990): 19–25; Mitchell Schwarzer, "Ontology and Representation in Carl Bötticher's Theory of Tectonics," *Journal of the Society of Architectural Historians* 52, no. 3 (September 1993): 267–80; Mitchell Schwarzer, *German Architectural Theory and the Search for Modern Identity* (New York: Cambridge University

Press, 1995); and Kenneth Frampton, *Studies in Tectonic Culture: The Poetics of Construction in Nineteenth and Twentieth Century Architecture* (Cambridge Mass.: MIT Press, 2001).

13. Kenneth Frampton, in his "Rappel a l'ordre," describes the etymology of the word: "Greek in origin, the term 'tectonic' derives from the term *tekton,* signifying carpenter or builder.... It appears in Homer, where it again refers to carpentry and to the art of construction in general. The poetic connotation of the term first appears in Sappho, where the *tekton,* the carpenter, assumes the role of the poet. This meaning undergoes further evolution as the term passes from being something specific and physical, such as carpentry, to the more generic notion of construction and later to becoming an aspect of poetry.... This etymological evolution would suggest a gradual passage from the ontological to the representational" (21).

14. In his 1990 essay, Frampton explained that the current architecture climate was reminiscent of that of the nineteenth century with its focus on "scenography": "Rather than join in a recapitulation of avant-gardist tropes or enter into historicist pastiche or into the superfluous proliferation of sculptural gestures, all of which have an arbitrary dimension to the degree that they are based in neither structure nor in construction, we may return instead to the structural unit as the irreducible essence of architectural form" (ibid., 20).

15. Schinkel wrote: "I observed a great vast store of forms that had already come into being, deposited in the world over many millennia of development among very different peoples. But at the same time I saw that our use of this accumulated store of often very heterogeneous objects was arbitrary" (Schinkel, qtd. in Goerd Peschken, *Das architektonische Lehrbuch* [Munich: Deutscher Kunstverlag, 1979], 150, trans. Alex Potts, in "Schinkel's Architectural Theory" in *Karl Friedrich Schinkel: A Universal Man,* ed. Michael Snodin [New Haven: Yale University Press, 1991], 50).

16. Schinkel, qtd. in Goerd Peschken, *Das architektonische Lehrbuch,* 54, trans. Alex Potts, "Schinkel's Architectural Theory," in *Karl Friedrich Schinkel: A Universal Man,* ed. Snodin, 49.

17. Karl Bötticher, *Die Tektonik der Hellenen* (The tectonics of the Hellenes), 2 vols. (Potsdam: F. Riegel, 1844, 1852).

18. Schinkel, qtd. in Goerd Peschken, *Das architektonische Lehrbuch,* 45, trans. Mitchell Schwarzer, in "Ontology and Representation in Carl Bötticher's Theory of Tectonics," 274.

19. A letter from Semper to his publisher, Eduard Vieweg, dated September 26, 1843, trans. Harry Francis Mallgrave, in "A Commentary on Semper's November lecture," *RES: Anthropology and Aesthetics* 6 (Autumn 1983): 24 (Peabody Museum, Harvard University).

20. "Prospectus: Comparative Theory of Building" (1852), in Gottfried Semper, *The Four Elements of Architecture and Other Writings,* trans. Harry Francis Mallgrave and Wolfgang Hermann (Cambridge: Cambridge University Press, 1989), 170. Additionally, Semper wrote, "Our science clearly has assumed a viewpoint similar to most other sciences that have been unable to advance from criticism and analysis to comparison and synthesis" (ibid., 169).

21. Ibid., 171.

22. For a discussion of the meaning of "purposeness," see Mallgrave, "A Commentary on Semper's November Lecture," 24.

23. Semper hoped to "facilitate an overall view of this field . . . [that would] permit an architectural theory of invention to be based on it, one that . . . [would avoid] both characterless schematism and thoughtless caprice" (Gottfried Semper, "Prospectus: Comparative Theory of Building" [1852], in Semper, *The Four Elements of Architecture and Other Writings,* 170).

24. Gottfried Semper, *Style in the Technical and Tectonic Arts, or Practical Aesthetics,* trans. Harry Francis Mallgrave (Los Angeles: Getty Research Institute, 2004), 86.

25. The complete title is *Précis des leçons d'architecture données à l'École royale polytechnique* (Paris: L'Auteur, 1802–5). For a recent edition, see *Précis of the Lectures on Architecture,* with graphic portion of the lectures on architecture by Jean-Nicolas-Louis Durand; introduction by Antoine Picon; translation by David Britt (Los Angeles: Getty Research Institute, 2000).

26. "Out of this chaos," Semper wrote, "the Descartes and Newtons, the Cuviers, Humboldts, and Liebigs created a new, so-called comparative form of science, animated by a world view (Weltidee)" (Semper, "Prospectus: Comparative Theory of Building," 170). Referring to Cuvier's exhibit of osteology in Paris, Semper continued: "Just as everything there develops and is explained by the

simplest prototypical form . . . in the same way, I said to myself, the works of my art are also based on certain standard forms conditioned by primordial ideas, yet which permit an infinite variety of phenomena according to the particular needs that affect them. . . . The parts, their combinations and deviations from the basic form would together convey the edifice's fundamental idea" (ibid., 176).

27. For a discussion of Pitt-Rivers, see Philip Steadman, *The Evolution of Designs: Biological Analogy in Architecture and the Applied Art* (Cambridge: Cambridge University Press, 1979), 83–95.

28. For a discussion of Semper's comparative theory, see Mari Hvattum, *Gottfried Semper and the Problem of Historicism* (Cambridge: Cambridge University Press, 2004). Hvattum's reasoning in relation to Semper was that "the new scientific legitimacy of biology and aesthetics alike relied on the possibility of viewing their respective subject matters as self-referential systems, whose full meaning could be grasped within the system itself. For scientific knowledge of such a system to be possible, none of its components could be hidden from view; the purpose of the organism must be regarded as its immanent property, available for observation and explanation" (ibid., 132).

29. As a professor of mechanical engineering at the Berlin Gewerbe Akademie and later as the rector of the Technische Hochschule in Berlin, Franz Reuleaux was actively involved in German culture. He served as the German ambassador to several world exhibitions, and following the Centennial Exhibition in Philadelphia, he wrote a book, *Briefe aus Philadelphia* (1877), on the poverty of German manufactured goods relative to those in the United States and England. He believed in the power of machines, embodying knowledge, to liberate man from the hardships of peasant life. In 1875, he published a book that was groundbreaking for its systematic classification of machine movements; it was translated a year later into English: *Kinematics of Machinery: Outlines of a Theory of Machines.* This volume followed his earlier *Constructor: A Handbook of Machine Design* (1861) and *Design for Mechanical Engineering* (1854). His publisher, Eduard Vieweg, also published Semper's work. Among the publisher's correspondence, 382 items were from Franz Reuleaux, beginning in 1852; this correspondence constitutes one of the most extensive of Eduard Vieweg and Sons.

30. Similar classifications of machines were attempted before Reuleaux, in the early nineteenth century, by Jean Nicolas Pierre Hachette and Charles Babbage. Their tabulations, as well as others, emphasized, however, the relations between elements in two dimensions, charting only fixed relations. Reuleaux's classification appeared during a time in which debate raged over the advantages of classroom teaching in engineering education, as compared with the traditional machine-shop apprenticeship. Reuleaux's system seemed to synthesize both, by promoting the study of scientific principles, engineering concepts, and mathematical formulas as well as concrete, hands-on simulations. For extensive information about Reuleaux, see Francis C. Moon, *The Machines of Leonardo da Vinci and Franz Reuleaux: Kinematics of Machines from the Renaissance to the 20th Century* (Dordrecht: Springer, 2007).

31. Many art and trade schools opened midcentury, first in England and later in Germany. Forty years later, Le Corbusier summed up the development of the Arts and Crafts movement in Germany in his *Étude sur le mouvement d'art décoratif en Allemagne* (1912; repr., New York: Da Capo, 1968). The Kunstgewerbe Museum opened in 1867, and its affiliated school offered courses in *Kunsthandwerk* and *Kunstindustrie.* Otto Lilienthal attended that school from 1867 to 1870. Gustav Lilienthal became interested in woodworking and metal techniques, as well as weaving and costume design, during his stay in Prague, after studying at the Bauakademie from 1869 to 1871. Later, working as an architect in London, he became acquainted with the arts and crafts collections at the South Kensington Museum (now the Victoria and Albert).

32. Gustav Lilienthal collaborated with the Georgenses on the second edition of *Die Schulen der weiblichen Handarbeit* in 1877 (Leipzig: Richter). The twelve volumes included: *Die Linienstickerei* (Tinted embroidery or linear embroidery); *Die Kanevas-Stickerei* (Gobelin); *Das Stricken* (Knitting); *Das Häkeln* (Crochet); *Knüpfen und Durchziehen* (Knotting and yarning); *Die Flechtarbeiten* (Braiding); *Mosaik und Applikation* (Mosaic and appliqué); *Die Plattstickerei* (Flat-stitch embroidery); *Das Spitzennähen* (Lace making); *Das Ausmalen* (Coloring); *Nähen und Zusshneiden* (Sewing and cutting); *Toilette und Dekoration* (Toiletry and decoration).

33. The main areas of study at the institute were the history of costume design and the different techniques of female handwork. Lilienthal attempted to help his students develop individual tastes, rather than simply reproducing ornamental motifs. He taught them to question each task in light of its purpose, materials, and appropriateness. He found inspiration for his lessons at the Altes Museum and Neues Museum, where he studied the paintings as well as the ethnographic collections. In particular, he was drawn to the collection of African handwork and the folk arts and crafts emanating from the nonindustrialized parts of Europe. For additional information on Lilienthal's involvement with handcrafts, see Heidi Braemer, "Reformerische Bemühungen um Kunstgewerbe und Kunstickerei," in *Gustav Lilienthal,* ed. Reichhardt, 33–60.

34. The education of future craftsmen was actively discussed in Germany in the 1870s. Material initiatives offered by the Prussian government helped initiate educational programs, and Gustav was hoping to receive such funding for his institute. He thus exhibited the work of his students in one of the Berlin exhibitions, which the crown prince attended. The prince promised to visit Lilienthal's school and help support his endeavors but, much to Lilienthal's dismay, failed to do so. Gustav Lilienthal ran the Continuing Education Institute from 1877 to 1880, when, following the building blocks debacle, he immigrated to Australia.

35. Lilienthal wrote: "In the area of Berlin . . . it will not be easy for those who have less money to construct a single-family house, and therefore one has to resort to the most rational methods of construction so that in regards to the cost of commute . . . one could compete with the urban property" (*Prometheus,* no. 54 [1890–91 (second year)]: 21, ed. Dr. Otto N. Witt). Lilienthal acknowledged, however, that his proposition could not be applicable to the lowest-paid worker, but to a middle-income working family.

36. Lilienthal and Lilienthal, *Die Lilienthals,* 57. Gustav Lilienthal answered his neighbors' taunts with a large sign, painted on his diminutive home's façade:

Wer nicht kann halten Mass,
Das Bauen lieber lass,
Schon dieser kleine Zwickel

Kost' hunderttausend Nickel.
(Whoever can't stay modest at all
Had better not build at all
Even this little gusset
Cost a hundred thousand nickels.)

37. "Die Burgen von Lichterfelde—Gustav Lilienthals Beitrag zur Berliner Architektur der Jahrhundertwende" (The Castles of Lichterfelde—Gustav Lilienthal's contribution to Berlin's architecture at the turn of the century) first appeared in *Der Tagesspiegel,* June 13, 1971, and was later reprinted in Julius Posener, *Aufsätze und Vorträge, 1931–1980* (Braunschweig, Wiesbaden: Vieweg & Sohn, 1981), 220.

38. Posener, *Aufsätze und Vorträge,* 220.

39. *Prometheus,* no. 54 (1890–91 [second year]): 22.

40. For more on Lilienthal's building techniques, see Wolfgang Schäche, "Gustav Lilienthal und das Bauen," 91–118.

41. *Prometheus,* no. 54 (1890–91 [second year]): 23.

42. Ibid.

43. In Lichterfelde, more than twenty of the thirty townhouses Lilienthal designed in the last decade of the nineteenth century are still standing. In late August 2001, Lilienthal's granddaughter, Anna Sabine Halle, invited me to visit Tiezenweg 5. The cool, semi-dark parlor was decorated with old photographs and the stuffed albatross Lilienthal had brought back from Brazil. Ms. Halle showed me unpublished family photographs (in one of which Gustav Lilienthal could be seen knitting, surrounded by his wife and five daughters) and told me many stories that illuminated the man's extraordinary personality.

44. In 1890, Otto Lilienthal introduced a profit-sharing system for the employees of his machine shop, becoming one of the first entrepreneurs in Germany to do so.

45. On Hertzka's Freeland, see Lewis Mumford, *The Story of Utopias* (New York: Boni and Liveright, 1922), 139. This utopian settlement would not necessarily require the overturning of existing institutions, Mumford explained, but rather would be established on a new territory, such as the Kenya Highlands in Africa.

46. Hertzka described the new "International Free Society," as "the establishment of a community on the basis of perfect liberty and economic justice—that is, of a community which, while it preserves the unqualified right

of every individual to control his own actions, secures to every worker the full and uncurtailed enjoyment of the fruits of his labour. For the site of such a community a large tract of land shall be procured in a territory at present unappropriated, but fertile and well adapted for colonization. The Free Society shall recognize no exclusive right of property in the land occupied by them, either on the part of an individual or of the collective community" (Theodor Hertzka, *Freeland: A Social Anticipation,* [London: Chatto and Windus, Piccadilly, 1891], 1). As Freeland was to be an agrarian socialist society, Mumford noted, "Hertzka reckons with the fact that in an industrial society, access to machinery is just as important as access to the land, since in a manner of speaking, all our modern activities, even agriculture, are parasitic upon machinery" (Mumford, *The Story of Utopias,* 141).

47. "The name *Freie Scholle* is a name for *Scholle im Freien*—'piece of land in the open' beyond the sea of houses of the metropolis, free as well from exploitation and profit-seeking" (Schäche, "Gustav Lilienthal und das Bauen," 107). According to Posener, in establishing the cooperative, Lilienthal was following the doctrine of Franz Oppenheimer, a practical reformer who, influenced by Hertzka, had written *Freiland in Deutschland*—also promulgating liberty through cooperative land settlements. Gustav Lilienthal himself, however, did not mention this. Freie Scholle was registered as a free corporation on November 25, 1895. The cooperative first purchased 30 acres next to Klein-Glienicke but was left with no money to build the houses. Two years later, it sold the land at a great profit (a capitalist move for a cooperative!), which enabled it to buy yet another plot and afford the construction of houses.

48. Anna Lilienthal recalled: "The good building sand that existed there suggested making use of this advantage, and Gustav Lilienthal constructed forms with which one could fabricate cement blocks and cement elements on site. With this move, one could keep the unemployed workers busy, and furthermore a large cost for the delivery of the stones was eliminated" (Lilienthal and Lilienthal, *Die Lilienthals,* 69).

49. Lilienthal left the board of the colony in 1903. Although the first houses built by Lilienthal are long gone, Freie Scholle still exists today.

50. The light system consisted of panels 5 centimeters

thick, while the heavy construction system consisted of panels 10 centimeters thick, with two layers of insulation. These walls were covered with Terrast cement with inlaid metal mesh and looked like plastered masonry wall panels. The vertical reinforcements of the light system were placed 25 centimeters apart; in the heavy system, they were set 50 centimeters apart. The ceiling of the light system was arched, made from flexible panels, joined together and covered with another layer of tar paper, thus making the ceiling completely waterproof. The ceiling of the heavy system, on the other hand, was constructed horizontally with beams and Terrast panels.

51. A page from the Terrast-Bauweise catalogue, reprinted in Schäche, "Gustav Lilienthal und das Bauen," 113.

52. Those included medals received at exhibitions and fairs: the International Fire Safety Exhibitions of 1901 in Berlin and 1903 in London, the Agricultural Exhibit of 1906 (Berlin), and the Marine and Colonial Exhibition of 1907 (Germany). Although the extent of the commercial success of the company remains unclear, three agrarian communities are known to have been built with the system: Hoffnungstal, Lobetal, and Gladental (Valley of Hope, Valley of Praise, and Valley of Grace, respectively). These were intended for the homeless and for former prison inmates, for whom the cooperative offered an opportunity for work as well as temporary housing. The best-known barrack built with the system was the "office building" for Siemens and Halske (predecessor of the company Siemens AG) in 1908. It was damaged by bombs in 1945 but remained in use as an office until 1980.

53. *Katalog der Terrast-Baugesellschaft,* in *Gustav Lilienthal,* ed. Reichhardt, 112. The development of the foundation system Lilienthal initiated in the Lichterfelde houses extended to the prefabricated systems as well. In the light system, the edge of the wall meeting the ground was anchored with a tightly woven metal mesh that, as the brochure explained, was attached to the panel to prevent penetration of the building interior by rodents. The heavy system, on the other hand, had continuous concrete foundations all around—thus the structure was completely closed off to the exterior and therefore had warmer floorboards. Furthermore, the catalogue stated, warmth was retained since "the empty space underneath the floor is connected to the space underneath the roof by the space between the walls" (ibid.).

54. Lilienthal and Lilienthal, *Die Lilienthals,* 105.

55. Ibid.

56. Étienne-Jules Marey, *La machine animale: Locomotion terrestre et aérienne* (Paris: G. Ballière, 1882), translated as *Animal Mechanism: A Treatise on Terrestrial and Aerial Locomotion* (New York: D. Appleton, 1874).

57. Otto Lilienthal also used photography to document his experiments. He photographed birds and the flying apparatus the brothers made, as well as their attempts to fly from 1891 onward. Other institutions sent their photographers to record Lilienthal's experiments as well.

58. Marey, qtd. in Paul Souriau, *L'esthétique du movement* (Paris: F. Alcan, 1889, 158), translated from the French by Tamar Zinguer.

59. Otto Lilienthal, *Birdflight as the Basis of Aviation: A Contribution towards a System of Aviation Compiled from the Results of Numerous Experiments Made by O. and G. Lilienthal* (London: Longmans, Green, 1911), xi. Although it is unclear whether the Lilienthals were aware of Marey's experiments during their youth, a reference to Marey in their 1889 book attests to their growing awareness of parallel developments and to their interest in situating their own work within them.

60. Ibid. Lilienthal added: "In order to escape the jibes of our schoolmates, we experimented at night time on the drill ground outside the town, but there being no wind on these clear star-lit summer nights, we met with no success" (ibid.). As their mother concluded that their frequent nightly experiments interfered with their schoolwork, the two were sent to separate technical schools to complete high school. They returned during every vacation to the storks and to flight.

61. Model no. 2, a contraption with beating wings, was made of palisander wood and large goose feathers sewn together: "For this purpose we had purchased all the feathers which were obtainable in our town, and this is no mean accomplishment in any Pomeranean town" (ibid., xiii).

62. For a detailed description of all the different machines leading to the successful glider, see Gustav Lilienthal, "The Evolution," in Otto Lilienthal, *Birdflight as the Basis of Aviation,* xi–xxiv.

63. In that seminal book, Otto Lilienthal exposed his findings—new at the time—concerning the structure of birds' wings, the buoyancy and resistance of air, and vari-

ous degrees of curvature, or camber, advantageous for lift and necessary for flight.

64. For additional details about Otto Lilienthal's gliders, their innovations and shortcomings, see Werner Schwipps, *Lilienthal* (Berlin: Arani-Verlag, 1979). For Gustav Lilienthal's contribution in particular, see Werner Schwipps, "Gustav Lilienthal und die Flugtechnik," in *Gustav Lilienthal,* ed. Reichhardt, 119–37.

65. From the time of Otto's death, Gustav Lilienthal became the spokesman for his brother's achievements. He published articles and hosted visitors interested in his brother's estate. In 1909, Orville Wright and Gustav Lilienthal were named honorary members of the Reichsflugverein, or Club for the German Flight Engineer.

66. Gustav Lilienthal proclaimed: "I still support this direction, which I had followed back then with my brother Otto, and recognize the final goal of aeronautical experimentation as being the bird-like flight. Because of my advanced years and my years of prior work, I gained the conviction that the hang-gliding system is a dead-end for flight engineering." Werner Schwipps, a historian of aviation commented: "One who is only slightly familiar with the development of flight technology will not be able not to smile at this statement [that ornithopters would work better than hang-gliders] . . . but that insight was not necessarily clear to everybody prior to World War I, after which experiments with airplanes with beating wings having no bearing or influence on contemporary flight technology, became completely marginalized" (Schwipps, "Gustav Lilienthal und die Flugtechnik in Reichland," in *Gustav Lilienthal,* ed. Reichhardt, 134).

67. Julius Posener, "Die Burgen von Lichterfelde—Gustav Lilienthals Beitrag zur Berliner Architektur der Jahrhundertwende" (1971), in Posener, *Aufsätze und Vorträge,* 222.

68. Ibid.

69. For the theories of play relating to Friedrich Froebel's Gifts, see chapter 1 of this volume.

70. Spencer quotes Charles Darwin, in fact, when he writes: "This survival of the fittest which I have here sought to express in mechanical terms, is that which Mr. Darwin has called 'natural selection, or the preservation of favoured races in the struggle for life'" (Herbert Spencer, *Principles of Biology,* vol. 1, [1865, 1898], 530–31).

71. *Die Spiele der Thiere* (Jena: G. Fischer, 1896) is first translated into English and published as *The Play of Animals* (New York: D. Appleton, 1898); *Die Spiele der Menschen* (Jena: G. Fischer, 1899) was published in English as *The Play of Man* (New York: D. Appleton, 1901).

72. Karl Groos, *The Play of Man* (New York: D. Appleton, 1901), 281.

73. "So may work become like play," Groos wrote, "when its real aim is superseded by the enjoyment of the activity itself." Then, it "can hardly be doubted that this kind of play is the highest and noblest form of work" (ibid., 400).

74. Ibid., 406.

75. Paul Souriau, *The Aesthetics of Movement,* trans. and ed. Manon Souriau (Amherst: University of Massachusetts Press, 1983), 7.

76. Groos, *The Play of Man,* 94.

77. Dolf Sternberger wrote about the modes of vision that opened up in a nineteenth-century world increasingly implicated with new technologies of travel: "Engines, especially trains and steamers, rails and the other daring constructions that smoothed their paths—tunnels, bridges, viaducts did not just alter that face of the landscape. In a new and novel fashion, they opened the world, the lands and the seas" (Dolf Sternberger, "Panorama of the 19th Century," *October* 4 [1977]: 10). About the bird's-eye view, see also Anthony Vidler, "Photourbanism: Planning the City from Above and from Below," in *A Companion to the City,* ed. Gary Bridge and Sophie Watson (Oxford and Malden, Mass.: Blackwell, 2000).

78. Writing about tall structures including the Eiffel Tower, Sigfried Giedion wrote: "This sensation of being enveloped by a floating airspace while walking through tall structures advanced the concept of flight before it had been realized and stimulated the formation of a new architecture" (Sigfried Giedion, *Building in France, Building in Iron, Building in Ferro-Concrete* [1928; repr., Santa Monica, Calif.: Getty Center for the History of Art and the Humanities, 1995], 102). Interestingly, Gustav Eiffel (1832–1923), the tower's architect, did not include the view as one of the tower's "raisons d'être," but instead listed the rational necessity of scientific measurements as well as aerodynamic and meteorological trials. Marey recounted: "With a courtesy for which I thank him, M. Eiffel has offered to me on the gigantic tower which he is erecting (at Paris) a post of observation. From that enormous height, birds photographed during a long flight will give photo-

chronographic images much more instructive than those which I have hitherto been able to obtain" (E. H. J. Marey, "The Mechanism of Flight of Birds," *Nature* 37 [February 16, 1888]: 369–74).

79. In relating to Tony Garnier's aerial views of his project "Cité Industrielle," Giedion described how that bird's-eye view embodied "the combination of ratio and vision that will perhaps most clearly silhouette the coming age" (Giedion, *Building in France, Building in Iron, Building in Ferro-Concrete,* 163).

80. Roland Barthes described that "new sensibility of vision" in his essay "The Eiffel Tower," written in 1953. There, he defined it as "an adventure of sight and of the intelligence." From above, he wrote: "the bird's eye view . . . permits us to transcend sensation and to see things *in their structure. . . .* To the marvelous mitigation of altitude, the panoramic vision added an incomparable power of *intellection:* the bird's eye view, which each visitor to the Tower can assume in an instant for his own, gives us the world to *read,* and not only to perceive; this is why it corresponds to a new sensibility of vision" (Roland Barthes, *The Eiffel Tower, and Other Mythologies* [New York: Hill and Wang, 1979], 8). Barthes notes that this view had been described fifty years prior to Eiffel's achievements, by romantic writers such as Victor Hugo, "as if they had anticipated the construction of the Tower and the birth of aviation" (ibid., 9).

81. Ibid.

82. Walter Benjamin, "Old Toys," in *Selected Writings,* ed. Marcus Bullock and Michael Jennings, vol. 2, *1927–1934* (Cambridge: Belknap Press of Harvard University Press, 1996), 100.

83. Ibid.

84. Groos, *The Play of Man,* 388–89.

85. Souriau, *The Aesthetics of Movement,* 7.

86. Ibid.

3. MECCANO, 1901, AND ERECTOR SET, 1911

1. A. C. Gilbert and Marshall McClintock, *The Man Who Lives in Paradise* (New York: Rinehart, 1954), 129.

2. *Saturday Evening Post,* October 18, 1913, 58.

3. Ibid.

4. *Saturday Evening Post,* October 4, 1913, 59.

5. Ibid.

6. Meccano is the only structural steel toy mentioned in European books, catalogues, and publications, despite the fact that Gilbert had opened offices in Europe.

7. Gilbert and McClintock, *The Man Who Lives in Paradise,* 119.

8. Ibid.

9. Mysto Manufacturing Company produced sets such as "Houdini's Paper Sack Escape," "Milk Can Escape," and more.

10. Gilbert and McClintock, *The Man Who Lives in Paradise,* 119.

11. Hornby's first invention—a failure—was a perpetual motion machine. His second one—another failure—was a siphon inspired by the meatpacking industry, intended to draw out the brine accumulating in a well from layers of dripping bacon (see Maurice Philip Gould, *Frank Hornby: The Boy Who Made $1,000,000 with a Toy* [New York: Meccano Company, 1915], 29–32).

12. Some passages of the biography are written as if spoken by Hornby (see ibid., 47–49).

13. Ibid., 51–52.

14. Ibid., 54.

15. Ibid., 53.

16. Ibid., 57.

17. Walter Benjamin, "Toys and Play" (1928), in *Selected Writings,* ed. Marcus Bullock and Michael Jennings, vol. 2, *1927–1934* (Cambridge: Belknap Press of Harvard University Press, 1996–2003), 118.

18. Erector Sets and Meccano are still very popular today, less among children than among older men—collectors who hold yearly meetings of the A. C. Gilbert Heritage Society. These collectors admit that their interests lie not in assembling the models but rather in assembling complete sets of the toys and in sharing their interest in "structural steel engineering."

19. The German company Märklin produced wind-up train toys starting in the 1890s. Despite their commercial success in Germany, it is interesting to note that Feininger, connected to artistic and architectural circles, chose to design a static train.

20. Dan Fleming, *Powerplay: Toys as Popular Culture* (Manchester: Manchester University Press, 1996), 148.

21. Patent no. 810,148, patented January 16, 1906, by Frank Hornby: Toy or Educational Device, application filed July 22, 1901.

22. This basic module of the perforated metal strip was copied by Meccano's competitors, who introduced slight variations (wider strips, two or three rows of holes, etc.).

23. Perforated metal strips similar to Meccano's were manufactured and sold separately by Gilbert as Erector Toy Builder. This "younger line" allowed for the assembly of primarily two-dimensional designs or smaller, less stable, three-dimensional ones. Perhaps as part of a marketing strategy, Gilbert used the numbers 0, 00, and 000 to label the sets resembling Meccano, and sold them at a low price—moves that positioned this product (and by extension Hornby's) as a less valuable precursor to the more "advanced" Erector Set. The nine products issued under that line in 1913 included, in addition to flat perforated strips, curved strips, angles, brackets, flanged and flat plates, pulleys, wheels, cranks, and hardware (screws, small nuts, and washers) as well as tools (wrenches and screwdrivers) necessary for erecting complex structures.

24. Patent no. 1,066,809, patented on July 8, 1913, by A. C. Gilbert: Toy Construction-Blocks. W.S. Patent Office, application filed on January 20, 1913.

25. Ibid.

26. In 1924, the Erector Set's girders were redesigned. Following the change in appearance of the lattice girders in real life, the parts were narrowed from 1 inch to ½ inch wide.

27. With Erector Outfit 0 of 1914, one could make 69 structures, all of which were two-dimensional. Model 69, the culmination of the series with that outfit, presented one three-dimensional construct: a 6-inch-square girder.

28. Gilbert and McClintock, *The Man Who Lives in Paradise,* 119–20.

29. Ibid., 1. The smallest set cost fifty cents and came in a cardboard box. The tool chest then cost twenty-five dollars. The sets grew very quickly with the years, building more models with an increasing number of parts. In 1915, set no. 1 built 88 models with 140 different parts and still sold for one dollar, while set no. 8 made 304 models with 1,800 different parts and still cost twenty-five dollars. The sets were expensive for the time. Set no. 4—the smallest set to contain a motor—was the most advertised set and the most popular; it sold for five dollars. Gilbert later recalled: "Nobody had ever advertised a five-dollar toy before in this country, and it really took courage. We had sets ranging in price from a dollar to twenty-five dollars,

but we featured the five-dollar set. People in the industry, who had thought that a dollar was a lot of money for any toy, believed we were crazy. But it worked, and started a new trend" (ibid., 131). A couple of months after the sets first appeared on the market, in January 1914, five dollars came to connote an extraordinarily high figure for a day's wages after it was granted to workers at the Ford Motor Plant to keep them from leaving the assembly line. The Ford factory had instituted the assembly line on April 1, 1913, forcing each man to execute the same task over and over again, and the labor turnover rate reached 380 percent by the end of the year. In October 1913, a 13 percent increase across the board set the minimum daily wage at $2.34. However, worker dissatisfaction, labor turnover rates, and signs of unionization kept rising. Henry Ford thus decided to narrow the gap between the salaries and profits of directors and the wages earned by the majority of workers—and set the extraordinarily high figure of daily earnings, thus "bonding" the enthusiastic workers to the factory. As an expensive new object that could be classified as something between a tool and an appliance, Erector promised the embracing of modernity in the house.

30. "Commence by placing a long screw through one or both ends of two girders," it instructed, "then separating the two[,] take another girder on the other side, pushing down into the grooves or channels." After a few more moves, one "put a nut on and tighten[ed] it up by means of a screw driver, binding all the parts firmly together," thus forming a square column girder (instruction manual, The Mysto Erector, 1916, 1).

31. Ibid.

32. Ibid., inside cover.

33. Gould, *Frank Hornby,* 95.

34. The American System of Manufactures was first put to practice in the Colt gun factories in Hartford, Connecticut, during the 1850s. It subsequently spread to other industries (namely sewing machine and bicycle production) and finally led to the mass production of the car. For more on this subject, see David A. Hounshell, *From the American System to Mass Production, 1800–1932* (Baltimore: Johns Hopkins University Press, 1984).

35. Gilbert and McClintock, *The Man Who Lives in Paradise,* 127.

36. Ibid. Gilbert also acknowledged the competition that existed at that point. About Anchor Blocks, he said,

"It was good, but there was a limit to what you could build and no motion." About Meccano, which he recognized as "the chief competitor of Erector," he wrote, "It was good, but it had no gears or pinions at that time, and no motor" (ibid., 127).

37. Gould, *Frank Hornby*, 95. The toy's creator "immediately began to dream of the great commercial success that would come because of his new invention and its great feature of interchangeability which no other toy had at that time" (ibid., 62).

38. From the first set onward, Erector came with a motor, which introduced movement to some parts. The motor was to be assembled by the player, which was no easy task. Different kinds of gear boxes allowing forward, reverse, and other motion enabled movement in all the mechanical models formed with Erector Sets. Nevertheless, the popularity of Erector was never gauged by its ability to move but rather by the variety of structures that could be created with its parts.

The engineering structures in the manuals of the early years included different kinds of bridges—single-girder bridges, single-track railroad trestles, and others—as well as tall structures such as multistory steel frames, elevator towers, windmills, weather vanes, and a sightseeing tower. Steel-frame structures included barns, some of which housed gear boxes (also made with Erector parts) thus yielding sawmills, machine shops, and well houses. There were models of heavy machinery involved in construction: rotary traveling crane, gantry crane, portable boom, revolving derrick, and more. Additional mechanical equipment included shovels, a hay stacker, pile drivers, and smaller machines, such as machine-shop equipment: drills, saws, and presses. Numerous railroad structures, such as telegraph and electrification towers, signal towers, and semaphores were also shown in the manuals, to be erected beside the numerous railroad wagons, trailers, and trolleys. Vehicles included a limousine, a sightseeing car, and an auto-dump wagon, as well as smaller types such as bicycles and wheeled chairs. Boats included a battleship, torpedo boat, and motor launch, while with Erector one could also make flying machines such as the Bleriot monoplane, a Wright biplane, and a dirigible. Different moving structures included playground equipment—seesaws, merry-go-rounds, and a Ferris wheel.

39. Small domestic objects included baskets of various kinds, an apothecary's balance, picture frames, and a coat hanger. There were also reduced-scale models—a sewing machine, a phonograph, and a cloth wringer—as well as full-scale household equipment, progressing gradually (through the use of additional girders) to include, among other things, a 36-inch-tall "Straight Back Chair" and a 30-inch-tall "Parlor Table." Mechanical objects included a clock and a vault door.

40. Henry Petroski, qtd. in Viva Hardigg, "The Poet Laureate of Technology," which appeared in *Prism Magazine,* a publication of the American Society for Engineering Education, *ASEE Prism* 9, no. 6 (February 2000): 24–26. Petroski also conducted a survey among "American business leaders who began their careers as engineers" and found that "many of them recall with fondness playing as children with chemistry sets and construction toys such as Lincoln Logs, Tinker Toys, and Erector Sets" (see Henry Petroski, "Work and Play," *American Scientist* 87, no. 3 [May–June 1999]: 208–12).

41. Viva Hardigg, "Engineering's Mr. Chips," ASEE *Prism* 8, no. 8 (April 1999): 26–28.

42. Sir Harry Kroto, qtd. in Adam Usher, "Why Britain Needs More Meccano and Less Lego," *Sunday Telegraph,* July 8, 2001.

43. In the United States, a few thousand women were employed in engineering by the 1920s; the number climbed to six thousand after World War II. For more on women, technology, and the engineering profession, see Ruth Oldenziel, *Making Technology Masculine: Men, Women, and Modern Machines in America, 1870–1945* (Amsterdam: Amsterdam University Press, 1999).

44. J. A. L. Waddell, "The Advisability of Instructing Engineering Students in the History of the Engineering Profession," *Proceedings of the Society for the Promotion of Engineering Education* 2 (1903): 193–217, qtd. in Oldenziel, *Making Technology Masculine,* 51.

45. Rudyard Kipling, "The Bridge Builders," in *The Day's Work* (London: Macmillan, 1898); Anna Chapin Ray, *Bridge Builders* (Boston: Little, Brown, 1909); Willa Cather, *Alexander's Bridge* (Boston: Houghton Mifflin, 1912). Ray's novel centers on a contest between two men— one is an engineer, the other, a writer—to win a woman's heart. The comments of the young woman's father are telling. About the writer, he remarks, "That fellow is very much a man, even if he does write books" (246). About

the engineer, the father says, "That's a man, all over," and his chosen profession "takes the best of a man's body and mind and soul" (246). The writer himself, in the novel, writes about his rival, the engineer: "What a man the fellow looked, dashing off like that. And after all, his was a man's profession, infinitely bigger, infinitely more virile than the mere knack of sitting in a corner and writing on a pad of paper" (116, qtd. in Ruth Oldenziel, *Making Technology Masculine,* 138).

46. "To become a Gilbert Master Engineer requires not only painstaking constructive effort, but originality and inventive skill" (B. C. Forbes, "Builds Novel Big Business at 36: Stirring Story in Which Magic Blends with Ideals, Grit and Achievement," *Forbes Magazine,* n.d. [probably 1921–22], 189, Gilbert Archives, Yale University Library).

47. "Gilbert Talk on Scientific Toys," newspaper clipping of unknown origin, n.d. (probably around 1918), reporting on Gilbert's talk at the Chicago Toy Fair, Gilbert Archive, Yale University Library. Gilbert would address his personal recommendation to the Master's Engineer's potential employer of choice, say, for a summer job. Gilbert realized that such rewards, carrying monetary value, could easily distract the boys from doing their homework. He therefore instituted a rule that no one could hold a Master Engineer Diploma without having earned an 80 or "above average" in his schoolwork.

48. Owen McLean, "Do What You Like—But Do It Better Than the Other Fellow," *American Magazine,* n.d., 115, Gilbert Archives, Yale University Library.

49. Gilbert and McClintock, *The Man Who Lives in Paradise,* 136.

50. Forbes, "Builds Novel Big Business at 36," 189.

51. Ibid.

52. Ibid.

53. Ibid.

54. Ibid. Other influential inventors who apprenticed in machine shops were also mentioned in the article and included George Eastman, who is said to have mixed the chemicals of his own photographic plates from the start, Thomas Edison, who spent more time in his shops than in his clerical departments, as well as presidents of large, successful enterprises, such as Charles Schwab, who started his career as an unskilled workman in a steel plant, and Coleman DuPont, who began as a worker in a coal pit.

55. Ibid.

56. Monte A. Calvert, *The Mechanical Engineer in America, 1830–1910: Professional Cultures in Conflict* (Baltimore: Johns Hopkins University Press, 1967), 13.

57. Ibid., 8.

58. Ibid., 7. The nineteenth-century "shop culture" gradually declined during the latter part of the century and lost its original role as the factories developed.

59. Forbes, "Builds Novel Big Business at 36," 189. Forbes added: "An organization whose ramifications are not only nation-wide but world-wide is doing this very thing. This organization is not a grammar school or a trade school or a high school or a university. It is a factory. It is a toy factory! Ridiculous? Not at all" (ibid.).

60. Gould, *Frank Hornby,* 50.

61. Ibid. Gilbert, in an interview with *Forbes Magazine* in 1930, recounted: "When I first attempted to market the earlier Erector set, I was told that most boys were more interested in tearing things to pieces rather than in making them. I replied that, on the contrary the real reason that makes the average boy want to take a mechanical contrivance to pieces is nothing more or less than one form of the expression of the instincts of the builder. He really wants to tear them to pieces so he can build them again" (reprinted in Gilbert, "Ask the Young," *Toy Department,* December 1930, 15 [probably a publication of A. C. Gilbert's Company], in Gilbert Archives, Yale University Library).

62. *Christian Herald,* December 1915. Both this ad and the following one in the *Ladies' Home Journal* were reported to have resulted in a large increase in sales. Charles W. Hoyt, the director of the agency handling all of Gilbert's advertising from its beginnings, reported on the ad's success in "The Advertising Romance of an Athlete: How Alfred C. Gilbert—a World's Champion—Broke Records in Toy Manufacturing," *Hoyt's Signal Tower* 1, no. 3 (December 1927): 1–3, Gilbert Archive, Yale University Library.

63. *Ladies' Home Journal,* December 1918. Also appearing in this issue is an advertisement for Gilbert's nurse's outfit. The small ad reads: "Girls too! I haven't forgotten the girls—here is a dainty and realistic set that appeals to the best instincts of the little mother—'Gilbert Nurse's Outfit.'" With apron, scissors, cap, armband, and more, this World War I–era costume included "everything for acting the real Red Cross angel of mercy."

64. "Kis-Lyn to Teach Model Building: Superintendent Announces Installation of Six Erector Sets in Industrial School," author and source unknown, n.d. (ca. 1916–17), Gilbert Archive, Yale University Library.

65. Forbes, "Builds Novel Big Business at 36," 190.

66. Letter cited ibid., 209.

67. After the war ended, Gilbert was instrumental in promoting the American toy industry. Describing German toys as noneducational "flimsy trinkets," he called for a ban on the import of German and other European items, thus effectively suppressing foreign competition in building toys. In 1919, he bought the rights to manufacture Anchor Blocks in the United States, and in 1929 he bought Meccano as well. In a twist of fate, the rights to manufacture Erector Set were sold to Meccano a few years after the Erector Company went out of business in 1964. Today Erector Set and Meccano are interchangeable names for the same toy, are part of the same company, and are manufactured in France. Now made of colorful plastic, they bear no resemblance to the original toys.

68. A. C. Gilbert, "Ask the Young," *Toy Department,* December 1930, 15.

69. Advertisement, Hoyt, "The Advertising Romance of an Athlete," 2.

70. Advertisement, *Ladies' Home Journal,* December 1918.

71. First full-page ad appearing in the *Saturday Evening Post,* November 28, 1914, and in *Collier's Weekly,* November 21, 1914, reprinted in Hoyt, "The Advertising Romance of an Athlete," 2.

72. Advertisement, *American Weekly,* November 27, 1927, and December 4, 1927, reprinted in Hoyt, "The Advertising Romance of an Athlete," 4.

73. Ithiel Town was a student of Asher Benjamin at the School of Architectural Composition in Boston. Town was considered a pioneer in American Revivalist architecture, forming a singular formal vocabulary, as he was said to be interested equally in construction and in composition. His better-known projects included Trinity Church (1813–16), the Center Church on the New Haven Green (1814), and the State Hospital (1833), all in New Haven, Connecticut; with Alexander Davis, he designed the New York Customs House in New York City (1842) and the Wadsworth Atheneum in Hartford, Connecticut (1842–44).

74. Ithiel Town, *American Journal of Sciences and Arts* 3 (1821): 158–66. Town added: "But in bridges and public buildings, it would seem, something better might be expected, if men scientifically and practically acquainted with such subjects, would step forward, in a disinterested manner, and determine between principles which are philosophical, and those which are not, and between modes of execution which are founded in practice and experience, and those which are founded in ignorance and inexperience."

75. Ithiel Town, cited in David Plowden, *Bridges: The Spans of North America* (New York: Norton, 1984), 38.

76. The earlier composite trusses had been designed by "inspired carpenters," as Plowden called them: Timothy Palmer (1751–1821), Lewis Wernwag (1769–1843), and Theodore Burr (1771–1822). All three builders had relied on their intuition rather than calculation in constructing their trusses and bridges.

77. Around 1840, Eli Whitney decided to build a dam and reservoir on the Mill River. He supposedly moved the bridge down a half mile, floating it on the river. He accomplished this task without removing or displacing a single timber, thanks to the strength and stability of the Town truss.

78. Town published Whitney's letter in "A Description of Ithiel Town's Improvement in the Construction of Wood and Iron Bridges," New Haven, 1821 (see Roger Hale Newton, *Town and Davis: Pioneers in American Revivalist Architecture, 1812–1870, Including a Glimpse of Their Times and Their Contemporaries* [New York: Columbia University Press, 1942], 44–45).

79. Town sent a network of people to scout the Northeast for bridges erected without a contract. Plowden notes: "His was the first stock design to be patented and produced by licensees or carpenters on a royalty basis." He calls Town's enterprise "the forerunner of the fabricating companies which were to dominate the bridge-building scene a half-century later" (Plowden, *Bridges,* 38).

80. Newton, *Town and Davis: Pioneers in American Revivalist Architecture, 1812–1870,* 19. Since the Town truss had no posts and was susceptible to warping and twisting, Town doubled the webs making up the truss to render it more suitable for use by the railroads. He was issued a patent for this improved system in 1835.

81. Arnold Koerte, *Two Railway Bridges of an Era: Firth*

of *Forth and Firth of Tay: Technical Progress, Disaster, and New Beginning in Victorian Engineering* (Basel, Boston, and Berlin: Birkhäuser Verlag, 1992), 15.

82. Ibid., 11.

83. Bruce Watson, "Hello Boys! Become an Erector Master Engineer!," *Smithsonian Magazine,* June 1999, 128.

84. For specifics on the Tay Bridge disaster, see Koerte, *Two Railway Bridges of an Era;* about railway travel and related fear of collapse, see Wolfang Schivelbusch, *Railway Journey: The Industrialization and Perception of Time and Space* (Berkeley: University of California Press, 1986).

85. Koerte, *Two Railway Bridges of an Era,* 48. "The multitude of identical parts indeed is reminiscent of North American bridges without however approaching their pragmatic sophistication" (ibid.).

86. See Newton, *Town and Davis,* 44. The steel counterpart of the Town lattice truss was first executed in Europe (see Plowden, *Bridges,* 37).

87. Koerte, *Two Railway Bridges of an Era,* 52–53.

88. Ibid., 84.

89. Construction on the Forth Bridge had already begun in 1878 according to a design by Bouch, but it was abandoned two years later after the report of the inquiry into the Tay Bridge disaster was issued. The bridge not only raised doubt about Bouch's ability as a bridge designer, but also questioned once more the behavior of suspension bridges under wind loads, and their use as railway crossings. Although a suspension bridge was a plausible option for crossing the Forth, public opinion was against it following the suspension bridge's association with Bouch, and a famous collapse of a suspension bridge in Angers, France, that killed 226 people. The principle of cantilever and central girder had already existed for some time. A "console girder"—a cantilever—crossing the Main River near Hassfurt was the first bridge of this type, designed twenty-three years before the Forth Bridge by Heinrich Gerber. Also, wooden cantilever bridges had existed in Tibet and China already in 1670. Nevertheless, many thought that the system was a modern invention, instituted by Fowler and Baker.

90. Koerte, *Two Railway Bridges of an Era,* 140.

91. Ibid., 183.

92. Ibid. There were many accidents during construction: fifty-eight workers perished while jumping playfully between the girders, high above the water, sometimes under the influence of whiskey. It was said that they were given confidence in their risky games by the stability of the structure.

93. The cantilever surpassed the Forth's by 90 feet, although the total span of the bridge was only one-half of the Forth's length.

94. *Manitoba Free Press* (Winnipeg, Canada), August 30, 1907, 1.

95. Plowden, *Bridges,* 175.

96. The contract in 1900 was awarded to the company that had submitted the lowest bid, which was then a common practice. The Quebec Bridge and Railway Company approached Theodore Cooper—then an illustrious civil engineer—to act as advisor to the design. The actual designer, however, was Peter Szlapka, the company's engineer. Nevertheless, like Bouch, Cooper died broken by his failure three months before the new Quebec Bridge was inaugurated, in 1919.

97. "Although the Quebec Bridge was in Canada, it was considered an American endeavor, and the responsibility for its design and collapse rested with the United States" (Plowden, *Bridges,* 174). As mentioned earlier (Oldenziel, *Making Technology Masculine,* 139 and footnote 43), the success of the male hero-engineer depicted in popular novels was analogous to the stability of their structures. The novels reiterated a common theme: "the parallel between a faulty design in bridge construction and the flawed character of the hero" was a popular theme (see ibid., 135).

98. Pin connections were more common in America; rivets were already used in Europe.

99. Plowden, *Bridges,* 175.

100. *Engineering News* 23 (19 April 1890): 373–74.

101. *Engineering News* 37 (11 February 1897): 93.

102. J. A. L. Waddell, *Bridge Engineering,* vol. 2 (New York: Wiley, 1916), 1540–41.

103. Westhofen explained: "When a load is put on the central girder by a person sitting on it, the men's arms and the anchorage ropes come into tension, and the men's bodies from the shoulders downwards and the sticks come into compression" (Wilhelm Westhofen, "The Forth Bridge," *Engineering* 49 [February 28, 1890], 218). The man sitting in the center, Kaichi Watanabe (1858–1932), was among the first Japanese engineers who had come to study in the west. He graduated from University of Glasgow in 1886 and worked on the construction of the

Forth Bridge as foreman. His participation in this model was meant to acknowledge the contribution of Japanese engineering to the development of the cantilever principle.

104. By the end of the nineteenth century, *Self-Help* had become a best seller around the world, including in the Middle East and the Far East.

105. This monumental work "was hailed as one of the most striking achievements of a mechanical age" (Asa Briggs, introduction to Samuel Smiles, *Self-Help, with Illustrations of Conduct and Perseverance* [London: J. Murray, 1958], 8).

106. Smiles, *Self-Help,* 305.

107. Ibid.

108. Ibid., 304–5.

109. Ibid., 61.

110. Ibid., 304–5.

111. Ibid., 336.

112. Gould, *Frank Hornby,* 114. Hornby's biography is interwoven with tales of Smiles's influence and reiterations of his thought: "Frank failed in his attempt to build an automatic syphon pumping device to empty the brine pit, but Samuel Smiles' books had taught him that failure was the most valuable thing in the world" (ibid., 36). He then tried to invent a box for bus conductors that would calculate the distance traveled by passengers and collect the appropriate fare: "But he was again doomed to disappointment. As he failed, he went over his favorite book and read again" (ibid., 38). It was thanks to *Self-Help,* Hornby acknowledged, that he knew "that although he had failed two or three, or four, or five times, yet there were the histories, the biographies of so many great men who had failed and failed and failed many more times than he had and yet who were the world's heroes today because they had kept on and on, until at last they achieved success" (ibid., 39).

113. Ibid., 115. Hornby also referred to the Boy Scout movement, founded in Britain in 1908 by Lord Baden Powell, as paralleling the "helpfulness" provided by his toy. "The Boy Scouts idea is to do a helpful deed every day. Meccano is built on the principle of helpfulness. That is on the true principle of self help. It gives every boy the opportunity to learn (while he is playing) how to do things that will help him to be successful when he becomes a man" (ibid., 112).

114. Ibid., 114.

115. Ibid., 115. Following Smiles, Hornby promoted mechanical dexterity as means for self-culture: "No matter what you are going to be when you grow to be a man, a knowledge of the principles of mechanics will help make you more successful" (ibid., 137). The aim of this training and intensive practice—achieved by playing with Meccano—is that the boy "can learn things that will count strongly in his favor and help him when he rubs against the real problems of later life" (ibid., 141). Such early training promises that, to the boy, "mechanics become second nature" (ibid.).

116. "A Young Man Who Earned £60,000 Last Year by Making Toys," *Efficiency Magazine,* 1924, 13, author and precise date unknown; an article with a similar self-help and success-related title by Arthur F. Jones, "Magic of Success in Persistence," *Brooklyn Eagle,* circa 1927, 5. Both articles in the Gilbert Archives, Yale University Library.

117. During the first year of its publication, there was a demand for more than a dozen editions.

118. Orison Swett Marden, *Rising in the World; or, Architects of Fate: A Book Designed to Inspire Youth to Character Building, Self-Culture and Noble Achievement* (New York: Success Company, 1900), preface.

119. The title of chapter 8 of *Rising in the World* is "Self Help: Self Made or Never Made. The Greatest Men Have Risen from the Ranks."

120. T. Benjamin Atkins, *Out of the Cradle into the World, or Self Education through Play* (Columbus, Ohio, and Boston: Sterling, 1895).

121. Ibid., 224.

122. Ibid., chap. 11.

123. Ibid., 217.

124. Ibid., 218.

125. Daniel Rodgers, *The Work Ethic in Industrial America, 1850–1920* (Chicago: University of Chicago Press, 1978), 7.

126. Ibid., 12.

127. It was during the late nineteenth century and early twentieth century that people became aware of neurasthenia and of the possibility of physical and nervous collapse. See also Anson Rabinbach, *The Human Motor: Energy, Fatigue, and the Origins of Modernity* (New York: Basic, 1990). The disease of neurasthenia—neurological complaints, including headache, insomnia, and melancholy—could be partly counteracted, advertisements claimed, by the use of the Electrical Vibrator, which the

A. C. Gilbert Company manufactured in the same factory as Erector Set. This proves that Gilbert was aware of social demands as they appeared in the popular press. As a marketing strategy, he would never admit that his intention with Erector Set was other than educational (i.e., a moneymaking scheme), but the choice he made of objects to manufacture, using the same small motor, testifies to his constant and ongoing involvement with current beliefs and fashions.

128. Rodgers, *The Work Ethic in Industrial America,* 95.

129. *Success Magazine* 11 (1908): 548–49.

130. Nathaniel C. Fowler Jr., *The Boy: How to Help Him Succeed* (New York: Moffat, Yard, 1912), 79, qtd. in Rodgers, *The Work Ethic in Industrial America,* 105.

131. Rodgers, *The Work Ethic in Industrial America,* 109.

132. George Ellsworth Johnson, *Education by Plays and Games* (Boston: Ginn, 1907), 98, qtd. in Bernard Mergen, "The Discovery of Children's Play," *American Quarterly* 27 (1975): 408.

133. Rodgers, *The Work Ethic in Industrial America,* 123.

134. John Dewey, "Play," in *A Cyclopedia of Education,* ed. Paul Monroe (New York: Macmillan, 1913), 725.

135. Karl Groos, *The Play of Animals* (New York: D. Appleton, 1898); and Karl Groos, *The Play of Man* (New York: D. Appleton, 1901). Both books were translated by Elizabeth L. Baldwin with the author's cooperation.

136. Dewey, "Play," in *A Cyclopedia of Education,* 726.

137. Ibid.

138. Ibid.

139. Ibid.

140. Ibid., 727.

141. Ibid.

142. Herbert Spencer, *The Principles of Psychology,* vol. 2, (1855; repr., Boston: Longwood, 1977), 630.

143. Ibid., 630–31.

144. Ibid., 631.

145. Ibid., 631–32.

146. Ibid., 647.

147. *Meccano Magazine,* 1926, 723.

4. THE TOY, 1951, AND HOUSE OF CARDS, 1952

1. John Leeper, "Exhibition for Children: Designed by Follis and Goode," *Arts and Architecture* 69, no. 12 (December 1952): 34–35. "Children do not want to look so much as to experience the material shown them, touching, moving it themselves wherever possible. . . . They must be regarded as participants, not spectators of the exhibitions" (ibid.).

2. *Interiors* 108, no. 6 (January 1949): 102–5.

3. The "standard building toy" to which the article referred was the Erector Set, which, the article claimed, still "mangled little fingers and produced castles whose miniature scale was more meaningful to the parents than to the child" (Industrial Design Section, *Interiors* 111, no. 2 [September 1951]: 10). Among the numerous articles devoted to design for children, see also "Toys to Grow With," *Everyday Art Quarterly,* no. 17 (Winter 1950–51); "Construction Toys," *Interiors* 113, no. 12 (July 1954): 16, 102, 104; and "Two Eames Sequels," *Interiors* 114, no. 2 (September 1954): 14.

4. "Construction Toys," 102. The prices at the time were said to be "98¢ for the House of Cards and $1.98 for The Little Toy which is pretty sensational in these days of dollar toys in the so-called 'dime stores'" (ibid., 104).

5. Industrial Design section, *Interiors* 111, no. 2 (September 1951): 10. The editorial board of *Interiors* mistakenly received a deck of House of Cards without slots cut on its sides. Before the instruction sheet arrived "with the official word on the slot, we held a conference and decided that the cards were perfect for fortune telling." About Giant House of Cards, they wrote: "We will go further and say that the 'giant' is beautiful and that it will appeal to adults" (ibid., 14).

6. "Construction Toys," 104.

7. *Vogue,* August 15, 1959, 127.

8. The Eameses' design for children included children's furniture such as molded plywood animals (1945), toy masks (1950), The Toy (1951), The Little Toy (1952), House of Cards (1952), Giant House of Cards (1953), The Coloring Toy (1955), The Alcoa Solar Machine (1957), Revell Toy House (1959), and The IBM Computer House of Cards (1970). The films incorporating toys were *Traveling Boy,* 11:45 min., color, 1950; *Parade,* 5:33 min., color, 1952; *Tops, or Stars of Jazz,* 3:01 min., black-and-white, 1957; and *Toccata for Toy Trains,* 13:28 min., color, 1957. All films were produced by the Office of Charles and Ray Eames, Los Angeles, California.

9. House of Cards was manufactured by Tigrett Enterprises from 1952 until 1961, when the company went out of business. It was reissued in the 1960s by the German

company Ravensburger, and again in 1986 by the Eames Office and the Museum of Modern Art. Today, more than a half century after its design, House of Cards is still vividly alive. Most images still seem up-to-date, reflecting a choice of objects that still surround us. The cards manifest all that has been written about Eames design: their "affection for objects," their love of "stuff," of "good design," and their creation of "functioning decoration." About "Functioning Decoration," see Pat Kirkham, *Charles and Ray Eames: Designers of the Twentieth Century* (Cambridge: MIT Press, 1998), 143–200.

10. Charles Eames, narration of opening segment of the film *Toccata for Toy Trains,* qtd. in John Neuhart, Marilyn Neuhart, and Ray Eames, *Eames Design* (New York: Abrams, 1989), 215.

11. "Building Toy," *Life,* July 16, 1951, 58.

12. Ibid., 60.

13. Publicity leaflet for The Toy, 1951, The Works of Charles and Ray Eames, Manuscripts Division, Library of Congress, Box 229. The Toy was manufactured by Tigrett Enterprises in Jackson, Tennessee, and was included in the Sears Roebuck catalogue for a few seasons. In 1951, it cost $3.50. An earlier working prototype of The Toy was comprised of only triangles. The Eameses added the rectangular elements to speed up the construction process and to enable players to build larger, taller forms. Tigrett Enterprises also manufactured The Little Toy from 1952 to 1961. A smaller version of The Toy, The Little Toy came with wire frames in the shape of triangles and squares that could be assembled to create, as the instruction sheet suggested houses, bridges, or rocket-launching platforms. Colorful cardboard panels connected to the frames. The Little Toy was advertised as creating small environments to play around, whereas The Toy was advertised as providing larger environments to play within.

14. Flexikite, for example, was manufactured between 1950 and 1951 and came in a cardboard tube. It was invented and patented by Francis and Gertrude Rogallo in November 1948. It had no rigid structure and led to the subsequent design of a parachute for NASA (Para Wing) by Francis Rogallo, an aeronautical engineer.

15. See letters of solicitation, The Works of Charles and Ray Eames, Box 104, Manuscripts Division, Library of Congress.

16. Of the two hundred kites exhibited at the Hallmark Gallery in New York City during the summer of 1968, seventy-one were loaned by Charles and Ray Eames. One year later, the Eameses sent ninety-seven of their kites to the Field Museum of Natural History in Chicago for the exhibition *The Wind in My Hands.*

17. *Polavision* was produced for the Polaroid Corporation by the Office of Charles and Ray Eames in Los Angeles, California, in 1978. In the film, short vignettes (each two-and-a-half minutes long) demonstrated aspects of everyday life.

18. The Case Study House Program, sponsored by John Entenza and *Art and Architecture* magazine, enlisted young architects to design and build low-cost, innovative architecture using new materials. Case Study House #8 was designed by Charles and Ray Eames for their own use, while Case Study House #9, its neighbor, was designed and built at the same time by Charles Eames and Eero Saarinen for John Entenza. Both houses used steel-frame construction, but in the Entenza House (#9) no beams or columns were expressed. For more on the Case Study House Program, see Elizabeth A. T. Smith, ed., *Blueprints for Modern Living: History and Legacy of the Case Study House* (Los Angeles: Museum of Contemporary Art; and Cambridge: MIT Press, 1989). For more on the Eames House specifically, see Neuhart, Neuhart, and Eames, *Eames Design,* 106–21.

19. "Life in a Chinese Kite," *Architectural Forum,* September 1950, 90.

20. Ibid.

21. Lawrence Hargrave (1850–1915) invented his kite in Australia in 1892 and put it to use in meteorological experiments (see Alexander Graham Bell, "The Tetrahedral Principle in Kite Structure," *National Geographic Magazine,* June 1903, 219–50).

22. Meccano was the British precedent of the American Erector Set that was manufactured by the A. C. Gilbert Company, New Haven, Connecticut, between 1913 and 1962 (see chapter 3 of this volume).

23. Although both Charles and Ray Eames are credited with the design of the Eames House, this article mentions Charles Eames alone as its architect ("Life in a Chinese Kite," 93–94, 96).

24. Ibid., 96. "One of Eames' many surprise discoveries as the house went up was that light steel is a distinct material, very different from its familiar, heavy parent" (ibid.).

25. Ibid. In summing up his work in the article, Charles Eames mentions his regret that he had not been influenced to a greater extent by the marine and aviation equipment with which he was familiar in the choice of materials for the house.

26. For more on the Eameses' practice of combining and recombining elements in their designs, see Beatriz Colomina, "Reflections on the Eames House," in *The Work of Charles and Ray Eames: A Legacy of Invention,* ed. Donald Albrecht (New York: Abrams in association with the Library of Congress and the Vitra Design Museum, 1997), 126–49.

27. At the time of the Cold War, there was little incentive to retool the Beech Aircraft Company in order to mass-produce the Wichita House.

28. R. Buckminster Fuller, *Designing a New Industry* (Wichita, Kans.: Fuller Research Institute, 1946).

29. Ibid., 2. The copy of *Designing a New Industry* with the dedication to the Eameses can be found in R. Buckminster Fuller, The Works of Charles and Ray Eames, box 30, folder 9, Manuscript Division, Library of Congress.

30. Fuller, *Designing a New Industry,* 2.

31. Ibid., 3.

32. Alden Hatch, *Buckminster Fuller: At Home in the Universe* (New York: Crown, 1974), 153.

33. John McHale, *R. Buckminster Fuller* (New York: Braziller, 1962), 29.

34. R. Buckminster Fuller, qtd. in Hatch, *Buckminster Fuller,* 153. Fuller explained: "All polyhedra may be subdivided into component tetrahedra, but no tetrahedron may be subdivided into component polyhedra of less than the tetrahedron's four faces . . . for we cannot find an enclosure of less than four sides" (R. Buckminster Fuller and E. J. Applewhite, *Synergetics: Explorations in the Geometry of Thinking* [New York: Macmillan, 1975], 335).

35. "The tetrahedron is the basic structural system, and all structure in the universe is made up of tetrahedronal parts" (Fuller, qtd. in Hatch, *Buckminster Fuller,* 153).

36. Fuller, according to McHale, *R. Buckminster Fuller,* 15.

37. Robert Marks, *The Dymaxion World of Buckminster Fuller* (Carbondale and Edwardsville: Southern Illinois University Press, 1960), 43.

38. Fuller assumed that the most economical structural energy web might be derived through the fusion of a tet-

rahedron and a sphere. The sphere encloses the largest amount of space with the smallest surface and is strongest against internal pressure, while the tetrahedron encloses the least amount of space with the largest surface and is strongest against external pressure (Fuller and Applewhite, *Synergetics,* 52–56, 319–30).

39. R. Buckminster Fuller, *Tetrascroll: Goldilocks and the Three Bears, A Cosmic Fairy Tale* (1975; repr., New York: St. Martin's, 1982).

40. Ibid., vii.

41. Wachsmann, together with Walter Gropius, founded the General Panel Corporation in September 1942 and developed a factory-made house with the aim of providing the postwar American market with industrialized suburban housing. The Packaged House engaged their attention between 1942 and 1951, and although it failed as a business endeavor, the architects' combined efforts created valuable prototypes for prefabricated housing (see Gilbert Herbert, *The Dream of the Factory-Made House: Walter Gropius and Konrad Wachsmann* [Cambridge: MIT Press, 1984]).

42. Konrad Wachsmann, *The Turning Point of Building: Structure and Design* (New York: Reinhold, 1961), 170.

43. Ibid., 12.

44. Ibid., 9.

45. Ibid., 186.

46. Robert Le Ricolais, "Les Réseaux à trois dimensions: À propos du project de hangar d'aviation de Konrad Wachsmann," *Architecture d'Aujourd'hui* 25 (July–August 1954): 10–12.

47. Ibid.

48. Wachsmann reported that a team of students and consultants worked on his design, which was developed mainly through models rather than drafting (Wachsmann, *The Turning Point of Building,* 186).

49. Ibid., 22–31. Kenneth Frampton called Wachsmann and Fuller "the technocrats of the Pax Americana" and wrote: "If there was a single techno-scientific genius admired by both men, it was surely Alexander Graham Bell. . . . Bell was seen by both men as the modern equivalent of the *uomo universale*" (Frampton, "I tecnocrati della Pax Americana: Wachsmann & Fuller," *Casabella* 542–43 [January–February 1988]: 40–45).

50. Alexander Graham Bell, "The Tetrahedral Principle

in Kite Structure," *National Geographic Magazine,* June 1903, 225.

51. Alexander Graham Bell, "Aerial Locomotion," *National Geographic Magazine,* January 1907, 11. Bell envisioned his apparatus as an extension of the system of "visible speech" that he invented in order to teach the deaf-mute to speak. But because all of Bell's predecessors who had tried to invent the telephone had failed, Bell's early apparatus was regarded with skepticism and was denigrated as a "musical toy," or at best a "scientific toy." Bell's success stemmed from his focus on the quality of the communicated sound, rather than merely its pitch.

52. Ibid., 11. At the time, Bell was president of the National Geographic Society and published many of his findings in *National Geographic Magazine.* He headed a group of five men—the Aerial Experiment Association—that, funded by his wife, Mabel Hubbard Bell, carried out countless well-recorded attempts to fly at Beinn Bhreagh in Nova Scotia.

53. Ibid., 10. The Wright brothers had flown their biplane successfully by 1903. Bell's probing of the idea of a plane made of tetrahedral cells was due in large part to his concern for the safety and stability of flight, which he felt the kite could increase. These reflections led him to the design of aerodromes (a term he preferred to "aeroplanes") and the development of hydrodromes, which he continued until his death in 1922 (J. H. Parkin, *Bell and Baldwin* [Toronto: University of Toronto Press, 1964], 17–18).

54. Bell, "The Tetrahedral Principle," 225.

55. Ibid., 224. Furthermore, Bell observed that the flatter the wings, the more unstable the arrangement in the air, as, with an upset, one side would lift while the other would depress. The more the wings are raised, the more they approach a perpendicular position and the more stable the arrangement is in the air. The dividing line between the two conditions is at 45 degrees; thus, the tetrahedron's angles, at 60 degrees, form a stable structure.

56. This was because the weight was increased to the power of three, while the surface, which was the kite's lifting vehicle, increased only to the square of the dimension.

57. Bell, "Aerial Locomotion," 12.

58. Ibid., 11.

59. Bell calculated that a structure twice the size, or 40 feet across, could sustain both a man and a motor while flying at low velocity.

60. Parkin, *Bell and Baldwin,* 441.

61. Bell, "The Tetrahedral Principle," 231.

62. The tower, which offered commanding views of Bras d'Or Lake and the surrounding hills of Cape Breton, was opened with an official ceremony on August 31, 1907, when guests, including women in long skirts, climbed more than one hundred steps to reach the observation deck at its pinnacle. It stood for about a decade before it was dismantled. During that time it was said to require hardly any maintenance (Parkin, *Bell and Baldwin,* 33).

63. Wachsmann, *The Turning Point of Building,* 31.

64. For a discussion of triangulated space-frames and their relation to networks of communication, see Mark Wigley, "Network Fever," *Grey Room* 4 (Summer 2001): 82–122.

65. Chardin employed the theme of the "house of cards" four times. A 1743 engraving entitled *House of Cards* was accompanied by verses that emphasized the insubstantiality of human endeavors, which Chardin said were as frail as a house of cards.

66. The best-known series, Le Petit Architecte, was published starting in 1862 by the Imagerie d'Épinal, Paris, and depicted French monuments as well as buildings from around the world. Elevations of buildings could be cut out and folded to form enclosures that were relatively stable. For more on *Le Petit Architecte,* see the exhibition catalogue *Potential Architecture: Construction Toys from the CCA Collection* (Montreal: Canadian Centre for Architecture, 1991), 21, 28.

67. This and the following quotes are taken from the "Instruction Sheet for the House of Cards," designed by Charles and Ray Eames and manufactured by Tigrett Enterprises, Jackson, Tenn., 1952. Like The Toy, House of Cards was produced until 1961, when the company went out of business.

68. The label on the box of Giant House of Cards.

69. In 1968, a second edition—of medium-sized cards, comprising thirty-two cards chosen from the picture and pattern decks and measuring approximately 4½ by 7 inches—was reissued by Otto Maier Verlag under the name Wolken Kuckucks Haus, or the Cloud Cuckoo's House, and appears also in Germany under the name Das bunte Katenhaus. In 1970, Giant House of Cards was reissued as well. Following this publication the cards received wide recognition in the press and numerous

prizes, among them, in 1971, the Bundespreis Gute Form. Seventy-eight reviews in total were written about House of Cards (see Works of Charles and Ray Eames, box 42, folder 2, Manuscript Division, Library of Congress). The extensive exchange between the publishing house and the design team on the minute details of the cards attests to Charles and Ray Eames's intense involvement in House of Cards fifteen years after its original design. The intense, businesslike, yet very friendly correspondence between the two parties over numerous years—and always on the subject of the cards—reflects the way the Eameses conducted business with a very personal touch. The client was actively participating in the creative process, caring equally for the craftsmanship and the final result, and seemed to enjoy the game.

70. For more on Computer House of Cards, see Neuhart, Neuhart, and Eames, *Eames Design,* 353.

71. Erwin Glonegger, of Otto Maier Verlag, to Charles Eames, September 8, 1969, Works of Charles and Ray Eames, box 42, folder 1, Manuscript Division, Library of Congress. These included requests from Fiat and Lufthansa, with which Eames complied, asking, however, that the companies create their own images. Eames refused a request by Telefunken, the German competitor of IBM at the time, to create a House of Cards similar to the Computer House of Cards. It is unknown whether such cards were eventually created by a European company.

72. Eames, Eames, Fuller, Saarinen and Entenza, eds., "Prefabrication," special issue of *Arts and Architecture,* July 1944, 20. The following note appears in the table of contents:

"This issue was prepared with the assistance of Herbert Matter, Charles and Ray Eames, Eero Saarinen, Buckminster Fuller. To all of the above, our grateful acknowledgement. THE EDITOR" (ibid.).

73. Eames, Eames, Fuller, Saarinen and Entenza, eds., "What Is a House?," *Arts and Architecture,* July 1944, 24.

74. Ibid., 25

75. Eames, Eames, Fuller, Saarinen and Entenza, eds., "What Prefabrication Is Not," *Arts and Architecture,* July 1944, 29.

76. Reyner Banham, *Los Angeles: The Architecture of Four Ecologies* (1971; Berkeley: University of California

Press, 2001), 227. "This is par excellence an architecture of elegant omission that takes Mies van der Rohe's dictum about *Weniger ist Mehr* even further than the Master himself has ever done" (ibid., 230).

77. The construction of Levittown was an attempt to mass–produce homes for returning veterans using prefabricated units. Using an assembly-line process, and industrial production methods, Levitt and Sons erected almost two hundred houses per week. The residential community of Levittown, on Long Island, developed between 1946 and 1951 and housed 82,000 people in 17,447 units. The cost of an entire home in 1951 was approximately eight thousand dollars, with only a ninety-dollar deposit required. For the history of Levittown, see Herbert J. Gans, *The Levittowners: Ways of Life and Politics in a New Suburban Community* (London: Penguin, 1967).

78. Tens of millions of government dollars went into developing the Lustron. Its failure was so monumental in terms of money lost and expectations dashed that it overshadowed all concurrent attempt at prefabrication. For more on the Lustron, see Thomas T. Fetters, *The Lustron Home: The History of a Postwar Prefabricated Housing Experiment* (Jefferson, N.C.: McFarland, 2002).

79. For more on the Acorn House, see "Prefabrication: The Acorn House," Building Types Study no. 161, *Architectural Record,* May 1950, 156-62; as well as Stanford Anderson, "The Acorn House: Lessons from the 'Complete Dwelling,'" *Architectural Review* 193 (November 1993): 68-69.

80. It was commissioned by the Kwikset Company, the hardware company responsible for most of the hardware in the Case Study Houses (see Neuhart, Neuhart, and Eames, *Eames Design,* 155; and Kirkham, *Charles and Ray Eames,* 138).

81. Gropius assigned the design of different units using the elements of the Packaged House as a project to his students at Harvard. For a very detailed study of the development of the system, see Herbert, *The Dream of the Factory–Made House.*

82. Fuller's experiments with paperdomes included the Cardboard House (1952); Plydome studies (1956); the Twenty-Nine-Foot-Diameter Plydome (1957); Paperboard Dome Patent (1959); Plydome Patent (1959). When coated with a thin layer of vinyl, the paperboard domes could

become water resistant. Plywood domes would assemble similarly yet would provide further strength and weatherproofing (see R. Buckminster Fuller, "The Cardboard House," *Perspecta*, no. 2 [1953]; 27–35; and R. Buckminster Fuller, *The Artifacts of R. Buckminster Fuller, The Geodesic Revolution Part I*, vol. 3 [New York: Garland, 1985], 237–38, 363–65, 386–88).

83. The experiment took place at the Department of Fine Arts, University of Georgia.

84. A similar pedagogical approach was employed in the two- and three-screen slide shows that Charles Eames created for the first-year course in architecture he gave at the University of California, Berkeley, in 1953 and 1954. "Continuities" and "connections" were expressed by disassembling environments—such as seascape, townscape, and the railroad—into close-up details and graphics, creating a whole through time and multiple parallel views. The Eameses' films also featured a similar breakdown of their subjects into smaller frames and conveyed a multiplicity of viewpoints. The Eames office had to engineer the electronic equipment to accommodate such presentations, as such equipment did not exist at the time.

85. Shannon published his article in two parts in the July and October 1948 issues of the *Bell System Technical Journal;* he later cowrote a book with the mathematician Warren Weaver that popularized the article and made it accessible to the nonspecialist (Shannon and Weaver, *The Mathematical Theory of Communication* [Urbana: University of Illinois Press, 1971], 3).

86. Ibid., 8.

87. Ibid., 9.

88. Ibid., 13.

89. Ibid., 12. "The quantity which uniquely meets the natural requirements that one sets up for 'information' turns out to be exactly that which is known in thermodynamics as *entropy*" (ibid.).

90. Beatriz Colomina, "Enclosed by Images: The Eameses' Multimedia Architecture," *Grey Room* 2 (Winter 2001): 6–28

91. Ibid., 22.

92. At the time, Banham, writing his dissertation, which was to become *Theory and Design in the First Machine Age,* emphasized the importance of futurism in the emergence of modernism, and aimed for a parallel mission for the Independent Group. He actively acknowledged the impact of science, technology, and mechanization on the history of design. As a former R.A.F. pilot, Banham—like Eames—was influenced by the aircraft industry. The historian Anne Massey reveals that "from his experience in the aircraft industry Banham knew that technology was never static and new techniques and materials were perpetually being incorporated into design" (Anne Massey, *The Independent Group: Modernism and Mass Culture in Britain, 1945–59* [Manchester: Manchester University Press, 1995], 51).

93. Ibid., 33.

94. Ibid., 92.

95. The photographs were divided, in the catalogue that accompanied the show, into categories that included Anatomy, Architecture, Art, Calligraphy, Date 1901, Landscape, Movement, Nature, Primitive, Scale of Man, Stress, Stress Structure, Football, Science Fiction, Medicine, Geology, Metal, and Ceramic. The catalogue listed all of the 122 images exhibited. In the catalogue, they were numbered in consecutive order, but in the show they were dispersed throughout the room and could not be easily identified.

96. The photographs, the description continues, "have been ranged in categories suggested by the material which underline a common visual denominator independent of the field from which the image is taken" (press release for *Parallel of Life and Art* [1953], Archives, Institute of Contemporary Art, The Tate, London). I am grateful to Virginia Walsh for providing this material.

97. For other contemporary displays similar in their spatial disposition to *Parallel of Life and Art,* see Virginia Walsh, *Nigel Henderson: Parallel of Life and Art* (London: Thames and Hudson, 2001), 99. These include Herbert Bayer's *Road to Victory* (1942) and *Airways to Peace* (1943) at the Museum of Modern Art, New York, as well as Ernesto Rogers's exhibit at the Triennale in Milan in 1951, which featured large photographic panels, positioned at striking angles to one another between floor and ceiling.

98. "Parallel Inventions" is the name of an article written by Peter Smithson regarding the role of the woman designer and her contribution to modernism (see Peter Smithson, "Parallel Inventions," *International Laboratory of Architecture and Urban Design,* Year Book, 1982–83,

46–51). For an analysis of "Parallel Inventions," see Beatriz Colomina, "Couplings," *OASE* 51 (Spring 2000).

99. Smithson, "Parallel Inventions," 51.

100. Frank O'Hara, "Memorial Day 1950," in *The Collected Poems of Frank O'Hara* (Berkeley: University of California Press, 1995), 17.

101. "Atomic Bomb over Nevada," *Life,* July 16, 1951, 51.

102. John Dewey, *Art as Experience* (1934; repr., New York: Berkeley Publishing Group, 1980), 278.

103. Johan Huizinga, *Homo Ludens: A Study of the Play Element in Culture,* trans. R. R. C. Hull (Boston: Beacon, 1955).

104. Ibid., 8.

105. Ibid.

106. Ibid., 10.

107. Ibid., 8.

108. Ibid., 89. Huizinga remarked that "in all Germanic languages, and in many others besides, play-terms are regularly applied to armed strife as well" (ibid., 40).

109. Ibid., 95.

110. Ibid., 10.

111. Ibid., 41.

112. *Arts and Architecture,* October 1950, 31.

113. Architecture and technology needed to develop simultaneously, Mies explained in the poem:

Our real hope is that they grow together,
that someday the one be the expression of
   the other.
Only then will we have an architecture worthy
of its name: Architecture as a true symbol of our time.
(*Arts and Architecture,* October 1950, 29)

114. Neuhart, Neuhart, and Eames, *Eames Design,* 99. Herman Miller worked in collaboration with Zenith—the airplane manufacturing company—and offered the resin chairs for sale for the first time in 1950—an edition of two thousand, in three different colors.

115. Charles Eames, "Design, Designer and Industry," *Magazine of Art,* December 1951, 321.

116. Ibid.

117. Ibid.

118. Dewey, *Art as Experience,* 281, 282.

CONCLUSION

1. This and all following quotes relating to "Blocks" are from the archives Works of Charles and Ray Eames, box 200, folder 7, Films—Blocks, Manuscript Division, Library of Congress.

2. A list accompanying the storyboard included Crandalls Blocks, Richters Blocks, puzzles, dominoes, alphabet cubes, Lincoln Logs, and other building blocks of different periods, materials, and forms, indicating that the Eameses' toy collection was substantial.

3. Friedrich Froebel, *Friedrich Froebel's Pedagogics of the Kindergarten: Or, His Ideas Concerning the Play and Playthings of the Child* (New York: D. Appleton, 1895), 3.

4. Roland Barthes, *Mythologies* (New York: Noonday, 1972), 54.

5. Ibid. Barthes laments the gradual disappearance of wood in toys, which, unlike metal or plastic, alters with time and gradually changes the relation between the object and the hand; if the toy "dies, it is in dwindling, not in swelling out like those mechanical toys which disappear behind the hernia of a broken spring" (ibid., 54–55).

6. Ibid., 54.

7. Froebel, *Friedrich Froebel's Pedagogics of the Kindergarten,* 106.

8. "The Philosophy of Toys," in Heinrich Von Kleist, Charles Baudelaire, and Rainer Maria Rilke, *Essays on Dolls* (London: Syrens, 1994), 24.

9. The first published English translation of Freud's *Jenseits des Lustprinzips* (1920) was *Beyond the Pleasure Principle* (New York: Boni and Liveright), 1922.

10. Sigmund Freud, *Civilization and Its Discontent,* in *The Complete Psychological Works of Sigmund Freud,* vol. 21, trans. J. Strachey (London: Hogarth Press, Institute of Psycho-analysis 1961), 119.

11. Freud's notion of play—recognizing aggressiveness and destruction—completed the arguments by Herbert Spencer and Karl Groos, who had underlined the biological necessity of play as a practice of adult acts necessary for growth.

12. Walter Benjamin, "Toys and Play," trans. Rodney Livingstone, in *Selected Writings,* vol. 2, *1927–1934,* ed. Michael W. Jennings, Howard Eiland, and Gary Smith (Cambridge: Belknap Press of Harvard University Press, 1999), 120, my emphasis. Benjamin claimed in 1928 that in

order to arrive at a new theory of play, which had not been done since Karl Groos wrote *The Play of Animals* in 1896 and *The Play of Man* in 1898, play gestures needed to be studied. Roger Caillois eventually did this in his *Les jeux et les hommes* of 1958.

13. Ibid.

14. Ibid.

15. Ibid.

16. Ibid.

17. See the entry "Habit" in *The Oxford English Dictionary.*

18. Montaigne, vol. 22, 1632, in *The Oxford English Dictionary* as citation for the entry "Habit."

19. Georges Teyssot, "Boredom and Bedroom: The Suppression of the Habitual," *Assemblage* 30 (August 1996): 53.

20. Walter Benjamin, "The Work of Art in the Age of Mechanical Reproduction," in *Illuminations, by Benjamin,* ed. Hannah Arendt (New York: Schocken, 1985), 217–52.

21. See Paolo Virno, "Childhood and Critical Thought," *Grey Room* 21 (Fall 2005): 7–12.

22. Roger Caillois, *Man, Play and Games* (Urbana and Chicago: University of Illinois Press, 2001), 32.

23. Ibid.

24. Ibid.

25. In all cases but the Eameses', the toys considered in this book were presented as playthings for children. The Eameses' toys were presented for both adults and children. The instruction pamphlet of The Toy addressed adults, who could make "large constructions, wall decorations or use it as a hobby." House of Cards was presented in design magazines with children manipulating it, but IBM adopted it early on for advertising.

26. Walter Benjamin, "Construction Site," excerpt of "One-Way Street," in *Reflections: Essays, Aphorisms, Autobiographical Writings,* trans. E. Jephcott, ed. P. Demetz (New York: Schocken, 1986), 69.

27. Giorgio Agamben, "In Playland: Reflections on History and Play," in *Infancy and History: Essays on the Destruction of Experience* (London: Verso, 1993), 70.

28. Claude Lévi-Strauss, *The Savage Mind* (1962; Chicago: University of Chicago Press, 1966), 12.

29. Ibid., 16–17.

30. Ibid., 17. Claude Lévi-Strauss adds: "The set of the 'bricoleur's' means cannot therefore be defined in terms of a project. . . . It is to be defined only by its potential use."

31. Ibid., 19.

32. Ibid., 21–22.

33. Agamben, "In Playland: Reflections on History and Play," 71.

34. In "In Playland: Reflections on History and Play," Agamben exposes the intricate relation between time, the calendar, and toys (67–68, 75).

35. Ernst Gombrich, "Meditations on a Hobby Horse, or the Roots of Artistic Form" was first published in *Aspects of Form: A Symposium on Form in Nature and Art,* ed. Lancelot Whyte (London: Lund Humphries, 1951), 209–28, and later in Ernst Gombrich, *Meditations on a Hobby Horse, and Other Essays on the Theory of Art* (London: Phaidon, 1963), 1–11.

36. Tristan Tzara, qtd. in Lawrence Alloway, "Dada 1956," in *Architectural Design,* November 1956, 374.

37. In 1951, members of the Independent Group in London curated the exhibition *Growth and Form,* which attempted to provide a renewed understanding of nature that was of interest at that time for the development of abstract form. Emphasizing organic and morphological processes and negating previous teleological explanations of the environment provided a basis for their criticism of the formal precepts of modernism. Following the exhibition, Ernst Gombrich reinforced that criticism in the symposium "Aspects of Form," in which he presented his essay "Meditations on a Hobby Horse, or the Roots of Artistic Form."

38. Gombrich, "Meditations on a Hobby Horse," 4.

39. Ibid., 8.

40. Ibid., 9.

41. Ibid., 11.

42. György Kepes, *The New Landscape in Art and Science* (Chicago: P. Thobald, 1956), 204–5.

43. Immanuel Kant, *Anthropology from a Pragmatic Point of View* (1798), trans. Mary J. Gregor (The Hague, Netherlands: Martinus Nijhoff, 1974), 73.

44. Ibid., 75.

45. Ibid. The reference here is to Laurence Sterne's *Tristram Shandy* (1760), vol. 1, chap. 7.

46. Erik Erikson, "Playing and Actuality," in Jean

Piaget and Maria W. Piers, *Play and Development: A Symposium* (New York: Norton, 1972), 691. Erikson's writings about toy constructions appeared in *Childhood and Society* (New York: Norton, 1950), which he later expanded and elaborated in his *Toys and Reasons* (New York: Norton, 1977).

47. Ibid. It could also be described as "free movement within prescribed limits," a spatial definition for the realm of play.

48. Adolf Behne, *The Modern Functional Building* (1923; repr., Santa Monica, Calif.: Getty Research Institute for the History of Art and the Humanities, 1996), 87.

49. Ibid.

50. "Again and always, I say that *we must hold ourselves in readiness,* throughout life and at every moment, to seize hold of the miracle inherent in things" (Le Corbusier, *Aircraft: The New Vision* (1935; repr., Paris: Fondation Le Corbusier, 1988), 8, emphasis in original.

51. Agamben, "In Playland: Reflections on History and Play," 71.

Illustration Credits

Akademie der Künste, Berlin, Konrad Wachsmann Archiv: fig. 103 (KWA-01-126 F 15), fig. 121 (KWA-01-570 BI.1)

Andrew Jugle Archives: fig. 63, fig. 66–69

Archives Otto-Lilienthal-Museum, lilienthal-museum.de: fig. 31 (F0761), fig. 38 (F0957), fig. 39 (Ka59/02), fig. 42 (F0771), fig. 43 (F0261), fig. 44 (F0028), fig. 45 (gl10), fig. 46 (takeoff, F0089; in flight, F0117), fig. 47 (F0787), fig. 48 (Lilienthal with ornithopter, F2097), fig. 50 (L3935)

T. Benjamin Atkins, *Out of the Cradle into the World or Self-Education through Play* (Columbus, Ohio: Sterling, 1895): fig. 84

Bestelmeiers Magazin (Nuremberg: G. H. Bestelmeier, 1803): fig. 25

John Blazejewski, Princeton University, photographer: fig. 91, fig. 126

Collection Centre Canadien d'Architecture/Canadian Centre for Architecture, Montréal; Acquired with the support of Bell Québec: illustration facing table of contents (TS2301.T7.PST58 1952), fig. 1 (TS2301.T7.W6 W54 1920), fig. 2 (TS2301.T7.G5 Z9 1919), fig. 3 (TS2301.T7.W6 J631 1930), fig. 6, fig. 10 (TS2301.T7.W6 M541 1870), fig. 26 (TS2301.T7.W6 Z98 1850), fig. 27 (set no. 12), fig. 32, fig. 61 (TS2301.T7.M4 M972 1914), fig. 62 (TS2301.T7.M4 M972 1914), fig. 64 (TS2301.T7.M4 M971 1915), fig. 65 (TS2301.T7.M4 M972 1914), fig. 86 (TS2301.T7.M4 M972 1914), fig. 97 (TS2301.T7.M4 M972 1914), fig. 111 (TS2301.T7.P3 J85 1891), fig. 112 (TS2301.T7.P3 I43 1900), fig. 114/frontispiece (TS2301.T7.P3 O43 1961)

Cornell University Libraries, Division of Rare and Manuscript Collections: fig. 35

Baron Georges Cuvier, *Leçons d'anatomie comparée,* vol. 5 (Paris: Crochard, 1805): fig. 33

Denver Art Museum, Herbert Bayer Collection and Archive: fig. 128

Deutsches Museum, © 2014 (photos): fig. 27 (sets no. 8 and 34), fig. 48 (ornithopter)

Dundee Library and Information Services, Scotland: figs. 73–74

Eames Office, LLC (eamesoffice.com), © 2014: fig. 89 (AW_CEn007), fig. 92 (TY_TYt193), fig. 93 (CR_RYs177), fig. 94 (EH_HMp011), fig. 101 (PE_Hop017), fig. 113, fig. 115 (TY_HDs012), fig. 120 (OA_KWp(Db)002), fig. 124 (LR_HCp05), fig. 127 (CH_PGp175, CH_PGp185)

Estate of R. Buckminster Fuller: figs. 98–100, figs. 122–23

R. Buckminster Fuller, *The Artifacts of R. Buckminster Fuller: A Comprehensive Collection of His Designs and Drawings,* vol. 3, *The Geodesic Revolution Part 1, 1947–1959,* ed. James Ward (New York: Garland, 1984): fig. 123

R. Buckminster Fuller, *Tetrascroll: Goldilocks and the Three Bears, A Cosmic Fairy Tale* (1975; repr., New York: St. Martin's, 1982): fig. 100

Jim Gamble: fig. 77

Jan Daniel Georgens, Jeanne Marie von Gayette Georgens, and Gustav Lilienthal, *Die Schulen der weiblichen Handarbeit* (Leipzig: Richter, 1877): fig. 36

Getty Images: figs. 80 and 83 (Hulton Archive), fig. 90 (Allan Grant, Time & Life Pictures), fig. 118 (Arnold Newman, Arnold Newman Collection)

Gilbert H. Grosvenor, "The Tetrahedral Kites of Dr. Alexander Graham Bell," *Popular Science Monthly* 64 (November 1903): fig. 105

George Hardy: figs. 28–30

Harvard Art Museums/Busch-Reisinger Museum; gift of Lufthansa German Airlines, 1989.69.8; photo © Imaging Department, President and Fellows of Harvard College: fig. 51

Harvard University, Houghton Library: fig. 21

René Just Haüy, *Traité de minéralogie,* vol. 5 (Paris: Bachelier, 1801): fig. 17

Nigel Henderson Estate, Tate, London, © 2014: fig. 125

Landesarchiv Berlin Rep. 200 Nachlass G. Lilienthal: figs. 36–37, fig. 41

Library of Congress: fig. 20 (LC-USZ62-41995, LOT 2979), fig. 129 (Charles Eames and Ray Eames Papers, box 200, folder 9, Manuscripts Division)

Otto Lilienthal, *Der Vogelflug als Grundlage der Fliegekunst* (Berlin: R. Gaerttners, 1889): fig. 45

Livre d'or de la conquête de l'air (Paris: Lafitte, 1909): fig. 49

Bert Love and Jim Gamble, *The Meccano System and the Special Purpose Meccano Sets, 1901–1979* (London: New Cavendish, 1986), with permission of Jim Gamble: fig. 57

Pat McElnea/Cooper Union Archives (photos): fig. 5, figs. 13–16 (gifts)

MIT Libraries: fig. 49

Moeller Fine Art, New York—Berlin/Artists Rights Society (ARS), New York/VG Bild-Kunst, Bonn, © 2014: fig. 58

National Geographic Creative: fig. 104 (Gilbert H. Grosvenor), fig. 108 (David Mccurdy), fig. 109 (Bell Collection)

National Library of Scotland: fig. 75

New Haven Museum: fig. 70

The New York Public Library, Astor, Lenox and Tilden Foundations: fig. 55 (Photography Collection, Miriam and Ira D. Wallach Division of Art, Prints and Photographs), fig. 87 (Science, Industry and Business Library)

Johann Heinrich Pestalozzi, *ABC der Anschauung* (Tübingen: J. G. Cotta'schen Buchhandlung, 1803): fig. 21

F. C. Phillips, *An Introduction to Crystallography* (New York: John Wiley and Sons, 1971): fig. 19, figs. 23–24

Photo by author: fig. 56

Augustus Pitt-Rivers, *Evolutionary Relationships of Australian Weapons* (1870), in A. Lane-Fox Pitt-Rivers, *The Evolution of Culture* (Oxford: Clarendon Press, 1906): fig. 34

Princeton University, Marquand Library of Art and Archaeology: fig. 88 (published with permission of Juliet K. Stone), fig. 96 (John Blazejewski, Photographer), fig. 117 (© David Travers; John Blazejewski, Photographer)

Princeton University Library, Rare Books Division, Department of Rare Books and Special Collections: fig. 8, fig. 11, fig. 33

The Quebec Bridge over the St. Lawrence River near the City of Quebec, Report of the Government Board of Engineers, vol. 1 (Canada Department of Railways and Canals, 1919): fig. 78

Johannes Ronge, *A Practical Guide to the English Kinder-garten* (1855; London: A. N. Myers, 1873): fig. 8, fig. 11

SCALA/Art Resource, NY: figs. 4 and 7 (© The Museum of Modern Art), fig. 110

Smithsonian Institution: fig. 71 (Archives Center, National Museum of American History), fig. 79 (Archives Center, National Museum of American History, Quebec Bridge Photograph Collection), fig. 94 (National Air and Space Museum, NAM A-38937-A), fig. 106 (Photo by Carl H. Claudy, Sr., National Air and

Space Museum, NASMSI 95-8650), fig. 107 (National Air and Space Museum, NASM 89-12607)

Steiger's Kindergarten Catalogue (New York: E. Steiger & Co., 1900): fig. 9

The Strong®, Rochester, New York: fig. 84

Swedenborg Foundation: fig. 18

Paul Tambuyser, Virtual Museum of the History of Mineralogy, http://www.mineralogy.eu: fig. 22

University of California, Berkeley, Library: fig. 76, figs. 81–82

University of Oxford, Bodleian Libraries, 247115e. 20: fig. 34

Gustav Voigt, *Kinematische Modells nach Prof Reuleaux* (A catalogue of the kinematic models of Prof. Reuleaux) (Berlin: G. Voigt 1907): fig. 35

Konrad Wachsmann, *The Turning Point of Building: Structure and Design* (New York: Reinhold, 1961): fig. 102

Edward Wiebé, *Paradise of Childhood: A Practical Guide to Kindergartners* (1869; Springfield, Mass.: Milton Bradley Company, 1923): figs. 12–16

Yale University Library, Manuscripts and Archives, A. C. Gilbert Papers, MS 1618: fig. 72

Index

Page numbers in italics refer to illustrations.

ABC der Anschauung (Büss), 46–47, *47,* 49

Acorn House (Koch), 177–78, *179*

aeronautics, 4, 15, 81. *See also* aviation

aesthetics, 10, 65, 67, 220n28

Agamben, Giorgio, 203, 205, 212, 239n34

agôn (competitive play), 11–12, 214n22

Albers, Josef, 3

Alpine Architecture (Taut), 5

American System of Manufactures, 101, 106, 226n34

anatomy, 67, *67*

Anchor Stone Building Blocks (Anker-Steinbaukasten), 3, 8, 77, 195, 197, 211; adult enjoyment of, 94; advertising for, *52,* 58, *59;* bird's-eye view of built environment and, 92, 95; collectors of, 203, 214n22; exercises in use of, 55–56; Friends of Anchor Club, 219n11; Gilbert and manufacturing rights in United States, 229n67; instruction manuals for, 54–55, *57,* 60, 62, 218n2; invention of, 53; legal dispute involving, 60, 61; Lilienthal brothers' flight experiments and, 84, 86, 91; materials of, 54–55, *55,* 218n3; Patent-Baukasten as original name for, 57, 61, 218n6; play affirming social conventions and, 89–90; production of, 56, 59–60, 62, 218n4; stacking assembly without connections/joints, 102; supplemental sets of blocks, 57–58, *58;* tectonics and, 63; as tools for progress, 70; as *Werkformen* devoid of ornament, 66; worldview associated with, 14

Animal Mechanism: A Treatise of Terrestrial and Aerial Locomotion (Marey), 81

"Another Toy to Tinker With" (*Interiors* magazine article, 1951), 145

Anschauung (sensory impression), 47–48

Anthropology from a Pragmatic Point of View (Kant), 208–9

Architectural Forum (journal), 154, *154,* 155

"Architecture and Technology" (Mies van der Rohe), 190, 238n113

Architektonisches Lehrbuch (Schinkel), 62, 64, 65, 66

Art as Experience (Dewey), 189, 192

arts and crafts, 70, 221n31

Aspen Design Conference (1951), 191–92

Atkins, T. Benjamin, 136

atomic bomb, 188–89, *189*

automobile culture, 147

aviation, 152, 154, 155, 224n66, 225n80, 234n25; Lilienthal brothers as pioneers of, 53; Marey's inventions and, 81

Babbage, Charles, 221n30

Bachelard, Gaston, 17

Baker, Sir Benjamin, 126

Banham, Reyner, 177, 186, 237n92

Barthes, Roland, 13, 92, 198, 225n80, 238n5

Baudelaire, Charles, 13, 199

Bayer, Herbert, 191, 192, 193

Bayko, 15

Behne, Adolf, 210, 211

Beinn Bhreagh (Nova Scotia) tetrahedral cell tower (Bell), 167, *168*, 235n62

Bell, Alexander Graham, 163–68, *163, 166, 168,* 235n49

Benjamin, Walter, 7, 13, 203, 214n12, 239n12; on habit (repetition) as essence of play, 200–201, 202; Märkisches Museum toy exhibit reviewed by, 16, 101, 215n33; on toys and miniature objects, 92, 94

Berlin, city of, 40, 53, 61, 221n35; Berliner Bauakademie, 70, 221n31; Berlin Gewerbe Akademie, 69, 220n29; Freie Scholle ("free piece of land"), 77, *78,* 86, 222nn47–48, 223n49; Kunstgewerbe Museum, 70, 221n31; Lichterfelde townhouses ("castles"), 73–76, *74,* 222n36, 222n43, 223n53; Lilienthal brothers in, 56, 59–60, 67, 73, 221n34; Märkisches Museum, 16; Mineralogical Museum, 45; Tempelhof Airport, 84, *86;* Terrast-Decke, 77–78, *80,* 223nn50–53

Bestelmeiers Magazin (mail-order toy catalogue), 53, *54,* 218n1

Beyond the Pleasure Principle (Freud), 200

Bill Deezy, 120

Birdflight as the Basis for Aviation (O. Lilienthal), 81, 83, 90, 224n63

birds, 88, 165, 216n49, 223n57, 225n78; aeronautical principles and movements of, 82, 224n66; anatomy of, 69, 81, 224n63; bird's-eye view, 91, 92, 95, 225nn79–80; flying machines modeled on, 83, 84, *85*

Blocks (proposed film, Eames and Eames), *194,* 195–96, 198, 202

Born, Max, 60–61, 219nn8–9

Bötticher, Karl, 62, 64, 65–66

Bouch, Sir Thomas, 126, 230n89, 230n96

boys, 99, 100, 101, 106, *113,* 228n47; Boy Scout movement, 231n113; construction-toy ads addressed solely to, *96, 97,* 111–12, *112,* 159; constructive/destructive duality of, 116–17, *118,* 120, 228n61; engineering/technology as masculine pursuits and, 112–15; Marden's Success Movement and, 135; sports and, 142

Boy Who Made $1,000,000 with a Toy, The (Hornby), 101

Bradley, Milton, 19–20, 24–25

Braque, Georges, 3

Bravais, Auguste, 51

Bravais lattices, 51, *51*

bricolage/bricoleurs, 204–6, 212, 239n30

bridges, 101, 102, 197; cantilever, 127–28, 230n89; collapse of real bridges, 124, 126, *126,* 128–31, *129,* 230n89; Erector Set models of, 106, *107,* 109, 227n38; fake collapse using Erector girders, *123;* trusses as, 120–21, *121, 123;* wooden bridges replaced by steel, 124. *See also specific bridges*

Briefe aus Philadelphia (Reuleaux), 220n29

Brosterman, Norman, 3

building blocks, 1–2, *54,* 62, 207–8, 212, 213n1; absence of preestablished meaning in, 198–99; bricolage and, 204; changes in built world and, 8; construction system for, 77; Froebel's Gifts as first systematic pedagogical use of, 38; of Fuller, 158; historical transformation of, 7; mass production of, 77; past experiences and play with, 189; proposed Eames film about, *194,* 195–96; stacking as essence of play with, 53; technological progress and, 76; tectonics and, 62

"Building Toy" (*Life* magazine article), 148, *148, 149,* 188

Büss, Christoff, 46–47

Caillois, Roger, 10, 11–12, 202–3, 214n22, 239n12

Canadian Centre for Architecture (CCA), 14–15

capitalism, 77, 103, 222n47

Cardboard House (Fuller), 181, *182,* 237n82

Card Houses: Upon a Novel Plan, Alphabetical and Zoological, Suitable for Children, *170, 170*

cards, decks of, 169–70, *169, 170*

Case Study House #8 (Eames and Eames), 154, *154,* 176, 233n18, 237n80. *See also* Eames House

Cather, Willa, 113

cave art, prehistoric, 206, 207

Centennial Exhibition (Philadelphia, 1876), 2, 20, 71–72, 220n29

"Chairs by Charles Eames" (*Arts and Architecture* layout), 190–91, *191*

Chardin, Jean-Baptiste, 169–70, 235n65

children, 3, 89; adults learning from experience of, 196; changing attitudes toward childhood, 1; freedom of play and, 10; television programming for, 16; as vital force for future of society, 9; worldview of, 206–12. *See also* boys; girls

chronophotography, 81

"Cité Industrielle" (Garnier), 225n79

Colin, Louise, 2

collectors, 12, 13, 214n22

Colomina, Beatriz, 155, 185

Comenius, Johann, 46

Communications Primer, A (Eames Office film, 1953), 184

communication theory, 183–85

comparative method, 67–69

"Comparative Theory of Buildings" (Semper), 66

Computer Glossary, or Coming to Terms with the Data Processing Machine, A (film, Eames and Eames, 1968), 174

consumerism, 62, 186

Continuing Education Institute for Women and Girls, 72–73, 221n34

Cooper, Theodore, 130, 230n96

Crandall Blocks, 218n1, 238n2

Critique of Pure Reason (Kant), 48

Crystal Chain correspondence, 5, 210, 214n10

crystallization, 39, 43

crystallography, 15, 20, 38, 39–40; Haüy's structural theory, 40–41; Law of Decrement, 41–42, 217n56; polar theory and, 42–43

Cuvier, Baron Georges, 67, 69, 220n26

Dada movement, 206–7

Dandanah, The Fairy Palace (Taut), 4–5, *6*, 214n11

Darwin, Charles, 88, 224n70

decoration, 63, 64, 152, *153*. *See also* ornament

De indagando formarum crystallinarum charactere geometrico principali (Weiss), 44

Designing a New Industry (Fuller), 157, 234n29

destruction, 132, 188, 189, 197; bricolage and, 204; constructive/destructive duality of boys, 116–17, *118*, 120, 228n61; destructive aspect of nature, 162; destructive aspect of play, 12, 142, 143, 198–202, 239n11

Dewey, John, 139, 140–41, 142, 189, 192

die-casting techniques, 102

dirigibles. *See* Zeppelins and dirigible balloons

Dissertation on the determination of the geometrical character of the principal crystalline forms (Weiss), 44

dolls and dollhouses, 6, 8

DuPont, Coleman, 228n54

Durand, Jean-Nicolas-Louis, 67, 217–18n87

Dymaxion House (Fuller), 156

"Dynamic Conception of Crystallization, The" (Weiss), 43

Eames, Charles, 2–3, 4, 8, 14, 145, 192; Aspen Design Conference lecture, 191–92; communication theory and, 184; death of, 195; experimentation with The Toy, 168–69; Fuller and, 157–58; on play as creation and destruction, 198, 199; prefabrication and, 174, 178–79; on purpose of The Toy, 150–51; UC Berkeley course taught by, 237n84

Eames, Ray Kaiser, 4, 8, 14, 145, *151*, 192; dancing in mask with Wachsmann, 160, *161,* 181; experimentation with The Toy, 168–69; Fuller and, 157–58; prefabrication and, 174, 178–79; work on House of Cards, 172, *173*

Eames House, 147, 155, 156, 234n23. *See also* Case Study House #8

Eames Office, 147, 179, 183

Eastman, George, 228n54

economics, 10, 62

Eden orchard cooperative, 77

Edgeworth, Maria and Richard L., 1

Edison, Thomas, 228n54

education, 1, 3, 10, 14, 20, 38. *See also* pedagogy

Education of Man, The (Froebel), 50

Efficiency Magazine, 135, 231n116

Eiffel Tower, 92, 101, 163, 224–25n78, 225n80; duplicated superimposition on Forth Bridge diagram, 131, *132;* encircled by flying machines, *91, 133;* toy replica of, 103

Émile, or On Education (Rousseau), 10, 217n72

Encyclopädisches Wörterbuch der kritischen Philosophie, 48

engineering, 67, 70, 81; machine shops and, 115–16, 228n58; manual skills of scientists and engineers, 134–35; as masculine enterprise, 112–15, 228n45, 230n97; Meccano advertisements and, 97, *98;* technological progress and, 101; women in engineering profession, 112–13, 227n43

Enlightenment, 8, 10

Entenza, John, 176, 233n18

entropy, 185, 237n89

Erector Set, 4, 8, 62, 92, 111–12, 232n3; advertising for, *96,* 97, 105–6, 111, 116–17, *118–19,* 120, 228n62, 229n63; box cover, 106, *107;* boys' constructive/destructive duality and, 116–17, *118,* 120; boys inspired to become engineers by, 111–12; bridge collapse simulated for Hollywood film using, *123;* as childhood toy of future scientists/engineers, 211–12; collectors of, 99, 203, 214n22, 225n18; difficulties and failures in play, 124; domestic objects modeled with, 109, 227n39; engineering as masculine profession and, 113–15; Erector Toy Builder, 226n23; experimentation with new technology and, 197;

Erector Set (*continued*)
  flying-machine models built with, 106, *108,* 227n38;
    girders of, 99, *100,* 104–5, *105,* 130, 226n26; instruction
    manuals for, 106, 109, *110,* 111, *111,* 122, *141, 155,* 227n38;
    Master Engineer Diploma, *112,* 114, 228nn46–47; Mec-
    cano interchangeable with, 229n67; motor used with,
    226n29, 227n38, 232n127; patent for, 104–5, *104;* ped-
    agogical aims of, 114–15; popularity of, 102, 225n18,
    227n38; prices of sets, 226n29; "real" construction sim-
    ulated by, 120; as "self-help" toy, 132, 137, 143; techno-
    logical breakdown and, 200; as transition from play to
    work, 141; versatility and part interchangeability of,
    106, 122; as "work toy," 139
Erector Tips (newsletter), 114, 116
Erikson, Erik, 209, 240n46
Ésthetique du mouvement, L' (Sourian), 90
Everyday Art Quarterly, 145
Evolutionary Relationships of Australian Weapons
    (Pitt-Rivers), *68*

Fabrik (Hoffmann), 4, 5, *5,* 214n11
factory system, 137
Feininger, Lyonel, 103, 226n19
Firth of Forth Bridge, 101, 124, 126–28, 163; demonstra-
    tions of stability of, 131–32, *132, 133;* Meccano model of,
    126, *127*
Firth of Tay Bridge, 124, *125,* 126, *126,* 130, 230n89
Flexikite, 233n14
flight and flying machines, 91–92, 106, 227n38. *See also*
    aeronautics; aviation
Forbes, B. C., 115, 116, 228n59
Ford, Henry, 115, 226n29
form, 49, 64, 219n15; child as maker-artist-conjurer of,
    208; decorative, 65; feeling and, 2; "form impulse," 38;
    tetrahedrons and, 169
Fox Blox, 147–48
Frampton, Kenneth, 219nn13–14, 235n49
Freie Scholle ("free piece of land"), 77, *78,* 86, 222nn47–
    48, 223n49
"Freilandbewegung" (Freeland movement), 76–77,
    222n46
Freiland: Ein sociales Zukunftsbild (Hertzka), 76–77
Freud, Sigmund, 200
Froebel, Friedrich, 2, 10, 71, 88, 196; educational principles
    of, 21, 26, 208, 215n4; on Gift nos. 1–4, 26, 27–30, 31, 33,
34; "Law of Opposites" in pedagogy of, 27, 28–29; Lil-
    ienthal brothers and, 56; Pestalozzi's method adopted
    by, 45, 49–50; philosophy of play and education, 14,
    26; on play as creation and destruction, 199; on power
    and independence of children, 38–39; progressive edu-
    cational system of, 20; teachers trained by, 19; on unity
    and interconnection of phenomena, 216n49; "Unity
    of Life" in pedagogy of, 27, 40, 45; Weiss as influence
    on, 45; women kindergarten teachers trained by, 19, 20,
    215n2. *See also* Gifts; Occupations
"From Weakness into Strength" (advertisement), 191, *193*
Frost King (tetrahedral kite), 167, *167*
Fuller, R. Buckminster, 3, 156–60, *157,* 168, 179, 191–92,
    234n38; paperdomes and, 181–82, *182, 183,* 237n82;
    prefabrication and, 174; tetrahedrons in work of, *157,*
    158–59, 234n38, 234nn34–35; Wichita House, *157,* 181,
    234n27
furniture, 145, *146,* 168; "Chairs by Charles Eames" (*Arts
    and Architecture* layout), 190–91, *191;* Erector Set models
    of, 109, *111*
Fürstliche Palast, Der (The prince's palace), 53, *54*

Garden City Letchworth, 86
garden suburbs, 86
Gartenhäuschen, Das (The little garden house), 53
gender differences, 12, 15, 20, 112–15, 228n45, 230n97. *See
    also* boys; girls
Genossenschaftswesen (cooperative systems), 77
geodesic dome, of Fuller, 159, 181
geometry, 50, 158, 187; of crystals, 41; of Kindergarten
    Gifts, 21, 22, 26, 38
Georgens, Jan Daniel, 71, *72*
Georgens, Jeanne Marie von Gayette, 71, *72*
Gerber, Heinrich, 230n89
Germany, 15, 38, 57; Arts and Crafts movement, 221n31;
    defeat in World War I, 9; *Naturphilosophie* move-
    ment in, 40; as toy-making capital before World War I,
    215n32. *See also* Prussia
Gibson Girl rescue kit, 152, *152*
Giedion, Sigfried, 224n78, 225n79
Gifts, of Froebel, 4, 15, 71, 195–96, 200; in childhoods of
    modernist pioneers, 2, 3; crystallographic studies and,
    39–40; as forebears of modernism, 211; "Forms of Life,
    Beauty, and Knowledge," *32,* 33–35, *35–37,* 37, 45, 197;
    Froebel's educational principles and, 26; Froebel's writ-

ings on, 25, 216n11; Gift no. 1, 21, *22*, 26, *27*; Gift no. 2,
21, *23*, 26–31, *28–31*; Gift no. 3, 21, *23*, 31–33, *32*; Gift no.
4, 22, *23*, 33–34, *35*; Gift no. 5, 22, *23*, 34–37, *36*; Gift no.
6, 22, *23*, 37–38, *37*; Gift no. 7, 22, *23*; Gift no. 8, 22; Gift
no. 9, 22; Gift no. 10, 22; grid drawing as pedagogical
method, 50–51; invention of, 8; pedagogy and, 10; "play
impulse" and, 38; ten types of, 21–22, *22–23*, 24; whole-
part relationships of, 21

Gilbert, Alfred C., 4, 14, 130, 225n6; American toy industry promoted by, 120, 229n67; autobiography of, 97,
99–100; boys addressed exclusively by, 112, 114; on boys'
constructive/destructive duality, 228n61; on competitors of Erector Set, 226n36; "self-help" literature and,
135, 137; toys manufactured for girls, 114, *119*, 229n63;
views on education, 114–15, 116

Gilbert Institute of Erector Engineering, *112*, 114

Girard, Alexander, 172

girls: Continuing Education Institute for Women and
Girls, 72–73, 221n34; Gilbert's toys manufactured for,
114, *119*, 229n63; The Toy and, 148, 150

Gombrich, Ernst, 206–8, 240n37

Groos, Karl, 88, 89, 94–95, 139–40, 224n73, 239n12

Gropius, Walter, 160, 214n10, 234n41, 237n81

Growth and Form exhibition (London, 1951), 239n37

Hachette, Jean Nicolas Pierre, 221n30

handicrafts, 8, 70–73, 221nn31–34

Hargrave, Lawrence, 164, 233n21

Hargrave box kite, 154, *164*

Haüy, Abbé René Just, 40–44, 217n56

Henderson, Nigel, 186, 187

Hertzka, Theodor, 76–77, 222n46

Hire, Philippe de la, 217n56

history, as object of play, 17, 205, 212

hobbies and hobbyists, 13, 203

hobbyhorses, 206–7, 208, 209

Hoffmann, Josef, 4

Homo Ludens (Huizinga), 10–11, 189–90

Hornby, Frank, 4, 99, 226n37; on destructive side of
boys, 116; first inventions of, 101, 225n11; influenced by
Smiles's *Self-Help,* 132, 134, 135, 231n112; inspiration for
Meccano, 100–101, *101*

House of Cards (Eames and Eames), 4, 169, *173*, 197,
236n69; change in process of design and, 192; communication theory and, 183–84; Computer House of Cards,

174, 233n8, 236n71; Eames Office design process and,
146, 147; Giant House of Cards, 172, 174, 232n5, 233n8,
236n69; instruction sheet for, *172*, 232n5; manufactur-
ers of, 233n9; *Parallel of Life and Art* exhibition and,
186–88; Pattern Deck and Picture Deck, 171–72, *172*;
player's freedom of choice and, 185; prefabrication and,
174, 176, 177; prices of sets, 232n4; as toy for children
and adults, 239n25

House of Cards, The (Chardin artworks), 169–70, *169*,
235n65

Huizinga, Johan, 10–11, 189–90, 238n108

Huygens, Christiaan, 217n56, 217n69

Ideas for a Philosophy of Nature (Schelling), 43

imagination, play and, 89–90, 141

imitation, 62, 89, 198, 199

Independent Group, 186, 187, 237n92, 239n37

industrialization, 4, 8, 9, 64, 141; housing and, 158, 176,
177; Industrial Revolution, 70; repetitive processes and,
202

"In Playland: Reflections on History and Play" (Agamben), 205

Institute for the Fostering of the Creative Activity, of
Froebel, 21

Institution for Self-Education, of Froebel, 21

Interiors magazine, *144*, 145, 146

Introduction to Crystallography, An (Phillips), *51*

Inventing Kindergarten (Brosterman), 3

Ives's Strukturiron, 120

Kahn, Louis, 169

Kandinsky, Wassily, 3

Kant, Immanuel, 42, 43, 48, 88, 208–9

Kepes, Gyorgy, *144*, 145, 208

Kepes, Juliet, *144*, 145

Kindergarten Gifts. *See* Gifts, of Froebel

kindergarten system: Centennial Exhibition (Philadelphia, 1876) and, 71; famous graduates of, 2–3; Gift no. 2
as basis of, 27; Institute for the Fostering of the Creative
Activity, 21; Institution for Self-Education, 21; opening of first kindergarten, 8, 19; proliferation in United
States, 19–20, 138; women as teachers of, 19, 20, 215n2

Kindergarten Verbot (Prussian decree, 1851), 19, 20, 71

kinematics, 69, *69*, 83

Kinsey's Ornamental Lock Block and Toy, 218n1

Kipling, Rudyard, 113

kites, 151–56, *152–55;* Bell's experiments with, 164–67, *166, 167,* 235n53, 235nn55–56; Hargrave box kite, 154, *164*

Kites (short film by Eames and Eames, 1978), 153

Klee, Paul, 3

Kleine Holzkenner, Der (The little wood expert), 53

Kroto, Sir Harry, 112

Kunstformen (art-forms), 65

Kunstgewerbe Museum (Berlin), 70, 221n31

Kwikset Company, 179, 237n80

Kwikset House (Eames and Eames), 178–79, *180*

"Law of Opposites" in Froebel's pedagogy, 27, 28–29

Leçons d'anatomie comparée (Cuvier), 67

Le Corbusier (Charles-Edouard Jeanneret), 2, 88, 211, 221n31, 240n50

Lee, Joseph, 138

Lego, 15–16

Leonardo da Vinci, 84

Le Ricolais, Robert, 162–63

Lévi-Strauss, Claude, 204–5, 239n30

Levittown houses, 177, 236n77

"Lichterfelde, castles of" (G. Lilienthal), 73–76, *74,* 222n36, 222n43, 223n53

"Life in a Chinese Kite" (*Architectural Forum* article, 1950), 154, *154, 155*

Lilienthal, Anna, 73, 79

Lilienthal, Gustav, 3, 53, 59–62, 221n35; in Brazil, 79, 84; flight experiments of, 81–84, *82, 83, 86, 87;* Freie Scholle cooperative colony of, 77, *78,* 222nn47–48, 223n49; handicrafts and, 70–72, *71, 72,* 221nn31–34; as illustrator of Froebel's manuals, 56, 88; immigration to Australia, 73, 221n34; Lichterfelde townhouses ("castles") of, 73–76, *74, 76,* 222n36, 222n43, 223n53; Modellbaukasten, 92, *93,* 171; playhouse designed by, 61, *61;* progressive educational projects of, 72–73, 221n34; social reform movements and, 76–77; tectonics and, 67; as teenager, *82;* Terrast-Decke developed by, 77–79, *80*

Lilienthal, Otto, 3, 53, 56, 59–60, 81; death of, 84, 224n65; at Kunstgewerbe Museum (Berlin), 221n31; Reuleaux and, 69–70; social reform movements and, 76–77, 222n44; tectonics and, 67; as teenager, *82*

Lilienthal brothers' flight experiments, 70, 81, 218n4; first attempts, 82–83, 223nn60–61; glider flights of Otto, 83–84, *85,* 90–91; ornithopter, 84, 86, *86, 87,* 224n66;

photography and, 223n57; Wright brothers and, 84, 224n65

Lincoln Logs (J. Wright), 5–6, *7,* 117n40, 195, 238n2

Little Craftsman, The (Pasadena Art Institute exhibition, 1952), 145, 232n1

Lives of the Engineers, The (Smiles), 134, 231n105

Log Cabin Play House, 218n1

Los Angeles: The Architecture of Four Ecologies (Banham), 177

ludus (play with binding rules), 12, 202

Lustron House, 177, 178, *178,* 236n78

machine shops, 115–16, 228n58

Man, Play and Games (Caillois), 10, 11–12

Man Who Lives in Paradise, The (Gilbert), 97

Marden, Orison Swett, 135, 137

Marey, Étienne-Jules, 81, 90, 223n59

Märkisches Museum (Berlin), 16

Massey, Anne, 187, 237n92

mathematics, 10, 39, 40

matter, 44, 49; crystalline, 40, 41; organization of, 39; polar theory of, 42, *42, 43*

Meccano, 4, 8, 62, 92, 225n6, 234n22; advertising for, 97, *98;* boys inspired to scientific careers by, 112; collectors of, 99, 203, 214n22, 225n18; Eames House compared to, 155; Erector Set interchangeable with, 229n67; experimentation with new technology and, 197; first model of, 101, *101;* Firth of Forth Bridge model made of, 126, *127;* Mechanics Made Easy as original name for, 103; patent for, 103–4, *103,* 226n21; perforated metal strips of, 104, 226nn22–23; popularity of, 102, 225n18; "real" construction simulated by, 120; as "self-help" toy, 132, 135, 137, 143, 231n115; technological breakdown and, 200; as transition from play to work, 141; versatility and part interchangeability of, 106, 226n37; as "work toy," 139

Meccano Magazine, 115–16, 143

Mechanical Engineer in America, 1830–1910, The (Calvert), 115

mechanical engineering, 4, 69, 70, 116, 220n29

"Meditations on a Hobby Horse" (Gombrich), 206–8, 240n37

"Memorial Day 1950" (O'Hara poem), 188

Mendeleev, Dmitri, 67

Merzbau (Schwitters), 210

Mies van der Rohe, Ludwig, 190, 236n76, 238n113

mimicry (simulation as play), 11, 12
mineralogy, 4, 40
Modellbaukasten (G. Lilienthal), 92, *93,* 171
Modern Functional Building, The (Behne), 210
modernism, 3, 17, 208, 211, 237n92
Mondrian, Piet, 3
"*Montage,* by Herbert Matter," 174, *175*
"Most Important Room, The" (Kepes and Kepes), *144,* 145
Mumford, Lewis, 86
Mysto Manufacturing Company, 100, 107, 225n9
Mythologies (Barthes), 198

nature, 38, 41, 51, 182; destructive aspect of, 162; geometry of, 199–200; kindergarten play and understanding of, 197; as only true source of teaching, 47, 217n72; Schelling's philosophy of, 39, 43
Nelson, George, 184, 191–92
net drawing (*Netzzeichnen*), 50
Neuer Kindergarten (journal), 71–72
neurasthenia, 232n127
New Landscape in Art and Science, The (Kepes), 208
Newton, Sir Isaac, 134

Occupations, of Froebel, 20, 25–26, 51, 71; braiding and weaving material (No. 14), 24, 26; cutting/combining of paper pieces (No. 13), 24; embroidering material (No. 12), 24; intertwining material (No. 17), 24; modeling material (No. 20), 24; paper folding (No. 18), 24; peaswork (Number 19), 3, 24, *25;* perforating material (No. 11), 24; slats for interlacing (No. 15), 24, 26; slats with many links (No. 16), 24; types of, 21, 24
O'Hara, Frank, 188
Oppenheimer, Franz, 222n47
ornament, 64, 65, 66, 75. *See also* decoration
Out of the Cradle into the World, or Self-Education through Play (Atkins), 136–37, *136*

Packaged House (Wachsmann and Gropius), 160, 180, 181, *181,* 234n41, 237n81
Pädagogik des Kindergartens, Die (Froebel), 38–39, 215n4
padia (uncontrolled play), 12
Paolozzi, Eduardo, 186, 187
Paradise of Childhood, A (Wiebé), 21–22, 24–25, *31,* 34
"Parallel Inventions" (Smithson), 238n98
Parallel of Life and Art exhibition (Institute of Contemporary Art, London, 1953), 185–88, *186,* 237n95, 238n96

Peabody, Elizabeth, 19
pedagogy, 12, 14, 62, 197; drawing and, 45–46, *45;* Erector Set and, 109. *See also* education
periodic table of elements, 67–68
Pestalozzi, Johann Heinrich, 20, 208; *Anschauung* concept and, 47–48; pedagogical drawing method of, 45–46, *45, 47,* 48–49
Petit Architecte, Le (Imagerie d'Épinal), *171,* 235n66
Petroski, Henry, 111, 227n40
photography, 6, 81, 206
physics, 10, 40
Pitt-Rivers, Augustus, 68
Plan Voisin (Le Corbusier), 88
plastic toys, 62, 229n67, 238n5; Bakyo, 15; Lego, 15–16; Plasticville, U.S.A., 148
play, 7, 17; adult liberty and, 94–95; aesthetic habits and, 3; building instincts and, 3; destructive aspect of, 142, 143, 198–202; in different cultures and contexts, 10; education and, 140–41; elevation of work over leisure, 137; evolutionary theory and, 88; functionalism opposed to, 210; imagination and, 89–90; imitative aspects of, 89; as ordering of materials, 189; pedagogy of, 38; "play impulse," 38; as preparation for work, 89, 224n73; science and, 88; as self-education, 136–37, *136;* self-help and healing associated with, 57; seriousness in oscillation with, 189–90; space of, 13; as strenuous activity, 138–39; as "tacit knowledge," 9
playground apparatus, *139*
Playground Association of America, 138
Polavision (Eames film for Polaroid Corp.), 153, 233n17
Posener, Julius, 74–75, 88, 222n47
Powerplay: Toys as Popular Culture (Fleming), 103
Practical Education (Edgeworth and Edgeworth), 1, 213n1
Practical Guide to the English Kinder-garten, A (Ronge), *27, 30*
Précis des leçons d'architecture (Durand), 67, 220n25
prefabricated systems: Acorn House, 177–78, *179;* Anchor Stone Building Blocks and, 197; at Freie Scholle, 77; House of Cards (Eames and Eames) and, 174; housing and, *180;* Levittown houses, 177; Lilienthal's panels, 62, 75, 76; Lustron House, 177, 178, *178,* 236n78; mass housing and, 175–78, *177, 178, 179,* 182–83, 234n41; Packaged House, 160, 180, 181, *181,* 234n41, 237n81; Terrast-Decke, 77–79, *80,* 223nn50–53
Principles of Psychology (Spencer), 89, 139

production, mass, 4, 9, 84, 103; American System of Man-
    ufactures and, 101, 106; factory system, 137; housing
    and, 182
production, means of, 3, 8, 60
progress, 14, 17, 70, 76, 109
Prometheus (periodical), 75
proportionality, 66
Prussia, 19, 40, 218n6, 221n34. *See also* Germany
psychology, 9, 12
Pushing to the Front, or Success under Difficulties
    (Marden), 135

Quebec Bridge, 128–30, *128, 129,* 230n93, 230nn96–97
Qu'est ce que le design? (C. Eames), 146–47, *147*

railroads: bridge collapses and, 124, 126, 130; electrified
    tracks, 99, *100;* New York, New Haven, and Hartford
    Railroad, 100, *100;* Town truss and, 122, 230n80. *See also*
    trains, toy
Ray, Anna Chapin, 113, 228n45
repetition (habit), play and, 200–202
representation, 49, 50, 206, 207; sensory and intuitive, 48;
    tectonics and, 63
Reuleaux, Franz, 69–70, 220–21n29, 221n30
Richter, Friedrich Adolf, 56–60, 70, 88, 219n11
Rising in the World (Marden), 135
Rodgers, Daniel, 137, 138
Rogallo, Francis, 233n14
Romé de L'Isle, Jean-Baptiste L., 217n56
roof gardens, 75
*Rough Sketch for a Sample Lesson for a Hypothetical
    Course, A* (C. Eames and Nelson), 184, *184*
Rousseau, Jean-Jacques, 10, 46, 217n72

Saarinen, Eero, 174, 233n18
Santos-Dumont, Alberto, "aerial banquet" of, *91, 95*
Savage Mind, The (Lévi-Strauss), 204
Schelling, Friedrich, 39, 42, 43
Schiller, Friedrich, 10, 38, 88, 214n15
Schinkel, Karl Friedrich, 62, 64–66, 219n15
Schulen der weiblichen Handarbeit, Die (Georgens), *71,*
    72, 221n32
Schwab, Charles, 228n54
Schwitters, Kurt, 210
science, 66, 67, 186

Self-Help (Smiles), 134–35, 137, 231n104, 231n112
Semper, Gottfried, 62, 64, 67, 72; on architectural inven-
    tion, 66, 220n23; on architecture compared to sciences,
    66, 220n20, 220n26
Shannon, Claude, 184, 185, 237n85
skyscrapers, 4, 102, 135, 197
Smiles, Samuel, 134–35, 137, 231n112
Smithson, Alison, 186, 187
Smithson, Peter, 186, 187, 188, 238n98
Smithsonian Institution, 152
Sonntagsblatt (Froebel's newspaper), 215n4, 216n11
Souriau, Paul, 90, 92, 95
souvenir buildings, 6
space, 91; enclosure of, 65; Kant's notion of, 48–49
Space City Project (Schultze-Fielitz), 169
Spariosou, Mihai I., 214n15
Spencer, Herbert, 88–89, 139, 140, 142, 224n70
Sphaira (Froebel), 40
Spiele der Menschen, Die (Groos), 89, 90–91, 139, 224n71,
    239n12
Spiele der Tiere, Die (Groos), 89, 139, 224n71, 239n12
Stephenson, George, 134
stereometry, 15, 38, 63, *63,* 66
Sternberger, Dolf, 224n77
Stil in den technischen und tektonischen Künsten, Der
    (Semper), 62
structure (vs. ornament), 65
style, architectural: changing nature of, 186–87; eclecti-
    cism of, 64; tectonics and, 63, 64
suburbs, American, 147, 148, 156
Success magazine, 135–36, 138
Sydney Harbour Bridge, Meccano model of, 143, *143*
symmetry, 33, 35, 40, 50; in architectural form, 66; of crys-
    tals, 42, 44, *44,* 51

Taut, Bruno, 4–5
technology, 8, 64, 99, 163; challenges presented by, 132;
    faith in, 143; histories of, 15, 211; information technol-
    ogy, 183; as masculine enterprise, 112, 114, 230n97; mili-
    tary, 191; progress and, 14
tectonics, 62–64, 66, 219n13
Tektonik der Hellenen, Die (Bötticher), 62, 65, 66
Terrast-Decke, 77–79, *80,* 223nn50–53
tetrahedron: architectural form in mid-twentieth century
    and, 169; Bell and, 163–68, *163, 164, 167, 168,* 235n53;